Lecture Notes in Computer Science 13300

More information about this series at https://link.springer.com/bookseries/558

Joanna Kołodziej · Matteo Repetto ·
Armend Duzha (Eds.)

Cybersecurity of Digital Service Chains

Challenges, Methodologies, and Tools

 Springer

Editors
Joanna Kołodziej
Naukowa i Akademicka Sieć Komputerowa -
Państwowy Instytut Badawczy (NASK-PIB)
Warsaw, Poland

Matteo Repetto
Consiglio Nazionale delle Ricerche
(IMAT-CNR)
Genoa, Italy

Armend Duzha
Maggioli Informatica
Santarcangelo di Romagna, Italy

ISSN 0302-9743   ISSN 1611-3349 (electronic)
Lecture Notes in Computer Science
ISBN 978-3-031-04035-1   ISBN 978-3-031-04036-8 (eBook)
https://doi.org/10.1007/978-3-031-04036-8

This Springer imprint is published by the registered company Springer Nature Switzerland AG
The registered company address is: Gewerbestrasse 11, 6330 Cham, Switzerland

Preface

Data is the key driver for the digital economy. Besides its clear business meaning, this statement accounts for most of the innovations and new paradigms introduced by the software industry in the last decade. As a matter of fact, the most remunerative business today is not the software per se, but the possibility to create value-added services for specific domains: industry, smart city, smart grid, e–Health, multimedia, etc. The real competitive advantage in this scenario is given by the agility to implement ever new digital value chains that emerge, evolve, and dissolve much faster than ever.

New computing models and software architecture have been progressively introduced to bring more agility in the creation and management of new digital services and products. The recurring buzzword that conveniently represents this attitude is "orchestration", meaning the capability to implement (semi–)autonomous systems that are able to evolve with self–properties (self-configuration, self-management, self-healing, self-protection, etc.). Concrete achievements in this respect consist of a number of management frameworks and interfaces for cyberphysical systems and telecommunication infrastructures, including TOSCA, ETSI NFV, and FIWARE. They actually allow us to compose digital resources from multiple domains (cloud, IoT, networks, data) into high-value services in a seamless way, without caring about technical details concerning hardware and software provisioning.

The downside of this evolution is represented by cybersecurity aspects, which have not yet been addressed in a satisfactory way. Despite the effort in making software-defined systems ever more smart and autonomous, cybersecurity processes still largely depend on human skill and expertise. Relying on individuals' ability for hardening, verification of security properties, attack detection, and threat identification is no longer practical, and it is clearly an unacceptable practice, especially when critical infrastructures and large chains are involved.

Motivated by this substantial imbalance between software management paradigms and cybersecurity models, the GUARD project has advocated the transition towards more agile security and privacy processes, which could follow the dynamics of modern digital infrastructures and services. The scope has extended to service integrity and data sovereignty, including, therefore, attack detection and data tracking aspects. The main objective is the introduction of similar models to those already used for software management, namely ones with the ability to *orchestrate* security capabilities in order to build advanced and agile detection and analytic processes. This book provides an overall review of the main concepts, architectures, technologies, and results from the GUARD project, covering both technical and non-technical aspects, i.e., legal and ethical issues.

Contents

Structured into ten complementary chapters, this book presents the current trends in service automation, data protection, attack detection and analysis, and business chain modeling, along with practical examples of using GUARD and similar platforms. The ethical issues related to the digital business chains are also discussed. The GUARD project partners co-authored all chapters along with GUARD collaborators from the PANELFIT H2020 project and the Cracow University of Technology, who have worked together through dedicated meetings, workshops, webinars, and conferences. The chapters are summarized below.

1. Nowadays, device-centric or infrastructural-centric conventional threat mitigation methods are primarily ineffective in coping with the multitude of digital objects and service topologies involved. In the first chapter, Carrega et al. present the GUARD architecture description and motivating reasons for its advantage to security operators. They focus on many architectural model aspects, such as containerization, elasticity, and programmability, making it a novel approach to defining a modern cyber security framework for building detection and analytics services for complex digital service chains.

2. In Chapter 2, Repetto and Carrega propose a new tool called bpfFlowMon that is useful for monitoring and analyzing network flows. The authors present the state-of-the-art network flow monitoring and motivate the selection of eBPF, which is the main focus of their tool. The tool requires minimal computational resources to enable application in virtualized environments, which is a relevant research problem. The evaluation presented in the paper compares the proposed mechanism with two standard tools for this purpose, namely Zeek and nProbe. The results show that the proposed tool yields similar performance to the baselines but significantly reduces memory and CPU consumption.

3. Kołodziej et al. provide a short state-of-the-art analysis of modern Intelligent Transportation Systems (ITSs), focusing mainly on monitoring, anomaly detection, and general security mechanisms. They also provide a simple classification of anomalies and survey promising machine learning detection methods. The practical implementation of the ITS in Wolfsburg (Germany) provided by the WOBCOM company is demonstrated at the end of the chapter.

4. In Chapter 4, Krzysztoń, Lew, and Marks develop the Net Anomaly Detector (NAD) system that uses classification machine learning techniques to detect anomalies in the network traffic. NAD was integrated with the GUARD platform as a security service component and detected attacks and anomalies in TCP/IP traffic and local (customers') networks, such as the LoRa network managed by WOBCOM company in one of the GUARD use cases.

5. Unknown cyber security attacks and anomalies in the network traffic are also discussed in Chapter 5. Skopik et al. define AMiner – an open-source tool for detecting log-based anomalies. All the machine learning algorithms implemented in AMiner are feasible for deeper analysis of the monitored system or network behavior, recognizing deviations from learned models and thus spotting a wide variety of even unknown attacks.

6. Szynkiewicz describes the implementation of a system to translate packet signatures into filtering rules for the eBPF framework. In particular, the solution is built around the network telescope traffic provided by the NASK Darknet Telescope. Thanks to this traffic, it is possible to collect data and detect attacks (e.g., DDoS).

Specifically, through this traffic analysis, it is possible to generate PGA signatures and automatically generate BPF code to parse likely malicious DDoS packets.

7. Wurzenberger et al. describe the approach used to implement an aggregation process to reduce the number of alerts that need to be reviewed by security analysts in the context of Intrusion Detection Systems (IDSs). In addition, all the implemented features are demonstrated by setting up an application example. The obtained results are presented using a dashboard that enables easy visualization and filtering operations management.

8. Blockchain technologies are currently viral in providing security for financial transactions and secure transmission of data and information in distributed computing environments. Blockchain was also initialized in the GUARD platform; however, more work is still required. Wilczyński and Kołodziej show in their chapter the blockchain algorithms, network, and all potential benefits from using them in several practical applications, including business chains. They have developed a new blockchain-based algorithm for scheduling tasks in distributed networks and environments, such as the GUARD platform. The blockchain mechanism in the scheduler allows improving the security aspect in data access and in scheduler itself.

9. Kozhuharova et al. provide a non–technical perspective on privacy and security aspects of modern computing paradigms. They focus on the ethical issues and define the concrete measures of protecting the privacy of data subjects that were implemented during the GUARD project lifetime with regard to the technology developed within it. What can serve as a primary recommendation, especially when creating new technologies, is to establish a list of requirements, including ethical ones, that the system must cover before any action is taken. It will ensure compliance with the ethical principles at the highest level and mitigate any adverse effect on the individuals.

10. A broader view on security and ethical aspects in general digital service chains is presented by Tronnier et al. in the last chapter of the book. The authors work on the PANELFIT H2020 project, a complementary project to GUARD. The main results from the provided analysis show that ethical challenges cannot be resolved in a general way and instead need to be discussed individually, taking into consideration the ethical principles that are violated in the specific steps of the service chains.

We hope that this book is of interest to the broad group of researchers, engineers, and professionals working in computer science and IT business units using intelligent modeling to support their interdisciplinary projects and applications in distributed cloud systems and data-intensive computing domains. We believe it contains a valuable survey of the recent modeling technologies and compelling use cases.

February 2022

Joanna Kołodziej
Matteo Repetto
Armend Duzha

Acknowledgements

We are grateful to all the contributors of this book, for their willingness to work on this interdisciplinary project. We thank the authors for their interesting proposals for the book chapters, their time and effort, and their research ideas, which makes this volume an interesting and complete state-of-the-art monograph of the latest research advances and technology development regarding next generation digital business chain support. We also would like to express our sincere thanks to the reviewers, who helped us to ensure the quality of this volume. We gratefully acknowledge their time and valuable remarks and comments.

Our special thanks go to the LNCS team of Springer Verlag for their patience, valuable editorial assistance, and excellent cooperative collaboration in this book project.

Finally, we would like to express our warmest gratitude to our friends and families for their patience, love, and support in the preparation of this volume.

 Funded by the Horizon 2020 Framework Programme of the European Union

Contents

A Reference Architecture
for Management of Security Operations
in Digital Service Chains

Alessandro Carrega[1] , Giovanni Grieco[2] , Domenico Striccoli[2],
Manos Papoutsakis[3], Tomas Lima[4], José Ignacio Carretero[5],
and Matteo Repetto[6]([✉])

[1] S2N National Lab, CNIT, Genoa, Italy
alessandro.carrega@cnit.it
[2] Politecnico di Bari, Bari, Italy
giovanni.grieco@poliba.it
[3] Foundation for Research and Technology – Hellas, Heraklion, Greece
paputsak@ics.forth.gr
[4] Mind & Sparks GmbH, Vienna, Austria
tomas.lima@mindsandsparks.org
[5] Fiware Foundation, Berlin, Germany
joseignacio.carretero@fiware.org
[6] IMATI, CNR, Genoa, Italy
matteo.repetto@ge.imati.cnr.it

Abstract. Modern computing paradigms (i.e., cloud, edge, Internet of
Things) and ubiquitous connectivity have brought the notion of pervasive computing to an unforeseeable level, which boosts service-oriented
architectures and microservices patterns to create digital services with
data-centric models. However, the resulting agility in service creation
and management has not been followed by a similar evolution in cybersecurity patterns, which still largely rest on more conventional device-
and infrastructure-centric models.

In this Chapter, we describe the implementation of the GUARD Platform, which represents the core element of a modern cybersecurity framework for building detection and analytics services for complex digital
service chains. We briefly review the logical components and how they
address scientific and technological challenges behind the limitations of
existing cybersecurity tools. We also provide validation and performance
analysis that show the feasibility and efficiency of our implementation.

Keywords: Cybersecurity architecture · Digital service chain ·
Detection · Analytics pipeline

1 Introduction

Around thirty years after its original definition, pervasive computing has become
a reality and probably has gone far beyond what could have been expected at that

© The Author(s) 2022
J. Kołodziej et al. (Eds.): Cybersecurity of Digital Service Chains, LNCS 13300, pp. 1–31, 2022.
https://doi.org/10.1007/978-3-031-04036-8_1

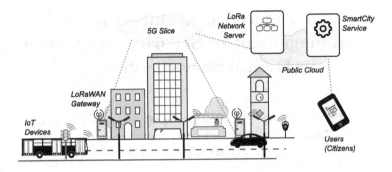

Fig. 1. An example of service chain for Smart City services.

time [29]. As a matter of fact, the integration of (invisible) computing capabilities into nearly all possible objects has only represented a part, yet relevant, of the implementation of this concept, while virtualization and ubiquitous connectivity have fully triggered the transition from device-centric to data-centric models. It therefore comes as no surprise that the more remunerative business in the digital economy is the creation of value added services for data retrieval, transformation, and sharing, no matter where and how processing is actually performed. This has been largely supported by a progressive (and still on-going) evolution from monolithic applications to service-oriented architectures, web services, and, more recently, service meshes [24].

Modern digital applications and services are increasingly designed and implemented according to microservice patterns, by composing (also denoted as *chaining*) digital resources (data, networks, cloud services, applications, and things) from multiple vendors on a growing scale; this allows to create, process, share, and consume data and content in a digital continuum, blurring the frontiers between application domains and breaking the current closed silos of information. Examples of digital resources include industrial and financial data sets, cloud infrastructures, lambda functions, storage services, smart devices in the Internet of Things, 5G network slices, LoRaWAN networks, and so on. An illustrative example is shown in Fig. 1. It depicts a possible chains of digital resources to create Smart City services. It includes Internet of Things (IoT) devices around the city (public transportation, traffic lights, public lightning, parking meters, etc.) connected to LoRaWAN gateways. The backbone is a leased 5G network slice, which interconnects the gateways to the LoRaWAN server deployed in the public cloud. In the same or a different cloud infrastructure, one or more applications implement the desired services (e.g., fleet and lightning management, free parking notification, traffic routing), maybe by interfacing with external datasets and users.

The loosely-coupled nature of micro-services allows to replace, duplicate, or remove part of them without affecting the operation of the overall application. As main result, digital services can be quickly provisioned in a matter of minutes or hours instead of days or weeks, can grow or shrink dynamically according to the evolving workload, can be easily deployed, replicated and migrated in multiple locations and even over heterogeneous infrastructures. This perfectly fits the dynamic and agile nature of modern business models, where digital services and business chains are expected to emerge, evolve, and dissolve much faster than traditional value-creating networks.

Unfortunately, cybersecurity mechanisms have largely been unable to keep the pace of this evolution towards data-oriented models. Indeed, they are still largely conceived to protect individual devices and specific infrastructures, either physical or virtual, but are largely ineffective to cope with complex dynamics, dispersion of data among the multitude of digital objects and infrastructures, non-deterministic, opaque and partially inscrutable service topologies [24]. Most issues come from privacy and integrity concerns. As a matter of fact, although the location and confidentiality of private and sensitive data are rather straight-forward to manage inside devices and infrastructures of a single provider, this is more difficult when resources from multiple providers are involved (e.g., cloud, storage, things, networks) [2]. Similarly, detection of cyberattacks in these conditions is extremely challenging, due to the lack of proper visibility over third party's infrastructures and services.

The GUARD framework was conceived as an evolutionary step in the design and operation of cybersecurity frameworks, towards data-centric models already implemented by modern computing paradigms [23]. It advocates the augmentation of service management interfaces with security capabilities, according to on-going efforts in IETF [13,19] and OASIS [1]. Further, it provides a way to leverage such extended interfaces for programmatically collecting data and feeding detection algorithms and security analytics, while providing the necessary agility to chase the dynamics of complex digital service chains. In this Chapter, we follow up on our preliminary architectural design [24] with a more concrete implementation of its core platform. We briefly describe the different components and the main benefits of the GUARD approach; we also provide validation and performance evaluation for the most critical parts of our platform.

The rest of the Chapter is organized as follows. We initially discuss related work in Sect. 2. We briefly review the overall GUARD framework in Sect. 3, while in Sect. 4 we describe the last version of the core platform architecture and its main components, namely the Context Broker Manager, the Security Controller, and the Dashboard. Then, we describe how the platform interacts with digital services and its internal workflows in Sect. 5. We report numerical results from our validation and performance analysis in Sect. 6. Finally, we give our conclusion and plan for future work in Sect. 7.

2   Related Work

The interconnection of digital resources from multiple heterogeneous domains (cloud, data sets, networks, IoT, etc.) creates complex systems of systems, which introduce more functions, management aspects, and security issues than the plain sum of the constituent components [25,26]. They represent a fertile ground for new forms of attacks, often leveraging advanced persistent threats (APT). Research efforts have largely focused on building complex analytics for spotting anomalies in large bulks of data, often leveraging big data techniques. Specific topics in this context include the heterogeneity of log data and events (e.g., structured, semi-structured, and unstructured samples) [11,31], scalability and multidimentional anomaly detection [17,21], the automatic generation of configurations from high-level policies [7,30], data handling architectures for Security Operation Centers [3,9], data collection strategies [18]. Besides, the concept of Security Monitoring-as-a-Service (SMaaS) was introduced, but it still remains bound to rigid architectures [10]. Notably, while many frameworks allow to create multiple analytics processes (e.g., Elastic Stack, Apache Metron), to the best of our knowledge there is no way to automate this configuration on dynamic systems-of-systems as digital service chains.

A meaningful step in this direction is the creation of standard interfaces to security functions. The I2NSF framework [13,19] defines YANG [5] data models for describing security capabilities and changing the configuration of network security functions with the RESTCONF/NETCONF protocols [4,6]; the framework also defines monitoring and reaction interfaces. Unfortunately, there is only a detailed data model for stateless packet filters, whereas other kinds of supported appliances (antivirus, IDS, web and Voice-over-IP firewall) have a much barer interface. The OpenC2 initiative [1] takes a different approach, focusing more on a standard set of commands rather than data models. Indeed, currently there is only an operation profile for the stateless packet filter [22], but the usage of this interface for other cybersecurity appliances requires far less extensions than I2NSF.

Identity management and access control always represent a big challenge in decentralized environments. Most of the emerging solutions exploit a decoupled mechanism, which aims at separating authentication and authorization functionalities in a harmonized fashion [16]. Many interesting solutions have been recently formulated in the scientific literature for identity management in multi-domain environments, like OpenID Connect and OAuth 2.0 [20,27,28]. They introduce the possibility to authenticate users within a federated ecosystem by means of a trusted Identity Provider. This is necessary to delegate security management to external providers, without sharing full access to the management interface.

3   The GUARD Framework

Recent advances in cybersecurity have largely focused on improved detection and correlation capability, in order to recognize advanced persistent threats and complex multi-vector attacks. In this respect, machine learning and other forms of artificial intelligence are often used for spotting anomalies in large bulks of data, which may be generated by zero-day attacks. Despite of the large effort in improving the detection and automating response and mitigation actions, the installation and configuration of protection systems is still largely a manual process, which takes time and needs continuous tuning every time the system changes (e.g., devices are added/removed/replaced, software is installed/updated/purged, new configurations are applied). Even if this approach has always been accepted for long-lived installations that are seldom modified or upgraded, it does not fit the agile nature of digital services that are quickly provisioned and changed.

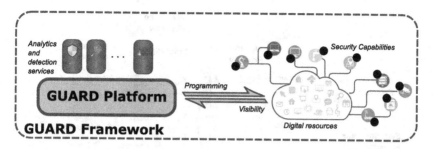

Fig. 2. Overview of the GUARD framework.

The GUARD framework is conceived as a new paradigm to implement detection and analytics processes for digital service chains. Its objective is to facilitate the creation and adaptation of such processes in fast-changing environments, by automating as much as possible the setup of security analytics pipelines. We define as *security analytics pipeline* the processing chain from security agents to detection algorithms, which includes the necessary tasks for data collection, transformation, filtering, indexing, analysis, correlation, and storage. This is implemented by the GUARD Platform, which acts as a sort of middleware between security agents and detection/analytics services, as depicted in Fig. 2.

The most innovative aspect of the GUARD framework is the multi-domain scope. Indeed, even if a digital service chain is created and managed by a single entity (denoted as *Service Provider*), it is usually composed by resources owned and operated by different *Resource Providers* [24]. Additionally, security aspects are often delegated to external parties, i.e., *Security Operators*, which have the skills, expertise, and technological assets to face a large number of diverse threats and attacks. The GUARD Platform is the tool that allows these operators to easily connect their analytics engines with their customers' services scattered across the Internet.

Monitoring a digital service chain is therefore extremely challenging, because security agents cannot freely be installed by Security Operators. A shift in mindset is necessary with respect to legacy paradigms, because security processes must build on embedded security capabilities rather than more conventional discrete security agents (even if a concrete agent will run anyway in most cases behind the abstraction provided by a security capability). Indeed, this transformation has already started, because many cloud providers already integrate security services in their offers, like firewalls, intrusion detection and prevention systems, antivirus software; these appliances work at the infrastructure layer, hence this approach ensures better visibility and safety than running them inside virtual resources (which is anyway unfeasible in case of containers and serverless computing).

An additional issue is represented by the delegation of security processes to external entities. Indeed, these operators should be granted access to the management interface of the resources involved in the chain, but this approach might not be recommended for confidentiality, safety, and privacy reasons.

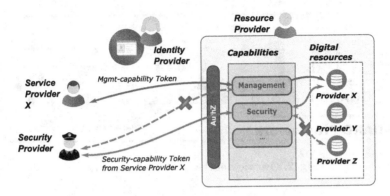

Fig. 3. Access control model for the GUARD Framework.

Fine-grained access control should instead be implemented in each digital resource to restrict their access to security-related capabilities only, preventing any other management action that could affect the continuity of the service. This requires scalable authentication and authorization schemes that give Security Operators limited access to digital resources (i.e., security capabilities) on behalf of the resource owner (see Fig. 3). Token-based mechanisms like OAuth2 [12] provide an effective solution to this problem, by avoiding the need to share secrets and to grant full control over the resources.

Although standard firewalling, antivirus, and intrusion prevention systems implemented by Resource Providers may be enough for some users, they are not probably enough for detecting and mitigating complex attacks. In this respect, we argue that security capabilities should include a "programmability" dimension, as shown in Fig. 2, that allows more flexibility in retrieving relevant security context (events, measures, data). Programmability may consist, for instance, in the possibility to select and chain multiple Logstash modules for data transformation; more interestingly, it may also entail the execution of custom code in a safe way (which means no vulnerability is introduced for the service and the whole infrastructure) [8].

4   GUARD Platform

The GUARD Platform is designed to implement a typical closed control loop for security enforcement, as shown in Fig. 4. In the upper part of the loop, a data handling pipeline is implemented, from data collection to detection, up to visualization; in the bottom part, control response strategies are applied for enforcement and mitigation actions. Detection and analytics can be performed both on real-time data, according to a streaming pattern, or on historical data, by offline analysis. As we already pointed out in the previous Section, the scope of the GUARD Platform does not include monitoring and inspection tasks, which are performed by local security agents embedded in digital services.

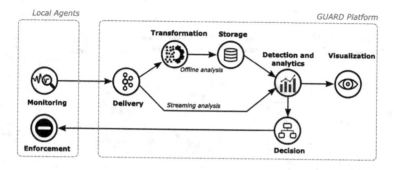

Fig. 4. The typical structure of a data handling pipeline for security analytics.

Figure 5 shows the software architecture of the GUARD Platform. The dark components are taken from typical Elastic Stack setup (though not all components are part of it), and represent a common solution for building a data handling pipeline that delivers data to one or more processing algorithms. The light boxes are GUARD components that implement the necessary feature to make this system flexible and adaptable to highly-dynamic computing environments. The Context Broker Manager provides an abstraction of security capabilities provided by Resource Providers. It uses data models to abstract the concrete implementation of security agents and the communication protocols; therefore, it offers to the rest of the system technology-agnostic access to monitoring and enforcement capability in local environments. The Security Controller is the smart component that takes decision based on control policies. Its main purpose is to trigger response and mitigation actions based on the evolving context (events, conditions) generated by the detection algorithms or directly by remote agents. It is expected to provide the necessary logic to resolve conflicts and to generate additional outputs by combining the set of provided rules. Additionally, the Security Controller is responsible for the setup of multiple security analytics pipelines within the Platform. Finally, the Dashboard is the user interface to visualize the service topology, security features, and data generated by agents and detection algorithms. The Dashboard also features an editor for creating analytics pipelines, starting from the list of available detection and analytics algorithms, as well as security capabilities of each digital resource.

One major contribution from GUARD is the definition of an API for exposing security capabilities. This goes in the direction of providing a uniform and common interface towards security agents, beyond the current set of heterogeneous services offered by different providers. Since the definition of such kind of interface is still an open issue and no implementations are available for on-going standardization initiatives [1,13], we built on existing management interfaces in the FIWARE domain and extended them to include security capabilities, as discussed in Sect. 5.1.

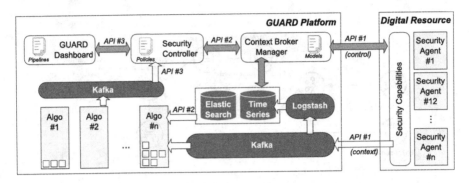

Fig. 5. Software architecture of the GUARD Platform.

4.1 Security Analytics Pipelines

One common issue in setting up detection services is the time needed to configure all the necessary elements. Although graphical user interfaces are often available for this purpose, manual operation for deployment and initial configuration are still required. We leverage the components of our architecture, as well as the interface to security capabilities, to bring more automation in this process, in order to better follow the dynamics of digital services. We introduce therefore the notion of *security analytics pipeline* (SAP), which includes the logical stages shown in Fig. 6:

- monitoring and inspection functions that are available in digital resources (Local Agent);
- aggregation, transformation, and enrichment tasks that are necessary to adapt the format of data generated by sources (agents) to what expected by consumers (algorithms);
- indexing and normalization operations before storing data;
- analytics and detection algorithms that are used to provide notifications and alerts;
- storage of data end events;
- analysis of events and conditions to undertake response and mitigation actions (Security Controller).

Figure 6 also shows typical configuration aspects for a SAP. They partially require input from Security Operators and partially can be automatically derived by the Security Controller. The definition of a SAP includes at least the following steps:

- The selection of one or more logical agents exposed by digital resources and their configuration. This provides raw data and measurements for further processing, or refined events if at least part of the detection is already implemented locally.

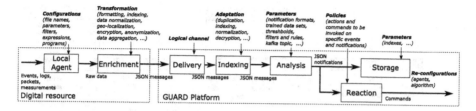

Fig. 6. The logical stages of a Security Analytics Pipeline.

- The selection of one detection/analytics service. This is an optional step, that correlates data and measurements for detecting known attack patterns or anomalies. In any case, all data will be dumped to a database.
- The definition of control policies for the Security Controller. These policies are kind of rules that define actions to be performed in response to given events, and after considering a set of conditions (e.g., current status).

Other stages of the pipeline (e.g., for data adaptation, transformation and indexing, delivery topics) should be automatically configured by the SC. However, this logic is only partially implemented and the intervention of the SC is currently mostly limited to the configuration of a dedicated Kafka topic for each SAP.

4.2   Context-Broker Manager

The Context-Broker Manager (CB-Manager) provides uniform access to heterogeneous security capabilities of different digital resources. There are two main aspects behind this abstraction:

- hiding the technological details and the heterogeneity of security capabilities in different domains;
- depicting a logical view of the whole service chain, including capabilities and the relationships between the different resources.

Each digital resource that exposes a management interface is considered an independent Execution Environment (ExecEnv). The main security aspects of each ExecEnv concern what kind of monitoring, inspection and enforcement processes are available to its user (collectively indicated as "security capabilities"), and what kind of relationship exists with other resources (e.g., a cloud service that keeps data in an external storage server; an application that uses an external data store). This information is retrieved from the interface towards digital services (we describe our implementation in Sect. 5.1, and then organized within the CB-Manager is a tree-like fashion, which root is represented by the service entry point (usually the service directly used by the user).

Service topology and security capabilities are abstracted in a data model that captures both the relevant parameters and the current configuration. The model is exposed through a REST interface, where POST/GET verbs on the endpoint

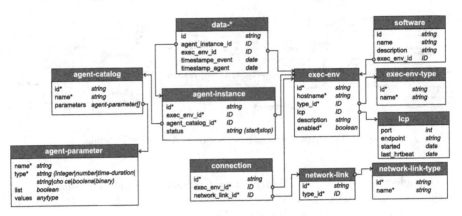

Fig. 7. Data model of the CB-Manager abstraction.

are translated by the CB-Manager in the corresponding operations on concrete elements.

Data Model. Figure 7 shows the Data Model diagram implemented by the CB-Manager abstraction. It captures both the service topology, security capabilities of each ExecEnv, and current configuration of local security agents. The service topology is represented in terms of Nodes and Edges. Nodes correspond to the ExecEnvs of each digital resource, while edges represent relationships (communication links, management or data interfaces, etc.).

The *exec-env* object contains the name of the digital resource, whereas the type_id denotes the type of ExecEnv. Examples of ExecEnv types include bare metal servers, virtual machines, containers, Platform-as-a-Service, IoT device. The *software* object contains the installed software in each ExecEnv, also including relevant fields (vendor, version, security patches, installation e.g., plain, chrooted, containerized, virtual machine, configuration options, etc.). This could be useful for risk assessment, to spot known vulnerabilities. Additionally, an endpoint for the security capability API is present, which is indicated as *LCP*. This name is taken from the component that implements this interface in our framework (see Sect. 5.1).

The definition of *network-link* includes an identifier and a type. All the possible network link types are defined in the *network-link-type* object. This can correspond to a physical link (e.g., Point to Point (Point 2 Point, LAN), a virtual link (IPSec, VxLAN, GRE, etc.), a network slice (as for a 5G network), a communication interface (protocol). Network links are connected to their ExecEnv by the *connection*; this approach is necessary to deal with multipoint communications, as in case of LANs. This object contains all the information regarding the configuration of the network link in the ExecEnv as, for example, the IP address (version 4 and/or 6), if the link is encrypted and how (which method, etc.).

The *data* object contains all the data exposed by the security capability of each ExecEnvs, in terms of security agent models. The different types of security agents and the corresponding configurable properties are registered in the *agent-catalog*. The model includes the list of parameters that can be configured, as *agent-parameter*. This nested object describes the parameter in terms of name and relative type. The *agent-catalog* does not need to hold a separate model for each different implementation; instead, the main purpose is to hide as many implementations as possible behind the same abstraction. For example, a "file log" monitoring agent is a quite general component, which parameters include the name of the files to monitor, the frequency of updates, the retrieval paradigm (differences or whole file); it may be implemented as Elastic FileBeat or by the native Kubernetes log retrieval command, but this is totally hidden by the CB-Manager abstraction. Clearly, the more specific the agent, the less parameters will be available for configuration.

The agents available in each ExecEnv are listed as *agent-instance* objects. Their properties can be read and changed, and this operation is reflected on their concrete implementation; in addition, they can be started and stopped. While the *agent-catalog* index is provided as part of the CB-Manager implementation according to the list of supported interfaces/agents, the *agent-instance* catalog is automatically populated by the discovery mechanism described in Sect. 5.1.

Control/Management API. Access to the Data Model is possible through a RESTful interface. This interface can be used both for management (i.e., including new agent models in the *agent-catalog*) and control (i.e., reading/setting parameters in the *agent-instances*.

The semantics of the CB-Manager API reflects the structure of the Data model. It is a REST server built with swagger that enables the standard CRUD operations. The HTTP syntax for requests includes therefore the following elements:

- HTTP method, which identifies the requested operation; supported values are: GET, POST, PUT, DELETE.
- Path, which identified the logical element to act on.
- Body, which contains a JSON object for passing arguments and options.

Responses are given with standard HTTP messages and status codes; they contain requested information in the body formatted as a JSON object.

The RESTful API is organized in three main path roots:

- *config*, which gives access to information about current instances and their configuration (Topology data);
- *catalog*, which contains the types of security agents that can be used in each ExecEnv (Catalog data);
- *data*, which gives access to the set of information collected by security agents (measures, events, etc. for historical data).

The first 2 elements support every HTTP method (subject to authorization and access control), since they refer to the overall service topology and its configuration; the last element only supports the GET method, as the injection of data with other methods than Kafka is not supported.

The *config* path is used to store the service topology and available agents. It is also used both to set and to retrieve the current configuration of available agents. When invoked with a PUT or POST method, the CB-Manager stores the required value and invokes the necessary interface to apply the new configuration to the remote agent. When invoked with the GET method, the CB-Manager only supplies the stored value, but does not query the remote agent, to improve performance. The CB-Manager does not solve configuration conflicts; this must be accomplished by the Security Controller, which implementation is more suitable for this function.

The *catalog* is a sort of driver repository for known agent types, since it defines the necessary commands to translate the capabilities into concrete configurations. Objects in the catalog are inserted by the system administrator, and then they are retrieved by the CB-Manager every time a configuration change is requested. The definition of the commands for each agent depends on the security capabilities exposed by digital service. The current implementation can i) load configuration files; ii) execute shell commands; and iii) forward HTTP requests to local agents.

The *data* path is used to retrieve data stored internally to the CB-Manager. It is conceived for offline analysis, since real-time data are collected more efficiently through Kafka. It is worth pointing out that the content of the data path is deliberately unspecified at this stage, because security operators are responsible to select the agents they need and the content and format of produced data, as well as any conversion and transformation that may be required to adapt such format to the input of relevant processing algorithms.

There are two ways to access elements from this REST API. If a single element is required and its identifier is known, it can be specified at the end of the path. This is the only allowed semantics to update elements (i.e., when using the PUT method). Otherwise, a query can be specified in the body of the request. Queries are performed by a JSON request that follows the SQL syntax[1].

4.3   Security Controller

The Security Controller (SC) automates management and control actions for SAPs. This is achieved by implementing behavioral guidelines that define the actions to be undertaken in response to specific events. In practice, this means that the SC configures and launches detection algorithms when it is necessary, listen for relevant data and events, and dispatches notifications to users.

Regarding its implementation, the SC is based on a rule engine that is able to express the logic behind the decision making due to the security policies as

---

[1] Elasticsearch guide – SQL language. URL: https://www.elastic.co/guide/en/elasticsearch/reference/current/sql-spec.html.

production rules. Drools [18] is the chosen rule engine applying and extending the Phreak algorithm. Drools is a Business Rules Management System (BRMS) solution. It provides a core Business Rules Engine (BRE) among others. It is open-source software, released under the Apache License 2.0. It is written in pure Java™, runs on any JVM and is available in the Maven Central repository too. Finally, SC integrates different sub-components required by the rule engine such as the knowledge base, the core engine, and the compiler.

Drools Engine in the SC is running continuously. Whenever a request reaches one of the SC's endpoints, an instance of the corresponding Java class is created and then inserted into the Drools working memory as a Fact. Facts are triggering Drools Rules that perform actions. For example, when a PUT request, with a JSON representation of a SAP in its body, arrives at the /startSecurityPipeline endpoint of SC (see Sect. 5.3), the following actions take place:

- An instance of the Pipeline Java class is created and some attributes that are meant for internal use are filled in, such as the uniqueID attribute of the said instance.
- The created instance is checked against a pipeline array list located locally in the file system. If there is no other instance with the same information, the newly created one is added in the array list. Otherwise, the pre-existed one is updated.
- The newly created/updated pipeline instance is then added into the Drools working memory.
- Based on the information carried by the pipeline instance, a number of instances of the AgentInstance Java class are created along with their configuration and are also inserted into the Drools working memory.
- A subset of the Drools rules is triggered due to the insertion of the new Drools Facts, invoking Java methods that send a request for each AgentInstance Fact to the appropriate Context Broker Manager endpoint.
- The endpoints' responses are then inserted as Drools Facts into the working memory triggering, this time, a different subset of Rules.
- The Java instances in the pipeline array list and the Smart Controller's log file are updated based on the Context Broker's responses.
- Drools Facts that are not necessary are retracted from the working memory.

The reason for storing Facts (pipeline array list) outside of the Drools Engine is two-fold: debugging purposes and pipeline status reporting.

Drools Rule Example. We have already mentioned that Drools rules perform actions. What follows is an example of such rule, which updates the status of incoming SAP based on the CB-Manager responses to the update-agent requests. Listing 1 depicts the *when* and *then* parts of the rule. The conditional elements in this case are all the agent instances of a pipeline and their corresponding responses received from the CB-Manager's update agent instance endpoint. The response of every one agent instance of the pipeline should report code 200 for the rule to be triggered. This is checked using the *forall* statement. One again we make sure that we check only the agent instances of a specific pipeline using the *from $agents* part of the *forall* statement.

```
1  rule "StartPipeline"
2  when
3    $pipeline: Pipeline(status=="start", $agents:=agents)
4    forall( $agent:Agent($agentId:=agent_catalog_id) from
        $agents
5      ContextBrokerUpdateAgentResponse($agentId:=subiectUuid,
        code==200)
6    )
7  then
8    KafkaProducerController.logger.info ("All agent instances
        of pipeline " + $pipeline.getId() + " - " + $pipeline.
        getUuid() + " have been successfully updated.");
9    $pipeline.storePipelineToContextBroker();
10   retract($pipeline);
11   KafkaProducerController.logger.info("Pipeline " +
        $pipeline.getId() + " - "  + $pipeline.getUuid() + " is
        retracted");
12   springBootkafkaAppApplication.pipelineArray.
        updatePipelineStatus($pipeline.getId(), "started");
13 end
```

Listing 1. StartPipeline Drools rule - The SAP status is updated and the pipeline is retracted from the working memory.

If the conditional elements are present in the working memory, the actions in the *when* part of the rule take place. The first action of this rule is to report in the log file that all agent instances of the specific pipeline have received a response with code 200. After that, a method of the pipeline Java class is called to store the pipeline with the new status in the Context Broker. The pipeline instance is then retracted from the working memory of the Drools Engine with the *retract* statement. This action is also reported in the log file. Finally, another Java method is called, part of the PipelineArray Java class that changes the status of the pipeline to "started". This attribute is retrieved when the SC is asked for the status of a pipeline.

4.4 Dashboard

The Dashboard is the Graphical User Interface (GUI) that simplifies the interaction between the end users (e.g., Security Operators) and the GUARD framework, by giving the user an easy way to apply configurations and interpret data and results. The Dashboard includes general features such as a secure authentication system with roles and permissions, profiles and account settings, as commonly required for this kind of tools. More interestingly, the Dashboard provides a schematic representation of the service topology, which helps the user to discover what difference resources are involved in the service, their relationships, and their security capabilities (see Fig. 8).

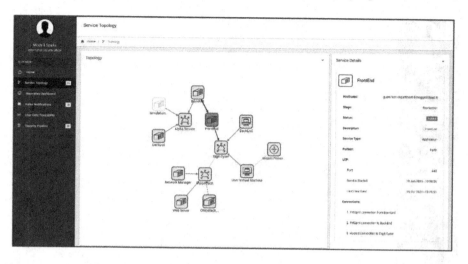

Fig. 8. Service topology visualization in the Dashboard.

The graphical visualization of service topology effectively supports the preliminary security analysis and risk assessment processes, which culminate in the design and instantiation of SAPs. These represent the main goal for the GUARD framework, therefore the Dashboard provides all functions to view, create, update, manage and remove them. The creation of a new pipeline requires to choose a name, select one or more agent instances among those reported by the CB-Manager, and (optionally) an analysis/detection algorithm that will be fed with monitoring data. The process includes the configuration of each agent (also including the possibility to upload configuration files) and the detection algorithm, as shown in Fig. 9; moreover, a set of rules can be inserted in the policy editor that automate response actions for events generated by the pipeline. Management operations include start, stop, and reload of the pipeline, which are concretely translated into management actions by the Security Controller (see the activation workflow in Sect. 5.3).

The Dashboard also provides situational awareness, by visualizing in the notification and anomaly view all relevant messages. They can be representative of relevant monitoring events from security agents or threat alerts from detection algorithms. Each event reports source, severity, description, data and date/time. Filtering allows to restrict the scope and not being overwhelmed by verbose agents. This notification feature allows to supervise the operation of the Security Controller and to undertake corrective actions that are not implemented by automation policies.

5   GUARD Operation

The functional components described in Sect. 4 interacts with additional elements to implement the functionality described for the whole framework. In

Fig. 9. Configuration of a pipeline.

the following, we describe the interaction with digital services and the identity management and access control subsytem.

5.1   Discovery and Management of Security Capabilities

One of the most challenging part of our framework is dynamic management of local monitoring and enforcement capabilities available in digital resources. To this aim, we implemented the Local Control Plane (LCP), which exposes a REST API that describes the main characteristics of an ExecEnv and its embedded security capabilities. This includes the relevant security context that is already part of the CB-Manager's data model, namely the type of ExecEnv, the installed software, links to external resources, etc. The LCP also represents the local control hook to configure and run security agents.

Table 1 shows the REST API exposed by the LCP, which is mainly consumed by the CB-Manager. The most relevant part is the information about child LCPs, namely LCPs of other digital resources that are chained. This is the case, for instance of a virtual machine that uses storage provided by a different provider, or an IoT agent that pushes data through a dedicated 5G network slice. By starting at the service entry point and recursively querying each LCP and its children, the CB-Manager can therefore discover the whole service topology. The concept

Table 1. The LCP API to expose security capabilities for a digital resource.

Path	Action
/self	Returns a simple identification of the resource, including the URL of the LCP, its identifier and name, the type of ExecEnv, and a human-readable description
/self/deployment	Returns the description of the ExecEnv, including the type of hardware (baremetal server, virtual machine, LXC or Docker Container), operating system, number of (virtual) CPUs, amount of RAM, disk devices and partition size, network interfaces and IP addresses
/lcp_parent	Returns the parent LCP(s) of this resource
/lcp_son/id	Returns the list of LCPs of subsidiary resources used by this ExecEnv. If an *id* is specified, only the corresponding LCP information is returned
/self/software	Returns the software run in this ExecEnv. The description includes the software name, vendor, connections to other software, and open network ports
/self/container	Returns the container name and the description of the hosted software (same information as previous object)
/agent/instance	Returns the list of security agents available in the ExecEnv. The description includes name, version, vendor, status (running, stopped, etc.), endpoint URL, identifier and description
/interactions	Returns the list of external resources used by this ExecEnv but without an LCP. This includes any kind of digital resource (cloud installations, applications, storage servers, network slices). It may also include a specific endpoint to retrieve additional details
/poll	Returns all the objects listed before, but formatted in a way that better fits the CB-Manager's data model

is schematically shown in Fig. 10, with reference to the example introduced in Sect. 1. Here, we see that VM1 hosts the "Smart City App", which is taken as the "entry point" of the service because it is the final service offered to citizens. VM2 hosts the "LORA Server", which collects data from IoT devices through a dedicated 5G slice. VM1 and VM2 run on resources provisioned by Cloud1 and Cloud2, respectively, which are not necessarily operated by the same provider not use the same technology. Additionally, the SmartCity App stores data on an external storage service. The different relationships between digital resources (e.g., application *hosted* in VM, VM *provisioned* on cloud, data *pushed* to server, etc.) are reflected in the parent-child relation between LCP instances, which can be discovered by recursive queries (not only at the root). This configuration must be provide by each Resource Provider. We argue that some providers might not expose security capabilities; this creates "blind spots" in the service which cannot be monitored (see, for example, the storage service in Fig. 10). Based on the

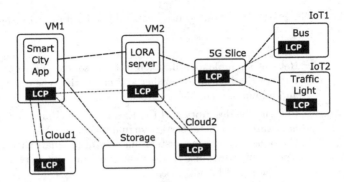

Fig. 10. Schematic representation of a service chain topology and logical tree built by the LCPs.

result of security and risk assessment, the Security Operator may suggest the Service Provider to look for alternative resources, which implement the required interface or provide stronger security guarantees.

Beside discovery, the LCP provides the list of available security capabilities, in terms of security agents that can be configured. Additionally, the description of the ExecEnv provides useful context information to point out vulnerabilities and potential threats, by performing queries to Common Vulnerabilities databases about the hosted software.

5.2   Identity Management and Access Control

The Identity Management and Access Control functionalities are provided by means of the Authentication & Authorization (AA) module. It defines secure authorization procedures for protecting the access to distributed resources in digital service chains. In particular, the module provides authentication services for system components and external agents. Furthermore, authorization services are configured to provide access control through the use of JSON Web Tokens (JWTs) and Access Control Lists (ACLs). JWT is an open standard that defines a methodology to transmit information between parties as a JSON object [15]. This information can be verified and trusted because it is digitally signed. JWT enables a security mechanism to rely on security policies based on Attribute-Based Access Control (ABAC) paradigm, which is based on granting or denying user requests based on both attributes of users and attributes of the object to be accessed to [14].

On the bases of the main architectural components, the AA module distinguishes two security zones: an internal GUARD domain, and an external zone in which there are local agents that offer security services.

The entities inside the GUARD Platform are protected through a centralized authentication mechanism, which ensures that components are recognized through a trusted internal Identity and Access Manager, so that operations

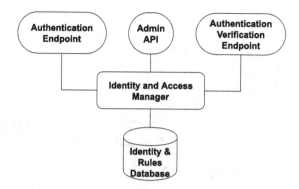

Fig. 11. AA Security Mechanism internal to the GUARD Platform to protect communications between GUARD internal components and security services.

can be confined according to an ABAC-based strategy. The authentication and authorization module of the GUARD Platform can be summarized in Fig. 11.

Protection of GUARD Internal Components. Regarding the protection of GUARD internal components and security services, the main components of the modules are presented hereby.

- *Identity & Rules Database.* It stores information relative to the users managed by GUARD and their attributes. This database is accessible by the Identity and Access Manager exclusively.
- *Identity and Access Manager.* It employs security routines and services to manage identities and the release of information in the form of a security token.
- *Admin API.* It is a REST and SOAP-based interface used for maintenance purposes. A web-based interface is also available that facilitates the administration of security policies by system administrators.
- *Authentication Endpoint.* It allows user identification through the exchange of security questions and challenges to prove the identity of the interacting service. If the service is correctly identified, the Identity and Access Manager releases an ABAC-based security token encoded in JWT.
- *Authentication Verification Endpoint.* It enables the verification of the security token signature if a resource protected by GUARD is serving an authenticated service. If the signature verification is correct, the protected resource can proceed to service authorization according to attributes present in the security token.

The entire service workflow of the AA Security Mechanism for the protection of internal services is presented in Fig. 12.

Protection for Entities External to the GUARD Platform. The entities external to the GUARD Platform need a decentralized protection, so a different

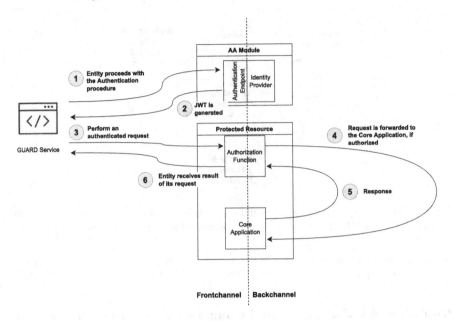

Fig. 12. Workflow of the AA Security Mechanism internal to the GUARD Platform.

approach is taken to ensure that mutual authentication is established and strong security policies can be applied between digital resources and the GUARD Platform. The security architecture and mechanism for users, LCP and Local Agents are illustrated in Fig. 13, and the main components of the AA module for the protection of the zone external to the GUARD Platform are described in what follows.

- **Identity Provider.** The Identity Provider (IdP) handles authentication procedures between services and GUARD users. It also defines the authorizations each actor has in the entire architecture by encoding the information in JWT. Before client authentication can be performed, an Identity Server must be configured in order to register the users that belong to the GUARD domain. This operation is permitted only by the system administrator and is performed through a Management Console with the administrator credentials. The configuration of the Identity Server includes also the assignment of the user roles, to allow or deny access to some applications or privileged operations, according to the ABAC mechanism.

  Once the user is created and registered by the Identity Server, the client can perform the authentication process. It consists of two phases: in the first, the user authenticates to the IdP with username and password; in the second, the IdP returns to the user a JWT, that is appended to the future requests made by the user, to demonstrate that it possesses certain attributes and is correctly authenticated to the system.

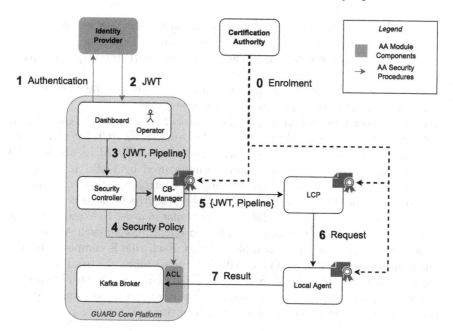

Fig. 13. AA Security Mechanism to protect communications between GUARD and LCP/Local Agents. Key actors are highlighted with bold characters.

– **Certification Authority.** In order to guarantee the authentication of LCP/Local Agents and their communications between CB-Manager and Kafka, a GUARD Public Key Infrastructure (PKI) with a Certification Authority (CA) is used to issue certificates for the mentioned actors. In this way it is possible to perform TLS mutual authentication procedures between these services.

– **Kafka Broker.** Kafka Broker has been configured to handle authentication with Kafka-enabled clients through TLS mutual authentication. X.509 certificates are used during the TLS handshake process to perform mutual authentication. So, the broker and clients certificates need to be enrolled and trusted. Kafka clients are represented by Local Agents that produce data to be sent to GUARD. Each entity involved in the secure communication must have keystore and truststore files to ensure that the mutual authentication is correctly performed. The keystore contains each machine's own identity. It is an archive which stores the private key and the public certificate signed by a CA. This certificate is also saved in the truststore and distributed among communicating parties, which contains the list of trusted certificates used to determine which entity or CA to trust. In this way, any certificate that was signed by the CA whose public key is in the truststore will in turn be trusted. This property is called the chain of trust, and it is particularly useful when deploying TLS on a large Kafka cluster. It is noteworthy that both the keystore and the truststore are protected by a password. Kafka listens on a dedicated port with TLS enabled and mutual authentication between broker and clients is performed through specific commands. During this phase, the SSL truststore and keystore are defined, together with the respective passwords.

Finally, once the broker is configured, Kafka clients have to be configured in order to communicate in a secure way with the broker.

- **Kafka Access Control List.** The Kafka Broker is configured to check client authorizations by means of an ACL. Kafka provides an ACL for each topic, allowing or denying Agents to perform operations on it. ACLs are handled by an "Authorizer", which is a server plugin used by Kafka to authorize operations. More specifically, the Authorizer controls whether to authorize an operation based on the identity and the resource being accessed. This ACL can be controlled by the Security Controller in order to express security policies at Kafka, thus confining the allowed operations for each Agent. The designed ACL works as a table of rules. Each rule is composed by the client identity written in its TLS certificate. Furthermore, the rule has a validity in time, for which, once it expires, the ACL denies any further communication with the Kafka client. Each client is authorized to perform a certain operation, i.e., read or write, on a determined topic of interest.

The Security Mechanism for the Protection of the External Components

Figure 13 is of great help to have a precise idea of the sequence of steps needed to describe the proposed security mechanism. More specifically, the procedure consists of the following phases:

1. **Enrollment Procedure.** The Enrollment Procedure is illustrated as *Step 0* in Fig. 13. The GUARD's trusted CA enrolls both the CB-Manager and LCPs by providing them a unique public identity encoded in X.509 format. This grants the possibility to mutually authenticate the exchange of the information between the CB-Manager and each LCP at *Step 4* and secure the communications between Agents and Kafka at *Step 6* of Fig. 13.

2. **Client Authentication.** Client Authentication is represented in *Step 1* and *Step 2* of Fig. 13. The entities involved in this phase are the GUARD client and the IdP. The GUARD clients can be of different kinds: they could be GUARD components (like the Dashboard depicted in Fig. 13) or human operators of the GUARD Platform. The client initiates the authentication procedure by contacting the IdP through its Authentication Endpoint. Once authenticated, the IdP returns a JWT with attributes characterizing that user for ABAC-based service authorization.

3. **Service Request and Response Mechanism.** Once the client is authenticated, each subsequent request to GUARD services and resources includes the JWT. Steps 3–7 of Fig. 13 show the sequence of operations executed to request and obtain a service. More specifically, in *Step 3* the client generates the security pipeline and appends the JWT obtained in the authentication process. This request is sent to the Security Controller, which ensures that the correct ACL policies (*Step 4*) are setup for Kafka messaging, and then forwards

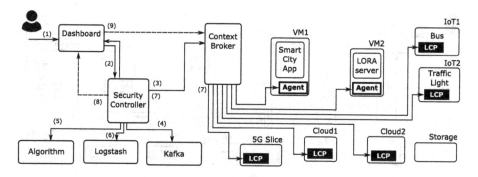

Fig. 14. Workflow for activation of a new security analytics pipeline.

the request to the CB-Manager. In *Step 5*, the CB-Manager is connected to the LCP through mutually-authenticated TLS connection. By leveraging the TLS session and its security services, the CB-Manager forwards the request to the LCP. The LCP has an authorization module that verifies the JWT validity and signature with the public keys of the IdP. If the token signature is correct, the authorization module then proceeds to decode user attributes and use them to detect if the request is valid and authorized for such service operations. These authorization procedures are performed by the LCP. If the request is legit and the user has a valid JWT with the right permissions, the LCP forwards the request to the appropriate Agent (*Step 5*). Finally, in *Step 6* the Agent produces the response and sends it to the Kafka Broker using mutual-authenticated TLS connection.

5.3 Workflows

There are two major workflows implemented by the GUARD Platform, one for creating new SAPs and one for response and mitigation.

Figure 14 shows the workflow for creating a new security analytics pipeline, with reference to the Smart City service illustrated in Sect. 1. The process is initiated by the Dashboard and then carried out by the SC, and consists of the following steps:

1. The user designs a security processing pipeline, by connecting data sources (security agents) with producers (algorithms). The process includes the configuration of both sources and algorithms, as well as the definition of control and reaction policies, as described in Sect. 4.4. The SAP is assigned a unique identifier and the Dashboard stores the SAP information centrally in the CB-Manager.
2. The SAP is encoded in a JSON message and sent to the SC using the REST interface available between the SC and the Dashboard.
3. The SC retrieves from the CB-Manager any necessary information that is referenced in the SAP (e.g., location and parameters of the algorithms, credentials).

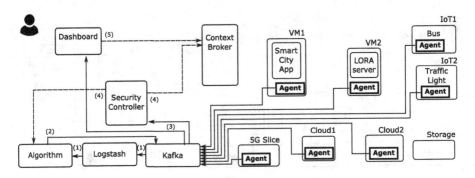

Fig. 15. Workflow for mitigation and reaction.

4. The SC creates a Kafka topic which will be dedicated to deliver data from sources to algorithms.
5. The SC configures and starts the requested algorithm, according to the message from the dashboard. In our implementation, we use a simple REST interface with a few commands to load one or more configuration files and start/stop the algorithm. This should cover a broad range of existing algorithms.
6. The SC downloads, installs, and configures any Logstash plugin which is required to run in the centralized platform. Currently, this step is not implemented yet.
7. The SC configures remote agents through the CB-Manager. The configuration received by the Dashboard is extended to include any necessary transformation and delivery task (currently, this is limited to the automatic generation and configuration of a dedicated Kafka topic). At this point, data are expected to start flowing through the pipeline. The SC also install all control policies included in the pipeline description, which describes what actions should be undertaken under the occurrence of specific events in given conditions. Finally, once the SAP has started correctly, the SC informs the success of the action to the Dashboard using the REST interface. The Dashboard stores both the descriptive template and the configuration of the actual instance of the security pipeline in the Context Broker, with the unique identifier assigned by the Dashboard.
8. Any error that may occur during the configuration process is reported to the dashboard, to inform the security operator that the process did not start.
9. After the security processing pipeline is operational, the security operator can retrieve its description from the CB-Manager, visualize it, and modify some parameters (e.g., frequency of collection, Logstash plugins, etc.). In this case, the dashboard retrieves the configuration of the active SAPs from the Context Broker.

Following its activation, the SAP becomes operational. A closed-loop control workflow is therefore implemented that takes decision based on the evolving context, according to the following steps (see Fig. 15):

1. Data starts flowing from configured agents to the intended algorithm.
2. When the algorithm detects something (attack, anomaly), it reports the information on a specific notification topic on the Kafka bus.
3. All messages published on Kafka (both data from agents and events from algorithms) are available to the SC and the Dashboard; in addition, they are stored in Elasticsearch for offline analytics.
4. Messages published in Kafka topics subscribed by the SC during SAP initialization (step 7 of the activation workflow) triggers the execution of the corresponding security policies. The Security Controller re-evaluate all the rules and tries to satisfy them. The result is usually an action of this kind:
   (a) re-configuration of one or more agents (to apply enforcement actions or to change some detection tasks);
   (b) re-configuration of the detection algorithm, in case for instance an early alarm would trigger more specific investigation.
5. (Optional) Similar reaction operations can be undertaken by the Security Operator through the dashboard, in case there are no suitable policy to handle the event.

6   Validation and Performance Analysis

We conducted validation and performance analysis to investigate the efficiency of both the data handling pipeline and control plane of the proposed framework. We mostly focused on virtualized environments, which are largely used for the implementation of digital services.

6.1   Data Handling Pipeline

When digital services are monitored remotely, the most critical part of the data handling pipeline is represented by the segment upstream the Kafka bus, involving the security agents and transmission over the Internet. We set up an experimental testbed with considered two pipelines: an Apache web server (monitored by Filebeat) and a MySQL database server (monitored by Metricbeat). Additionally, we consider a Logstash instance for data enrichment and transformation. Both the main service and the corresponding agents are standalone containers that run in the same pod. In case of Filebeat, the agent periodically scans the logs generated by Apache and checks for new records to be sent to the CB-Manager. In our testbed, Logstash adds a timestamp to each log records, and this implies more processing in case of larger workload.

All pods are deployed in a local testbed, made of 3 Kubernetes nodes equipped with 2x Intel Xeon CPU E5-2660 v4 @ 2.00 GHz with 14 cores and hyperthreading enabled, 128 GB RAM, 64 GB SSD storage. The local connection is a plain 1 Gbps Ethernet. We used the default configuration for all containers (1 vCPU, 250 MB RAM).

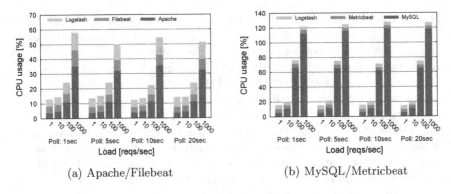

(a) Apache/Filebeat   (b) MySQL/Metricbeat

Fig. 16. Cumulative CPU usage by all containers in the same pod.

The evaluation was conducted by varying the following parameters:

- the *period of collection*, which affects the latency to access the context and in some cases the volume of traffic generated over the network (for Metricbeat, because it reports the current status at each request), from 1 to 20 seconds;
- the *rate of requests* to the Apache and MySQL servers, which in some cases increase the volume of logs generated (Apache function, which records every access), from 1 to 1000 requests/s. We used jmeter[2] and mysqlslap[3] to generate a variable amount of requests for Apache and MySQL, respectively.

We initially consider the impact of security agents on the main business logic (namely Apache/MySQL). Figure 16 shows that the overhead of the agents is rather limited (below 10% of the available CPU) in all conditions but for the largest number of requests. Indeed, the relative impact on MySQL is much lower, especially at high-load because this application uses more CPU cycles. We conclude that the impact of agents remains quite limited (below 10%), which is acceptable in most practical cases. By comparing Filebeat and Logstash, we conclude that the latter has a higher overhead, even in case of simple operations (i.e. timestamping).

Memory allocation of the security components has a large impact on the main business logic, especially due to Logstash, as shown in Fig. 17. Our understanding is that the current implementation of Logstash is not suitable for lightweight operation in cloud-native applications, because its memory footprint is often bigger than the main application. In general, it would be preferable to directly write to the Kafka bus with Filebeat, if additional transformation operations are not strictly necessary.

Finally, we consider the delay introduced along the pipeline, up to the Logstash instance deployed in the GUARD Platform.

Figure 18(a) shows the latency to gather data from the Apache log file by Filebeat, to move data from the Filebeat to the local Logstash instance, and to

---

[2] https://jmeter.apache.org/.
[3] https://mariadb.com/kb/en/mysqlslap/.

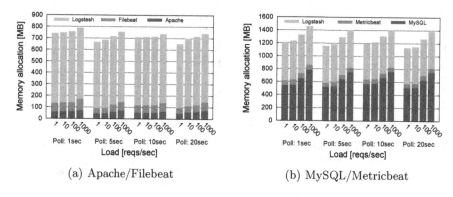

Fig. 17. Cumulative memory allocation for the pod.

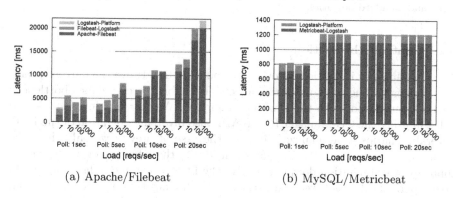

Fig. 18. Cumulative latency for the pipeline up to Logstash instance in the GUARD Platform.

transfer data to the GUARD Platform. The latency is generally shorter than a few seconds, and it is mostly affected by longer polling intervals. Indeed, there are two main consequences when varying the parameters under investigation. On the one hand, higher workloads result in more lines in the log file, hence bigger messages to be sent. On the other hand, longer sample times also result in more data lines and, most of all, in larger delay in the delivery of older lines. The second effect is predominant, since the transmission of larger packets does not affect significantly the latency with high-speed links.

Similarly, Fig. 18(b) shows the latency to move data from Metricbeat to Logstash and to transfer data to the GUARD Platform. The latency is generally around one second, and this time does not increase with the workload or the polling interval. The reason is that the same amount of information is collected in this situation (metrics), independently of the workload and polling interval. In any case, we note that a greater latency in data collection is not a specific performance limitation of the agents, but it may have side effects on the timely of the detection. The polling interval must therefore be selected case-by-case depending on the specific needs of the detection process.

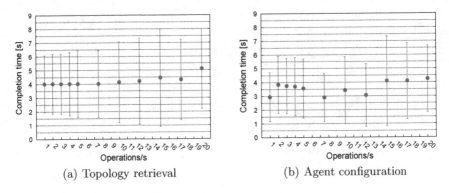

(a) Topology retrieval　　　　　　　(b) Agent configuration

Fig. 19. Latency of common operations on the CB-Manager. The picture shows mean value and standard deviation.

6.2 Control Abstraction

The CB-Manager is queried by other components to retrieve the current topology and change the configuration of agents. Therefore, it represents a bottleneck for the operation of both the Dashboard and SC. We therefore investigated the delay in using the CB-Manager REST API, also involving operation of the LCP. Several scenarios were analyzed, but for the sake of brevity we only show the results for two of them. We therefore consider i) the latency to get the service topology (this operation does not involve the LCP, because the discovery workflow is performed with lower frequency); ii) the latency to configure and start an agent (which is the common part to the activation and reaction workflows). Both operations are made of multiple HTTP requests (12 for getting the topology and 10 for configuring the agent) and corresponding responses from the CB-Manager.

The evaluation was done using Apache JMeter, to generate a variable load of operations per seconds, from 1 to 20. Figure 19 shows that it takes on average a few seconds to complete an operation with the CB-Manager. In case of topology retrieval, there is slight increment of the latency with more concurrent operations per second; the trend is less clear for the other scenario. Overall, the latency is quite good for control and management purposes.

7 Conclusion

In this Chapter we have described the GUARD architecture to create detection and analytics pipelines for multi-domain distributed digital service chains. Our implementation demonstrate the feasibility of the overall concept, by providing the necessary interfaces and authentication and authorization mechanisms to perform monitoring and inspection tasks in Third Party's digital resources. We have also demonstrated that common agents entail a low overhead in the execution of the main business logic, so their implementation does not lead to major costs for resource providers.

Future work will be addressed to investigate monitoring and inspection mechanisms that fit modern computing paradigms. Indeed, we argue that the implementation and proper isolation of local security agents remains a responsibility of Resource Provider, which must guarantee this does not turn into a security vulnerability. Additionally, PaaS and serverless environments are challenging to be monitored by legacy agents and tools. Our work will focus on the possibility to create monitoring and inspection tasks at run-time, by leverage the concept of code augmentation in a safe way.

Acknowledgment. This work was supported in part by the European Commission under Grant Agreement no. 833456 (GUARD).

References

1. Open command and control (OpenC2). OASIS standard, language Specification Version 1.0, Committee Specification 02, November 2019
2. Alt, F., Zezschwitz, E.: Emerging trends in usable security and privacy. J. Interact. Media **18**(3), 189–195 (2019)
3. Bienias, P., Kołaczek, G., Warzyński, A.: Architecture of anomaly detection module for the security operations center. In: IEEE 28th International Conference on Enabling Technologies: Infrastructure for Collaborative Enterprises (WETICE), Napoli, Italy, 12th–14th Jun 2019 (2019)
4. Bierman, A., Bjorklund, M., Watsen, K.: RESTCONF protocol. RFC 8040, January 2017. https://tools.ietf.org/html/rfc8040
5. Bjorklund, M.: YANG - a data modeling language for the network configuration protocol (NETCONF). RFC 6020, October 2010
6. Bjorklund, M., Schoenwaelder, J., Bierman, A.: Network configuration protocol (NETCONF). RFC 6241, June 2011. https://tools.ietf.org/html/rfc6241
7. Bringhenti, D., Marchetto, G., Sisto, R., Valenza, F., Yusupov, J.: Towards a fully automated and optimized network security functions orchestration. In: 4th International Conference on Computing, Communications and Security (ICCCS), Rome, Italy, 10th–12th October 2019 (2019)
8. Caviglione, L., Mazurczyk, W., Repetto, M., Schaffhauser, A., Zuppelli, M.: Kernel-level tracing for detecting stegomalware and covert channels in linux environments. Comput. Netw. **191**, 108010 (2021)
9. Chamiekara, G.W.P., Cooray, M.I.M., Wickramasinghe, L.S.A.M., Koshila, Y.M.S., Abeywardhana, K.Y., Senarathna, A.N.: AutoSOC: a low budget flexible security operations platform for enterprises and organizations. In: National Information Technology Conference (NITC), Colombo, Sri Lanka, 14th–15th September 2017, pp. 100–105 (2017)
10. Elsayed, M.A., Zulkernine, M.: Towards security monitoring for cloud analytic applications. In: IEEE 4th International Conference on Big Data Security on Cloud (BigDataSecurity), Omaha, NE, USA, 3rd–5th May 2018, pp. 69–78 (2018)
11. Elsayed, M.A., Zulkernine, M.: PredictDeep: security analytics as a service for anomaly detection and prediction. IEEE Access **8**, 45184–45197 (2020)
12. Hardt, D.: The OAuth 2.0 authorization framework. RFC 6749, October 2012. https://www.rfc-editor.org/rfc/rfc6749.txt

13. Hares, S., Lopez, D., Zarny, M., Jacquenet, C., Kumar, R., Jeong, J.: Interface to network security functions (I2NSF): problem statement and use cases. IETF RFC 8192, July 2017. https://www.rfc-editor.org/rfc/pdfrfc/rfc8192.txt.pdf

14. Hu, V., et al.: Guide to Attribute Based Access Control (ABAC) Definition and Considerations. Special Publication (NIST SP) 800-162, National Institute of Standards and Technology (NIST) (2019)

15. Jones, M., Bradley, J., Sakimura, N.: JSON Web Token (JWT). RFC 7519, May 2015

16. Lang, B., Wang, J., Liu, Y.: Achieving flexible and self-contained data protection in cloud computing. IEEE Access **5**, 1510–1523 (2017)

17. Laue, T., Kleiner, C., Detken, K.O., Klecker, T.: A SIEM architecture for multidimensional anomaly detection. In: 11th IEEE International Conference on Intelligent Data Acquisition and Advanced Computing Systems: Technology and Applications, Cracow, Poland, 22nd–25th September 2021, pp. 136–142 (2021)

18. Lin, H., Yan, Z., Chen, Y., Zhang, L.: A survey on network security-related data collection technologies. IEEE Access **6**, 18345–18365 (2018)

19. Lopez, D., Lopez, E., Dunbar, L., Strassner, J., Kumar, R.: Framework for interface to network security functions. IETF RFC 8329, February 2018. https://tools.ietf.org/pdf/rfc8329

20. Lynch, L.: Inside the identity management game. IEEE Internet Comput. **15**(5), 78–82 (2011)

21. Nespoli, P., Papamartzivanos, D., Marmol, F.G., Kambourakis, G.: Optimal countermeasures selection against cyber attacks: a comprehensive survey on reaction frameworks. IEEE Commun. Surv. Tutor. **20**(2), 1361–1396 (2018)

22. Open command and control (OpenC2) profile for stateless packet filtering, version 1.0, Committee Specification 01, July 2019

23. Repetto, M., Carrega, A., Duzha, A.: A novel cyber-security framework leveraging programmable capabilities in digital services. In: Proceedings of the Fourth Italian Conference on CyberSecurity (ITASEC20), Ancona, Italy, 4th–7th February 2020, pp. 201–211 (2020)

24. Repetto, M., Carrega, A., Rapuzzi, R.: An architecture to manage security operations for digital service chains. Futur. Gener. Comput. Syst. **115**, 251–266 (2021)

25. Repetto, M., Striccoli, D., Piro, G., Carrega, A., Boggia, G., Bolla, R.: An autonomous cybersecurity framework for next-generation digital service chains. J. Netw. Syst. Manag. **29**(37) (2021)

26. Sage, A., Cuppan, C.: On the systems engineering and management of systems of systems and federations of systems. Inf. Knowl. Syst. Manag. **2**(4), 325–345 (2001)

27. Shehab, M., Marouf, S.: Recommendation models for open authorization. IEEE Trans. Dependable Secure Comput. **9**(4), 583–596 (2012)

28. Vapen, A., Carlsson, N., Mahanti, A., Shahmehri, N.: A look at the third-party identity management landscape. IEEE Internet Comput. **20**(2), 18–25 (2016)

29. Weiser, M.: The computer for the 21st century. Sci. Am. **265**(3), 94–105 (1991)

30. Yang, J., Jeong, J.: An automata-based security policy translation for network security functions. In: International Conference on Information and Communication Technology Convergence (ICTC), Jeju, South Korea, 17th–19th October 2018, pp. 268–272 (2018)

31. Zuech, R., Khoshgoftaar, T.M., Wald, R.: Intrusion detection and big heterogeneous data: a survey. J. Big Data **2**, 3 (2015)

Monitoring Network Flows
in Containerized Environments

Matteo Repetto[1]([⊠])[iD] and Alessandro Carrega[2][iD]

[1] Institute for Applied Mathematics and Information Technologies (IMATI),
CNR, Genoa, Italy
matteo.repetto@ge.imati.cnr.it
[2] S2N National Lab, CNIT, Genoa, Italy
alessandro.carrega@cnit.it

Abstract. With the progressive implementation of digital services over virtualized infrastructures and smart devices, the inspection of network traffic becomes more challenging than ever, because of the difficulty to run legacy cybersecurity tools in novel cloud models and computing paradigms. The main issues concern i) the portability of the service across heterogeneous public and private infrastructures, that usually lack hardware and software acceleration for efficient packet processing, and ii) the difficulty to integrate monolithic appliances in modular and agile containerized environments.

In this Chapter, we investigate the usage of the extended Berkeley Packet Filter (eBPF) for effective and efficient packet inspection in virtualized environments. Our preliminary implementation demonstrates that we can achieve the same performance as well-known packet inspection tools, but with far less resource consumption. This motivates further research work to extend the capability of our framework and to integrate it in Kubernetes.

Keywords: Network flow monitoring · Cloud computing · eBPF · Cloud-native applications

1 Introduction

With the growing adoption of cloud technologies and Internet of Things (IoT) in the implementation of digital services, monitoring and inspection tasks for security purposes are becoming more challenging, because legacy cybersecurity appliances might not be straightforward to deploy and operate in these environments. Typical issues include limited computing and memory resources, unavailability of software and hardware acceleration frameworks, heterogeneity of the execution environments, and cloud-native software paradigms. For instance, in a Kubernetes environment, monitoring files in a different container of the same pod is tricky, and becomes unfeasible in different pods. Similarly, the networking model is based on a mesh pattern instead of common bus, and the implementation of the Container Network Interface (CNI) [8,14] does not allow to inspect all the traffic from a single location.

J. Kołodziej et al. (Eds.): Cybersecurity of Digital Service Chains, LNCS 13300, pp. 32–55, 2022.
https://doi.org/10.1007/978-3-031-04036-8_2

Packet inspection is a typical problem in the domain of cybersecurity, although it is really challenging in high-speed networks. To overcome this issue, hardware and software acceleration is often used, together with sampling techniques to monitor network packets at line speed, but these artifacts are usually unavailable in cloud infrastructures and IoT devices. Moreover, they usually provide many monitoring, inspection, and transformation features, resulting in a non-negligible resource footprint. This overhead is perfectly acceptable for monitoring big infrastructures for a large number of threats, but it becomes unnecessarily overwhelming when the analysis is restricted to threats for a specific service. This is the case, for instance, of the collection of basic features to apply Machine Learning algorithms [16].

We believe that recent advances in code augmentation techniques for the Linux kernel, represented by the enhanced Berkeley Packet Filter (eBPF), have a great potential to create packet inspection processes for cloud native applications that are efficient, portable across infrastructures, and programmable. In this respect, we investigated the feasibility and performance of implementing network flow monitoring with eBPF in virtualized services. For this purpose, we designed bpfFlowMon, a simple tool that collects common statistics that are necessary for flow analysis. The preliminary implementation considers the most common use-cases, by parsing IPv4/6, ICMP, TCP, and UDP headers; future releases will support additional protocols and will provide native integration with Kubernetes. Our work represents a valuable contribution to the implementation of security agents for the GUARD framework, since bpfFlowMon fits containerized and serverless computing environments better than existing tools while basically providing the same set of information elements (namely, traffic characteristics and measures). This extends the scope of detection services that make use of traffic features, for instance the MLDDoS detector [16].

Our approach only leverages the eBPF technology which is already built-in in any recent Linux kernel (4.19 and 5.x), which is the common options for all installations. This ensures predictable performance in environments provided by different providers, hence giving more freedom in the deployment and migration processes. We carried out extensive performance evaluation of our tool, and compared it with well-known appliances, namely nProbe and Zeek. Our evaluation shows that CPU usage and memory footprint of our implementation are almost one order of magnitude lower than the selected alternatives, while reporting the same level of information.

The rest of the Chapter is organized as follows. We provide a brief understanding of the flow monitoring problem in Sect. 2, including the tools taken for reference and the usage of eBPF for monitoring and inspection. Then, we describe the bpfFlowMon tool in Sect. 3 and report performance evaluation and comparison in Sect. 4. We also discuss the limitations and open issues of our approach in Sect. 5. We also provide a short survey of the current scientific literature about the usage of eBPF-based tools for security purposes in Sect. 6. Finally, we give our conclusion in Sect. 7, which includes the road away.

2 Flow Monitoring

Flow monitoring provides a high-level view on network traffic, by grouping packets into logical communications (i.e., "flows"), which can be used for management, debugging, and security purposes of both local and wide area packet networks. Packets can be mapped to flows according to many characteristics (e.g., field values in protocol headers, ingress/egress interface, next hop - see RFC 3954 and 3917 [3,15]); a very common approach is the identification of flows based on the network and transport endpoints, namely the 5-tuple composed of source network address, destination network address, protocol, source transport port, and destination transport port. For each flow, aggregate statistics are measured, as total number of bytes/packets exchanged, average rate of bytes/packets, duration of the flow, average latency and jitter, relevant flags and field values seen.

Despite the relative simplicity of this definition, tracking network flows is a cumbersome process because all packets must be parsed in order to extract the relevant fields and to detect the begin/end of the flow. In fact, performing this operation at line speed is extremely challenging especially in case of small packets and link rates of 10 Gbps and above. For this reason, typical implementations usually rely on dedicated hardware, sometimes integrated in the same network devices; in addition, sampling is often used in network equipment with fast interfaces (usually above 1 Gbps). Flow monitoring appliances can directly visualize data to users or forward it to remote processes, where further processing may occur; in this second case, there are specific protocols to exchange this information (NetFlow [3], IPFix [4], sFlow [13]).

2.1 Existing Tools and Limitations

There are different tools available for packet inspection and flow analysis. Some of them mostly work as "simple" network probes that just collect the necessary measures and make them available for further processing, either locally or to a remote location. Besides proprietary implementations in network equipment, nProbe[1] is a pure software flow exporter compatible with NetFlow/IPFIX. It has Deep Packet Inspection (DPI) capabilities and support for over 250 applications; however, the set of measurements and data that can be collected are hard-coded in the application and cannot be extended for specific needs. Unfortunately, nProbe is not open-source, even if there is a free version with some limitations on capabilities and usage.

Other tools provide a complete framework for flow and packet analysis. Zeek[2] (formerly Bro) is fully open-source and it provides a flexible framework that is easy to extend by a scripting language. Zeek does not export flow descriptors, but it only creates compact transaction logs, file content, and fully customized output, suitable for manual review analyses by a Security and Information Event Management (SIEM) system.

---

[1] https://www.ntop.org/products/netflow/nprobe/.

[2] https://zeek.org/.

Packet processing at line rate is a challenging task, especially on general-purpose hardware, because of the delay introduced by packet copies, interrupt handling and context switches. Many monitoring tools improve their efficiency by using software acceleration frameworks that bypass the built-in kernel networking stack and give direct access to hardware queues (e.g., PF_RING, Netmap, DPDK, OpenOnLoad). Both nProbe and Zeek, for instance, use PF_RING to increase performance. Unfortunately, all these technologies are not par of vanilla kernel releases and require modification of the running kernel; therefore, both the availability and the effectiveness of such technologies in virtualized environments is questionable, especially in the case of public infrastructures.

Even if the volume of traffic within a virtualized service could be processed without acceleration frameworks, the deployment of traditional network monitoring appliances might not be efficient or straightforward, especially in container runtime environments, where they should be deployed in every pod for ensuring full visibility. In such scenarios, it is important to reduce as much as possible resource consumption (CPU, memory and storage), to make the deployment process faster and to decrease the cost in case public cloud infrastructures are used.

2.2   The Extended Berkeley Packet Filter

Monitoring the behavior of an Operating System and its applications has always been a hot topic both for performance and security reasons. User-space applications can easily monitor the integrity of files, the behavior of the system users and other applications (by looking at logs). However, support from the kernel is necessary to gain visibility over its operation, including the processing of network packets and the execution of system calls and other internal functions. Kernel monitoring has been based for long on third-party extensions; unfortunately, this approach requires notable effort to update and re-compile additional modules every time the kernel changes, not to mention the difficulty to support many different kernel versions and the risk of introducing instability.

The extended Berkeley Packet Filter (eBPF) was introduced as a flexible and *programmable* mechanism to monitor kernel activity. It extends the scope of original BPF (sometimes denoted as "classical" BPF – cBPF) from network packets to software functions as well, by introducing a common interface to easily access multiple kernel subsystems. Its implementation consists of an embedded virtual machine that executes a specific set of instructions, which scope is deliberately restricted to avoid harming the kernel itself. eBPF gives access to multiple data sources present in the kernel, by attaching eBPF programs to "probes" (kprobes, uprobes) and "tracepoints" (USDT,[3] kernel tracepoints, lttng-ust[4]), as well as to "network hooks" (XDP,[5] TC[6]). Differently from other tools that use the same

---

[3] Userland Statically Defined Tracing.
[4] Linux Trace Toolkit Next Generation Userspace Tracer.
[5] eXpress Data Path.
[6] Traffic Control.

hooks (e.g. LTTng or SystemTap), a key added-value of eBPF is that it does not require any additional kernel modules. This allows augmenting the running kernel with custom code in a safe way, without the need to load additional modules or to recompile the whole kernel.

The execution of eBPF programs is triggered by specific events of each hook (i.e., the reception of a network packet for XDP/TC, the invocation of a function for other software probes) and their size is limited to a few instructions for safety and performance reasons. As a matter of fact, they are only expected to collect raw measurements and events, as well as to perform enforcement actions. Such data can be stored in shared data structures (*maps*) between the kernel and the user-space; further processing and delivery to intended recipients can therefore be implemented more effectively in userland applications. For more complex tasks, which exceed the limit of the stack size, a *tail call* mechanism is available that allows to chain multiple programs while sharing the context, in order to perform the task in multiple stages. Interestingly, eBPF can trace kernel functions but cannot drop their execution, whereas this is instead possible for network packets.

A development toolchain is available that allows writing programs in C code, which are then compiled into the eBPF assembly. Programs are then verified and compiled into bytecode only at loading time, to ensure that they are loop-free and do not access data outside of their boundary. Developing eBPF applications is not trivial for beginners, but common operations are available through more user-friendly frontends, like the BPF Compiler Collection (BCC[7]) and the bpftrace interpreter.[8]

2.3   eBPF for Monitoring, Inspection, and Enforcement

Though it was originally conceived for investigating performance issues, eBPF is also valuable for security monitoring, network filtering and for tracing, profiling, and debugging the software (see the related work discussed in Sect. 6). Many commercial and open-source frameworks have already integrated eBPF, including Suricata,[9] Sysdig Falco.[10]

eBPF programs can also be used to better support the integration of security features in containers. For observability, ntop and InfluxData have partnered to offer eBPF monitoring for containers, while Netdata is offering out-of-the-box eBPF monitoring for system and application monitoring.[11] Differently from these frameworks that focus on observability, Cilium[12] uses eBPF to provide secure network connectivity and load balancing, leveraging the ability of eBPF to filter and drop packets based on rules. Kubectl-trace is a Kubernetes command line

---

[7] https://github.com/iovisor/bcc.

[8] https://github.com/iovisor/bpftrace.

[9] https://suricata.readthedocs.io/en/latest/capture-hardware/ebpf-xdp.html.

[10] https://sysdig.com/blog/sysdig-and-falco-now-powered-by-ebpf/.

[11] https://containerjournal.com/topics/container-management/using-ebpf-monitoring-to-know-what-to-measure-and-why/.

[12] https://cilium.io/.

front end for running bpftrace across worker machines in Kubernetes cluster. However, to the best of our knowledge, there is no solution yet to activate metric capturing during the deployment of a containerized application with Kubernetes or equivalent [2].

3   A New Flow Monitoring Tool: bpfFlowMon

To investigate the feasibility, limitations, and performance of monitoring network flows by eBPF, we implemented a tool named bpfFlowMon[13] composed of the following components:

- an eBPF *Flow Inspector* for the TC hook (namely, the queue management system associated to each network interface), which builds a raw table of unidirectional flows seen in a specific direction (either ingress or egress);
- a userland *Flow Handling* application that periodically scans the raw flow table, merges and removes unidirectional flows belonging to the same conversation once terminated, and exports them.

Additionally, a *Flow Management* daemon is also present for loading/unloading the eBPF and userland programs. The logical separation between packet inspection and flow handling perfectly fits the design pattern for eBPF programs, leading to an efficient approach. The overall structure of our eBPF-based flow monitoring implementation is sketched in Fig. 1.

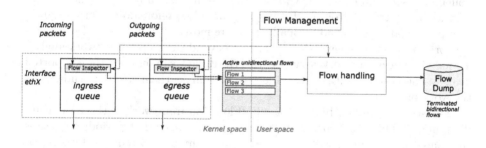

Fig. 1. Software architecture of bpfFlowMon.

The implementation of the Flow Inspector is rather simple, according to the specific nature of eBPF programs. It is basically a parser of network packets, from Ethernet up to TCP/UDP headers. As already noted beforehand, this preliminary implementation was mostly conceived for performance investigation, so the support for additional protocols and deep-packet inspection is left for future extensions. Unfortunately, the code for parsing Ethernet/IP/TCP/UDP headers already consumes all of the small stack available to eBPF programs, and

---

[13] https://github.com/mattereppe/bpf_flowmon.

this does not include all possible options. Future extensions must address this issue, for example by decomposing the Flow Inspector into different programs for each protocol, and by chaining them with the *tail call* mechanism. Since the number of stacked protocols for each packet is rather limited, this approach should not increase significantly the processing delay. An alternative approach could be to forward the relevant header portion to the userspace, and to parse there the fields, similarly to what happens in the Zeek framework. This would bring more flexibility in defining parsing and aggregation tasks, but would likely increase resource usage, as shown for Zeek in Sect. 4.2.

The Flow Monitoring program follows common practice for flow analysis. Each flow is identified by the 5-tuple $<src\_ip\_addr,\ dst\_ip\_addr,\ proto,\ src\_port,\ dst\_port>$, where the last two parameters are only present where applicable.[14] We point out that this definition identifies "unidirectional" flows; in general, for each *forward-direction* flow $<addr1,\ addr2,\ proto,\ port1,\ port2>$ there will always be a *backward-direction* flow $<addr2,\ addr1,\ proto,\ port2,\ port1>$ with IP addresses and protocol ports inverted. To keep the implementation simpler, our eBPF program identifies unidirectional flows and stores them in a shared map, but does not merge them. Indeed, looking for a complementary flow at each packet reception would unnecessarily waste time and CPU cycles, because this aggregation is not requested for the computation of any metric.

For each flow, both its identifier and a relevant set of measurements are stored in the shared map. This set includes all the necessary measurements to derive the same NetFlow/IPFIX flow information elements as nProbe for IP and UDP/TCP fields.[15] Other metadata concerning routing information, BGP domains, inspection engine, DNS resolution are not taken into account because they are not retrieved from packet inspection and therefore do not bring significant performance issues; additionally, they are mostly useful in case of wide-area networks and management issues, which is beyond the scope of network analytics for virtualized network services [16,17]. Table 1 summarizes the supported fields at the time of writing; the objective is to make them easily extendable as the work progresses.

The second building block of the bpfFlowMon framework is the Flow Handling utility. This is a C program running in user-space that periodically scans the shared map of unicast flows, merges them, dumps and removes terminated flows. The usage of the C language instead of the BCC framework is mostly motivated by the need for more efficiency, especially with a large number of flows. This is evident when comparing resource usage given in Sect. 4.2 with similar analysis we did on a BCC tool for the detection of steganographic channels in network headers [21].

As common practice, flows are considered terminated either after explicit messages (FIN or RST flags have been seen for TCP) or an inactivity timeout (which works for both TCP, UDP, and ICMP). The choice of the inactivity

---

[14] The *src_port* field is used with a different meaning for ICMP protocol, to identify the message type.

[15] https://www.ntop.org/guides/nprobe/flow_information_elements.html.

Table 1. Information elements for bpfFlowMon.

Name	Context	Meaning
first_seen	General	Epoch of the first packet of this flow (ns)
last_seen	General	Epoch of the last packet seen so far (ns)
jitter	General	Cumulative delays between packets
pkts	General	Cumulative number of packets
ifindex	General	Capture interface
version	IP	Version (4/6)
tos	IP	TOS/DSCP (IPv4) or Traffic class (IPv6)
fl	IP	Flow label (IPv6)
bytes	IP	Cumulative number of bytes
min_pkt_len	IP	Smallest IP packet seen in the flow
max_pkt_len	IP	Biggest IP packet seen in the flow
pkt_size_hist[6]	IP	[0]: pkts up to 128 bytes; [1]: pkts from 128 to 256 bytes; [2]: pkts from 256 to 512 bytes; [3]: pkts from 512 to 1024 bytes; [4]: pkts from 1024 to 1514 bytes; [5]: pkts over 1514 bytes
min_ttl	IP	Min TTL (IPv4) or Hop limit (IPv6)
max_ttl	IP	Max TTL (IPv4) or Hop limit (IPv6)
pkt_ttl_hist[10]	IP	[0]: pkts with TTL $= 1$; [1]: pkts with TTL > 1 and TTL ≤ 5; [2]: packets with TTL > 5 and ≤ 32; [3]: packets with TTL > 32 and ≤ 64; [4]: packets with TTL > 64 and ≤ 96; [5]: packets with TTL > 96 and ≤ 128; [6]: packets with TTL > 128 and ≤ 160; [7]: packets with TTL > 160 and ≤ 192; [8]: packets with TTL > 192 and ≤ 224; [9]: packets with TTL > 224 and ≤ 255
next_seq	TCP	Last sequence number seen (used for computing retransmissions)
last_id	TCP	Last ipv4 identification value for last_seq
cumulative_flags	TCP	Cumulative TCP flags seen in all packets so far
retr_pkts	TCP	Total number of retransmitted packets
retr_bytes	TCP	Total number of retransmitted bytes
ooo_pkts	TCP	Total number of out-of-order packets
ooo_bytes	TCP	Total number of out-of-order bytes
min_win_bytes	TCP	Min TCP window
max_win_bytes	TCP	Max TCP window
mss	TCP	TCP max segment size
wndw_scale	TCP	TCP window scale

timeout affects the accuracy of flow identification. More in detail, short timeouts may result in the same conversation to be seen as two separate flows; on the other hand, long timeouts may result in more conversations merged into a single flow and delay flow reporting.

When two unidirectional flows are merged together, the result is a full conversation; its forward direction is conventionally assumed by taking the source according to the first packet seen. Informative elements (i.e., measures taken by the eBPF program) are kept separate for the forward and backward direction, since this is a typical requirement from analytics and detection algorithms. This represent an extension with respect to, e.g., nProbe, which only provides aggregate metrics for both directions. The current version dumps flows to text files (or to the standard output), either in plaintext or JSON format.

Finally, there is also a Flow Management component, which takes care of loading the eBPF programs and starting the userland utility. It attaches the eBPF program to the ingress and/or egress queue of one or more interfaces, and configures user-space options (polling parameters, filename and folder for dumping, etc.). The purpose is to support different scenarios, where the virtual function acts either as end node or forwarding device. The current implementation of this component facilitates the integration with SysVinit and Systemd for automatically starting and stopping the whole framework.

4   Evaluation

Evaluation of the proposed approach was carried out by comparing both how accuracy and performance vary with respect to existing tools. In the first case, we investigated if and under what conditions there are deviations in the detected flows with respect to nProbe. In the second case, we compared the maximum transfer rate and the overhead in terms of resource consumption, including both CPU time and memory with respect to i) the baseline scenario (where no monitoring tool is run), ii) to nProbe, and iii) to Zeek.

Since our main application target are virtualized services, we performed our experiments in Virtual Machines (VMs). In this way we can account for any limitations that packet acceleration software experiences in virtualized environments. The next step would be the validation with containers, by transforming the current management script into some Kubernetes artifact (e.g., Daemon-Set[16] or new operator). However, we do not see any reason to expect different performance in a containerized setup.

Evaluation was carried out under the same testbed topology built in an OpenStack installation: one sender that generates packets, one receiver that performs measurements, one intermediate node that runs the flow monitoring tool. Flows were monitored on both interfaces of the intermediate node, which is a typical condition in case multiple interfaces are present. All nodes ran on the

---

[16] A Kubernetes DaemonSet is a resource object that ensures that a given pod is instantiated in each cluster node. See the documentation: https://kubernetes.io/docs/concepts/workloads/controllers/daemonset/.

same hypervisor, 2x Intel Xeon CPU E5-2660 v4@2.00 GHz with 14 cores and hyperthreading enabled, 128 GB RAM, 64 GB SSD storage. The configuration of the three OpenStack servers is reported in Table 2.

For investigating accuracy, we used Pcap traces available from the Internet, which include a mix of ICMP, TCP and UDP traffic. More specifically, we used two network traces of different size designed to test IPFIX/NetFlow, indicated as smallFlows and bigFlows.[17] For performance we generated network packets with iperf3,[18] while varying the main parameters that might affect the inspection process.

Table 2. Configuration of OpenStack servers used for testing.

Node	vCores	vRAM	vStorage
Sender	1	1 GB	16 GB
Receiver	1	1 GB	16 GB
Forwarder	4	2 GB	32 GB

4.1 Accuracy

We define the "accuracy" of a flow monitoring tool as its ability to assign individual packets to the correct flow. This association should not be ambiguous, because it is based on the value of a few header fields. However, wrong classification sometimes occur due to the presence of connectionless protocols without an explicit signaling (UDP, SNMP, ICMP, etc.), abnormal flow termination, as well as delayed or duplicated packets that arrive after the estimated termination of the flow.

We preliminary investigated if and how the flows detected by bpfFlowMon differ from what reported by nProbe. The two tools perform almost the same way, and most differences are only due to different configuration settings. For instance, the flow inactivity timeout, namely the time to wait without seeing any packet before considering the flow closed, largely affects the reporting. With a small value, the risk is that a single flow is seen as two separate flows, when the gap between the transmission of consecutive packets is large enough. On the other hand, with a large value the risk is that two independent flows are seen as the same conversation; however, this is unlikely with TCP, because the end of the connection is also detected by the header flags (both in case of normal closing and aborting/resetting). Besides the inactivity timeout, we also found some differences in the granularity of flows for ICMP and SNMP, the usage of protocol flags and additional header fields to recognize the end of the flow, and the presence of routing options.

---

[17] Both traces are available at https://tcpreplay.appneta.com/wiki/captures.html.
[18] https://iperf.fr/.

In the following, we summarize our main findings in this respect.

ICMP. Notably, bpfFlowMon uses the ICMP Type field as source port (even if this may look like an abuse of the classification), so it distinguishes between different ICMP flows involving the same couple of peers. Instead, nProbe sets both protocol source and destination ports to 0, hence failing to give indication about the type of ICMP messages.

From our experiments, bpfFlowMon successfully correlates ICMP requests with responses, while the same behavior is not guaranteed for nProbe (we observe several cases where two separate flows are reported).[19]

TCP. Resetting a TCP connection might have side effects, because this operation does not usually imply mutual agreement from the peers. The challenging aspect is that multiple reset packets may be sent, in case the remote peer continues to acknowledge previous packets. Under this (not so uncommon) circumstance, nProbe terminates the flow on the first reset, so any following reset/ack packet is accounted as a different flow. Our implementation partially mitigates this problem, because the userland utility only dumps a flow after scanning the map of unidirectional flows, which happens periodically. This way, any additional (re-)transmission in a short timeframe is counted as part of the previous flow.[20] This largely avoids the incorrect reporting of tiny flows with a few ack/reset packets.

In a similar way, it is possible that duplicated packets are received after the exchange of FIN messages, and get counted as different flows. In this case, the problem was observed for bpfFlowMon, due to the fact that the map of active flows was scanned just after the exchange of FIN messages.[21] The problem could be easily solved by waiting for the inactive timeout before purging the flows, but this brings two drawbacks: i) the dumping is delayed (and this may be a problem, if we are trying to identify malicious flows in real-time), and ii) two consecutive flows might be merged together (the split between user and kernel space tasks does not allow to easily take into account the presence of two consecutive flows with the same 5-tuple).

UDP. We didn't observe relevant differences between nProbe and bpfFlowMon for UDP traffic, but we noticed a potential flaw with source routing. As a matter of fact, both nProbe and bpfFlowMon are transparent to the source routing option, so they are somehow cheated because they only see the "inner" intermediate node and not the final destination of the packet. This means that if only

---

[19] This is the case, for instance, for packets numbered 108593 and 108755 (according to Wireshark) in the bigFlows trace.

[20] This happens, for instance, for TCP stream number 19032 (as reported by Wireshark), again from the bigFlows trace.

[21] This was observed for TCP stream number 16749 (as reported by Wireshark), again from the bigFlows trace.

part of packets belonging to the same flow are sent with the loose source routing option, whereas the remaining are not, bpfFlowMon reports two separate flows (and nProbe does the same).[22] This, in some way, affects the statistics of traffic towards given destinations.

In this case, we used a third tool to better investigate this problem, namely tshark, the terminal-based version of Wireshark. Interestingly, this tool is able to parse the full range of options and reports a single flow towards the correct destination, as after all Wireshark does too.

SNMP. We found another unexpected behavior in case of SNMP flows. This time, the oddity was found for tshark, which reported two separate UDP flows for the same SNMP conversation, even if also Wireshark grouped the messages in the same flow.[23] We guess this might be due to some interpretation of the SNMP, but we didn't investigate the issue in detail because deep packet inspection is out of scope for our work and our tool behaves well in this scenario.

4.2   Performance and Overhead

Performance and overhead were investigated by considering both the impact on packet transmission as well as resource consumption. We considered both UDP and TCP flows, by varying the main parameters that are expected to affect packet processing:

– packet size and transmission rate for UDP flows;
– maximum segment size (MSS) for TCP streams.

For packet size, we considered 4 values that are representative of the following cases:

– 16 bytes is the smallest value allowed by iperf, and this is the worst condition for packet forwarding;
– 1470 bytes is representative of the biggest Ethernet packets, also accounting for the presence of tunneling in the underlying virtual network;
– 8192 bytes is the reference size for jumbo frames in Ethernet, which is a common situation in all installations;
– 65507 bytes is the maximum size allowed by UDP and the best condition for packet forwarding, but it is only feasible on loopback interfaces (therefore, it can only be used when VMs are running on the same host).

For the transmission rate, we considered a broad range of different load conditions, from 10 Kbps to the unfeasible (at least for our installation) rate of 10 Gbps. For the MSS, we again selected 4 values that this time are representative

---

[22] This was observed for UDP stream 1164 (according to Wireshark numbering), from the bigFlows trace.

[23] This happens for UDP stream 3604 (again, according to Wireshark numbering), bearing an SNMP conversation from the bigFlows trace.

of: the smallest value accepted by iperf3 (88 bytes), the minimum value that should be used on IP links (536 bytes), the typical value used for Ethernet links (1460 bytes) and jumbo frames (8192 bytes).

For comparison, we took both nProbe and Zeek, briefly introduced in Sect. 2. In addition, we assumed the transmission without flow monitoring tools as the "baseline," which is the best value we can achieve in the target scenario, without the usage of hardware or software accelerators and other modifications of the vanilla OpenStack installation. In case of nProbe, we run the application both with and without PF_RING, to verify software acceleration is ineffective in a standard virtualized setup. Beside that, we note that a single nProbe instance can get packets from multiple interfaces when PF_RING is used; however, two separate instances must be when this module is not used. For completeness, we point out that multiple instances of our eBPF program and Zeek are also run, one for each interface.

To make the comparison fair, we collected the same set of information fields (IP protocol version, IP source and destination addressed, L4 protocol, L4 source and destination ports, flow start/end timestamp, flow duration, forward/backward packets, forward/backward bytes), and we dumped the information to file. Experiments were run for 10 min each, so to mitigate as much as possible interference with other parallel activity, both in the network and within the guest/host systems.

Impact on Packet Transmission. Our analysis focuses on the parameters reported by iperf3, namely the transmission rate, packet error rate and jitter. Figure 2 shows how the measured bitrate at the receiver changes for different settings of packet size and transmission bitrate for UDP flows. There are not meaningful differences between the different mechanisms, even if nProbe with PF_RING performs slightly better in case of bigger packets.

Figure 3 measures the percentage packet loss at the receiver under the same conditions. As expected, packet loss is higher with smaller packet sizes and faster transmission rates. Both bpfFlowMon and nProbe without PF_RING perform almost the same way as the baseline scenario, whereas the behavior of nProbe with PF_RING and Zeek is much more unpredictable. Zeek seems to perform better than other tools almost in all conditions, but it suffers a packet loss close to 100% in case of 65507-byte packets at the fastest transmission rate. We do not have a clear motivation for this anomaly, but for sure it is persistent across many replicas of the experiment.

The last UDP measurement is the average packet jitter, shown in Fig. 4. The variation in the inter-packet delay is negligible for practical applications (below 0.1 ms), and it is likely to be highly affected by external factors (including perturbations in the generator and the receiver). Similarly to previous indexes, there is no tool which wins over all in every condition.

Oddly, in the baseline scenario we achieved worse performance than with flow monitoring, and this is rather unexpected, especially when compared to bpfFlow-Mon and nProbe without PF_RING. We do not think these are measurement

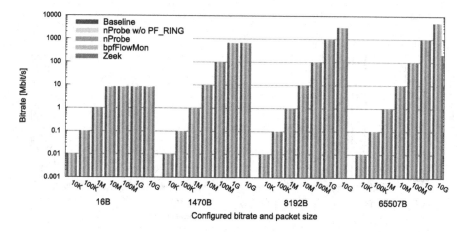

Fig. 2. Measured bitrate at the receiver, while varying packet size and the transmission bitrate for a UDP flow.

errors, since the same behavior is present in all conditions and occurred even when replicating the experiments.

Finally, we show in Fig. 5 the transmission rate achievable by TCP when generating packets for the whole duration of the experiment. Not surprisingly, higher bitrates are possible with larger MSS, because this has a beneficial impact on the TCP flow control mechanism. Again, no meaningful differences are visible between the considered tools, even if in this case the baseline scenario achieves slightly higher bitrate, in line with what expected.

By looking at the performance indexes reported in this Section, we can conclude that our eBPF-based mechanism does not affect packet transmission in a significant way.

CPU Usage. CPU and memory usage are important to understand what is the impact on the operation of other applications. We expect significant differences in the usage of CPU between bpfFlowMon and the other tools, due to the different architectural design. As a matter of fact, Zeek and nProbe are basically user-space applications. The default capture driver for Zeek is libpcap,[24] whereas nProbe builds on the PF_RING module in kernel space, falling back to libpcap if PF_RING is not available. On the other hand, our bpfFlowMon tool leverages in-kernel eBPF programs, hence the usage of CPU from kernel and userspace is expected to be rather different.

This is largely confirmed by the breakdown of CPU usage reported in Figs. 6, 7, 8 and 9 for a UDP flow, with different payload size. Our measurements show much higher CPU usage for user-space (*%user*) in case of nProbe and Zeek, especially for small packet sizes (which is the worst scenario for packet processing),

---

[24] There are alternative capture drivers that can be used with Zeek, including raw sockets, libpcap, and PF_RING. We only considered libpcap in our study.

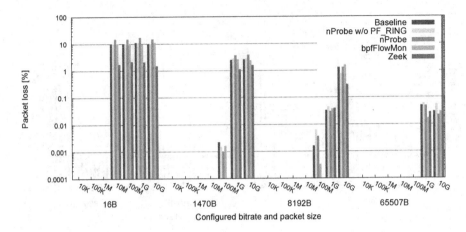

Fig. 3. Measured packet loss at the receiver, while varying packet size and the transmission bitrate for a UDP flow.

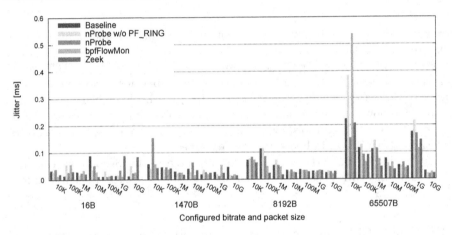

Fig. 4. Measured packet jitter at the receiver, while varying packet size and the transmission bitrate for a UDP flow.

whereas bpfFlowMon always brings a small overhead with respect to the baseline. However, the CPU consumption in user-space is not directly compensated by a corresponding lower kernel usage (% *system*), even in case of low traffic; this can probably be ascribed to the usage of polling in both PF_RING and libpcap. When the traffic increases, the benefit of PF_RING is evident, but the total overhead is still far beyond our eBPF-based tool. Overall, we note that the time spent in other states (%*nice*, %*iowait*, %*steal*) is negligible.

Similar considerations hold in case of TCP, which measurements are shown in Fig. 10.

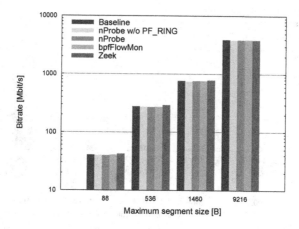

Fig. 5. Measured bitrate at the receiver, while varying the MSS for a TCP flow.

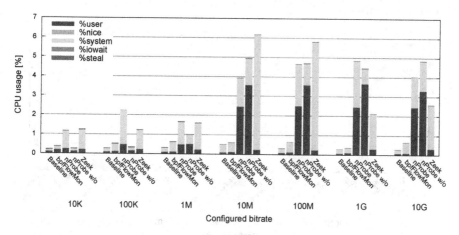

Fig. 6. Cumulative CPU usage measured at the intermediate node for a UDP flow. Payload size is 16 bytes.

Memory Allocation. When comparing the different considered in our investigation, the first thing to consider is the need for additional kernel modules. Indeed, nProbe requires the PF_RING kernel module (which is proprietary and not released as open-source), whereas bpfFlowMon needs the cls_bpf module (which is part of the vanilla kernel); Zeek does not require any kernel extension (even if PF_RING support is available as option). We note that the size of the PF_RING module in our configuration is 737.280 KB, while the cls_bpf is only 24.576 KB.

Going on, the next step is memory consumption in user space (not including, therefore, the kernel modules). We consider the Virtual Memory Size (VMS), the Resident Set Size (RSS), the Proportional Set Size (PSS), and the Anonymous share (Anon). The first corresponds to the overall address space allocated by

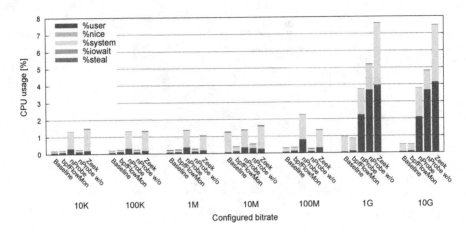

Fig. 7. Cumulative CPU usage measured at the intermediate node for a UDP flow. Payload size is 1470 bytes.

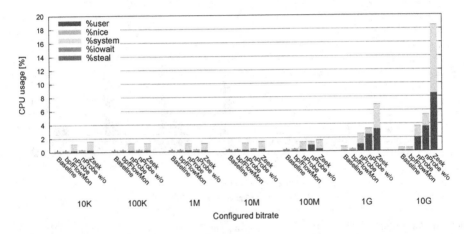

Fig. 8. Cumulative CPU usage measured at the intermediate node for a UDP flow. Payload size is 8192 bytes.

the program, the second is the real size of physical memory allocated (including shared libraries), the third is again the physical memory but with proportional attribution of shared libraries (namely, their memory allocation is divided by the number of programs that use them), and the forth is memory mappings not backed by a file. The amount of memory is further broken down according to the corresponding mapping type (e.g., file, library, stack, heap, process, socket, etc.), to give the more picture of memory usage. Figure 11 shows that Zeek has the largest memory address space (VMS) of all considered tools, even if its real memory usage (RSS) is comparable with nProbe, especially when the latter runs without the PF_RING module. The reason is that nProbe can only monitor one

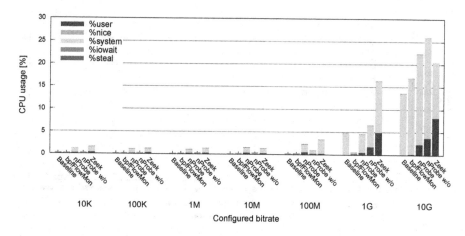

Fig. 9. Cumulative CPU usage measured at the intermediate node for a UDP flow. Payload size is 65507 bytes.

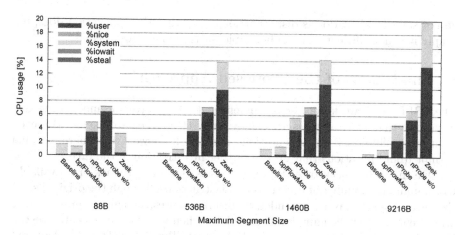

Fig. 10. Cumulative CPU usage measured at the intermediate node, for a TCP flow.

network interface, so to keep the comparison functionally equivalent with the other cases we have to run two parallel instances, one for each interface. This is necessary to see all traffic intended to the host. If additional network interfaces are monitored, the memory usage will scale accordingly. The same issue applies to Zeek: in this case, we do not have to manually start two instances, but they are anyway launched when multiple interfaces are selected in the configuration file. Memory consumption of our tools is negligible with respect to nProbe and Zeek (only a few kilobytes); actually, it cannot even be seen due to the scale of the graph. We remark that the larger memory required by Zeek and nProbe is also due to the many features available in these applications. In general, we

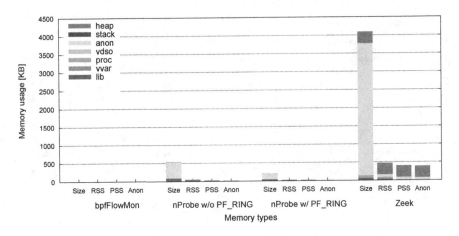

Fig. 11. Memory allocation for the different user-space tools.

do not say this allocation is disproportionate to what the application does, but simply it is not efficient when only simple measurements are needed.

5 Limitations of the Proposed Approach

The eBPF framework represents an efficient alternative for monitoring and inspection than existing tools, especially for virtualized environments. However, both our preliminary implementations and the framework in general are not exempt from limitations that devote further investigation in the future.

One main drawback of eBPF programs is the limited stack size available, which limits the number of functions and instructions. Though the original stack size of 512 bytes may be extended in future releases, parsing several network layers remains a challenging issue, especially when variable options are present. We were able to parse common fields in IPv4/IPv6/UDP/TCP headers, but inspecting all TCP options requires at least to drop support for one IP version. To overcome this limitation, next releases of bpfFlowMon will leverage the *tail call* mechanism, which allows to invoke a chain of eBPF programs. This approach would bring the opportunity for deep packet inspection, and it is also expected to improve the flexibility and composability of the system, as new parsers can be easily added to the base framework.

Another well-known drawback is the eBPF verifier that, on the one hand ensures there are no loops and the program always terminates, but on the other hand still has many limitations, including high rate of false positives, poor scalability, and lack of support for loops [7]. As a matter of fact, the verifier does not scale to programs with a large number of paths, its algorithm is not formally specified, and no formal argument about its correctness is given; as a matter of fact, multiple bugs have been already discovered.[25] Programmers have to "infer"

---

[25] https://www.openwall.com/lists/oss-security/2017/12/21/2.

the way that the verifier performs sanity checks, for their code to be accepted. This is a major problem, because developers often waste a lot of time for this process, e.g., by inserting redundant sanity checks on pointers. This definitely represents a major barrier for quickly extending the framework, especially when parsing headers with a number of variable options. A better verifier, grounded in state-of-the-art verification theory and practice, would enable a wider range of eBPF use cases and would dramatically simplify the development process [7].

6   Related Work

There are several examples in the literature of usage of eBPF technology for monitoring and inspection tasks. One possible application is to augment the context for flow monitoring, by providing additional data that cannot be retrieved in packet headers. Deri et al. [5] note that existing monitoring and tracing tools (Sysdig, Falco, Cilium) mostly lack the ability to match network with system events in order to provide complete visibility both at system and network level, while preventing unwanted network communications to take place similar to what IPSs currently do. Based on this consideration, they extend their existing tool *ntopng* with events generated by *libebpfflow*, a library that enriches network-layer data (e.g. source and destination IP addresses) with system metadata (e.g. source and destination processes and system users). Their objective is to support the definition of custom policies to drop unwanted connections, by affecting the return value of the kernel functions that are used to create network flows. However the Linux kernel supports override returns only on a small group of functions, which does not include the ones concerning network activities. For this reason, the kernel has been patched to enable this mechanism for network communications. A major limitation of this approach is that only local processes and users are visible through eBPF. As a future work, small ePBF probes will be created and disseminated in the network with the aim of circumventing this limitation and have visibility also on remote clients and servers.

A more common application is to improve the efficiency of dropping malicious DoS attacks. eBPF can be used to break up the conventional packet filtering model in Linux, moving the inspection process in the XDP, where ingress traffic can be processed before the allocation of kernel data structures which comes along with performance benefits [10]. This provides a first line of defense against traffic that is in general unwanted by the host, e.g., spoofed addresses or Denial-of-Service flooding attacks [1]. Independent studies have shown that XDP can yield four times the performance in comparison to performing a similar task in the kernel using common packet filtering tools [18], and can be even integrated with existing well-known management interfaces (i.e., iptables) [11]. This approach is made even more interesting given that dedicated platforms for packet filter offloading based on FPGAs like HyPaFilter [6] and hXDP [19] or SmartNICs supporting eBPF [12] have emerged.

In the context of network tracing, Suo et al. [20] propose a framework where a master node translates user inputs into configuration files, eBPF agents are used to monitor network packets of specific connections at given tracepoints (e.g., virtual network interfaces), and measurements are centrally collected and analyzed. vNetTracer supports instrumenting kernel functions, return of kernel functions, kernel tracepoints and raw sockets through kprobe, kretprobe, tracepoints and network devices, hence providing a monitoring tool that works across the boundary of single domains.

Beside parsing and inspection, eBPF has also been used to support the redirection of the traffic to existing monitoring appliances. In [9] the authors propose an eBPF-based implementation for duplicating packets at the OpenvSwitch. They tackle the use case of monitoring the traffic between VMs without specific hardware appliances for duplicating packets. Their analysis shows that duplicating packets with an eBPF program in the TC hook achieves better throughput than native Port Mirroring of OpenvSwitch, especially in case of large packets.

Finally, there are also examples of management systems that are able to deploy eBPF programs and collect measurements, beyond the limited capability of the tools discussed in Sect. 2. Cassagnes et al. [2] designed a system for deploying eBPF programs and collect their measurements in containerized userspace applications. They used tools like Prometheus, Performance Co-Pilot, and Vector, and developed specific eBPF programs and their userland counterparts for monitoring the garbage collector, identifying HTTP traffic, and IP whitelisting. Nevertheless, they are only able to spot local information, and a global end-to-end view on distributed applications is still missing.

7 Conclusion

In this Chapter, we have proposed an alternative approach for network flow monitoring, based on eBPF technology. Our work was mainly motivated by the need for efficient yet effective solutions for virtualized environments, where hardware/software acceleration techniques are not available or largely ineffective, and resource usage is a performance and cost matter.

The extensive performance and functional validation demonstrated that our tool performs as well as other more traditional approaches, but with a far smaller resource utilization footprint. Indeed, almost the same set of information elements is available for L3/L4 headers as state-of-the-art solutions, but with great savings in terms of CPU usage and memory allocation. We do not claim that our bpfFlowMon outperforms nProbe and Zeek, especially in terms of functionality and absolute performance for physical systems. However, we have demonstrated that a more lightweight and portable approach is possible, especially for monitoring the traffic of virtualized applications in public cloud infrastructures.

There are a number of aspects that we are considering as part of our future research work. First of all, the aforementioned architectural change, from one single program to multiple programs linked by the tail call mechanism. This would also simplify the possibility to dynamically create eBPF code based on the required measures, since only the relevant protocols could be included. Second, we are interested in integrating our tool in Kubernetes CNI, likely Calico or Cilium, to demonstrate that it could be used by different users without confidentiality and privacy concerns (i.e., each user should only be able to inspect its own traffic). Third, beyond specific aspects related to the eBPF technology, the current userland utility is rather limited in terms of export interfaces. It only dumps flows to file, both in plaintext and JSON; this can be easily composed with other common agents (FileBeat, Logstash) for sending data to the centralized platform, but it would also increase the overhead. Exporting data directly to Kafka is an additional feature that is worth integrating in the next release. All these extensions would allow to expose the our monitoring tool as an additional agent in the GUARD ecosystem, and to make it controllable by an external analytics platform.

Acknowledgment. This work was supported in part by the European Commission under Grant Agreement no. 786922 (ASTRID) and no. 833456 (GUARD).

References

1. Bertin, G.: XDP in practice: integrating XDP into our DDoS mitigation pipeline. In: Netdev 2.1, The Technical Conference on Linux Networking, Montreal, Canada, 6–8 April 2017 (2017). https://netdevconf.info/2.1/papers/Gilberto_Bertin_XDP_in_practice.pdf
2. Cassagnes, C., Trestioreanu, L., Joly, C., State, R.: The rise of eBPF for non-intrusive performance monitoring. In: 2020 IEEE/IFIP Network Operations and Management Symposium (NOMS 2020), Budapest, Hungary, 20–24 April 2020 (2020)
3. Claise, B.: Cisco systems netflow services export version 9. RFC 3954, October 2004. https://www.rfc-editor.org/rfc/rfc3954.txt
4. Claise, B., Trammell, B., Aitken, P.: Specification of the IP flow information export (IPFIX) protocol for the exchange of flow information. RFC 7011, September 2013. https://www.rfc-editor.org/rfc/rfc7011.txt
5. Deri, L., Sabella, S., Mainardi, S.: Combining system visibility and security using eBPF. In: Proceedings of the Third Italian Conference on Cyber Security (ITASEC 2019). cEUR Workshop Proceedings, Pisa, Italy, 13–15 February 2019, vol. 2315, pp. 50–62 (2019)
6. Fiessler, A., Hager, S., Scheuermann, B., Moore, A.W.: HyPaFilter-a versatile hybrid FPGA packet filter. In: ACM/IEEE Symposium on Architectures for Networking and Communications Systems (ANCS 2016), Santa Clara, CA, USA, 17–18 March 2016 (2016)
7. Gershuni, E., et al.: Simple and precise static analysis of untrusted Linux kernel extensions. In: Proceedings of the 40th ACM SIGPLAN Conference on Programming Language Design and Implementation (PLDI 2019), Phoenix, AZ, USA, 22–26 June 2019, pp. 1069–1084 (2019)
8. Hausenblas, M.: Container Networking - From Docker to Kubernetes, 1st edn. O'Reilly Media, Sebastopol (2018)
9. Hong, J., Jeong, S., Yoo, J.H., Hong, J.W.K.: Design and implementation of eBPF-based virtual TAP for inter-VM traffic monitoring. In: 2018 14th International Conference on Network and Service Management (CNSM), Rome, Italy, 5–9 November 2018 (2018)

10. Høiland-Jørgensen, T., et al.: The express data path: fast programmable packet processing in the operating system kernel. In: Proceedings of the 14th International Conference on Emerging Networking EXperiments and Technologies (CoNEXT 2018), Heraklion, Greece, 4–7 December 2018, pp. 54–66 (2018)
11. Miano, S., Bertrone, M., Risso, F., Bernal, M.V., Lu, Y., Pi, J.: Securing Linux with a faster and scalable iptables. ACM SIGCOMM Comput. Commun. Rev. **49**(3), 2–17 (2019)
12. Netronome: Avoid kernel-bypass in your network infrastructure. Blog post, January 2017. https://www.netronome.com/blog/avoid-kernel-bypass-in-your-network-infrastructure/
13. Phaal, P., McKee, N., Panchen, S.: InMon corporation's sFlow: a method for monitoring traffic in switched and routed networks. RFC 3176, September 2001. https://www.rfc-editor.org/rfc/rfc3176.txt
14. Qi, S., Kulkarni, S.G., Ramakrishnan, K.K.: Understanding container network interface plugins: design considerations and performance. In: 2020 IEEE International Symposium on Local and Metropolitan Area Networks (LANMAN), Orlando, FL, USA, 13–15 July 2020 (2020)
15. Quittek, J., Zseby, T., Claise, B., Zander, S.: Requirements for IP flow information export (IPFIX). RFC 3917, October 2004. https://www.rfc-editor.org/rfc/rfc3917.txt
16. Sanchez, O.R., Repetto, M., Carrega, A., Bolla, R.: Evaluating ML-based DDoS detection with grid search hyperparameter optimization. In: IEEE International Conference on Network Softwarization, Tokyo, Japan (Virtual), 28 June–2 July 2021 (2021)
17. Sanchez, O.R., Repetto, M., Carrega, A., Bolla, R., Pajo, J.F.: Feature selection evaluation towards a lightweight deep learning DDoS detector. In: IEEE International Conference on Communications, Montreal, Canada (Virtual), 14–23 June 2021 (2021). https://zenodo.org/record/4967143#.YMtxw26xXUI
18. Scholz, D., Raumer, D., Emmerich, P., Kurtz, A., Lesiak, K., Carle, G.: Performance implications of packet filtering with Linux eBPF. In: 30th International Teletraffic Congress (ITC 30), Vienna, Austria, pp. 209–217 (2018)
19. Spaziani Brunella, M., et al.: hXDP: efficient software packet processing on FPGA NICs. In: 14th USENIX Symposium on Operating Systems Design and Implementation (OSDI 2020), 4–6 November 2020, pp. 973–990 (2020)
20. Suo, K., Zhao, Y., Chen, W., Rao, J.: vNetTracer: efficient and programmable packet tracing in virtualized networks. In: IEEE 38th International Conference on Distributed Computing Systems (ICDCS), Vienna, Austria, 2–6 July 2018, pp. 165–175 (2018)
21. Zuppelli, M., Carrega, A., Repetto, M.: An effective and efficient approach to improve visibility over network communications. J. Wirel. Mob. Netw. Ubiquit. Comput. Dependable Appl. (JoWUA) **12**(4), 89–108 (2021). https://doi.org/10.22667/JOWUA.2021.12.31.089

Intelligent Transportation Systems – Models, Challenges, Security Aspects

Joanna Kołodziej[1,3](✉) ⓘ, Cornelio Hopmann[2], Giovanni Coppa[2],
Daniel Grzonka[3] ⓘ, and Adrian Widłak[3] ⓘ

[1] Naukowa i Akademocka Sieć Komputerowa - Państwowy Instytut Badawczy
(NASK-PIB), ul. Kolska 12, 01-045 Warszawa, Poland
`joanna.kolodziej@nask.pl`
[2] WOBCOM GmbH im WNT, Heßlinger Strasse 1-5, 38440 Wolfsburg, Germany
`{Cornelio.Hopmann,Giovanni.Coppa}@wobcom.de`
[3] Department of Computer Sciences, Cracow University of Technology,
ul. Warszawska 24, 31-155 Cracow, Poland
`{joanna.kolodziej,daniel.grzonka,adrian.widlak}@pk.edu.pl`

Abstract. As cars and other transportation devices become increasingly interconnected, mobility takes on a new meaning, offering new opportunities. The integration of new communications technologies in modern vehicles has generated an enormous variety of data from various communications sources. Hence, there is a demand for intelligent transportation systems that can provide safe and reliable transportation while maintaining environmental conditions such as pollution, CO2 emission, and energy consumption. This chapter provides an overview of the Intelligent Transportation Systems (ITS) models. Briefly, it discusses the most important features of the systems and challenges, mostly related to the security in data and information processing. Fast anomalies detection and prevention of external attacks may help solve the problems of traffic congestion and road safety to prevent accidents. The chapter contains the description of the realistic Smart Transportation System developed by the Wobcom company and implemented in Wolfsburg (Germany). That system is also used for practical validation of the security service components of the platform created in the GUARD project.

Keywords: Smart Transport · Smart City · Artificial intelligence ·
Anomaly detection · LoRa networks

1 Introduction

Modern transport systems aim at an optimal flow of goods and people, which significantly impacts the quality of life in any society. Technological developments in transport modes, population growth and changes in population density, increasing urbanisation - all these factors generate new challenges for the management of modern transport systems. Poor traffic organisation causes numerous traffic

J. Kołodziej et al. (Eds.): Cybersecurity of Digital Service Chains, LNCS 13300, pp. 56–82, 2022.
https://doi.org/10.1007/978-3-031-04036-8_3

jams, hindering the efficient use of transport infrastructure and increasing travel time, air pollution, and fuel consumption.

The rapid development of research, technology and information tools for electronics, communication and control systems, sensor networks and the processing of enormous data sets has contributed to a real revolution in modern public and private transport management and the development of effective strategies for both road infrastructure and management systems and the efficient use of existing infrastructure. The use of modern Information and Communication Technology systems (ICT) has significantly improved (and in many situations even enabled) the transfer of accurate traffic data, implementing control measures, varying the level of uncertainty and randomness that characterised conventional, manually managed transport networks. Successful implementation of Intelligent Transportation Systems (ITS) requires a good understanding of both locally and globally, and the impact of related phenomena and possible traffic anomalies, such as generation and propagation of shock waves, initiation of congestion, etc. Human relations are also an essential factor that must be considered in designing such systems.

ITS is nowadays a global important market. Figure 1 shows the calculation and estimation of this market size in the period of 2018–2025.

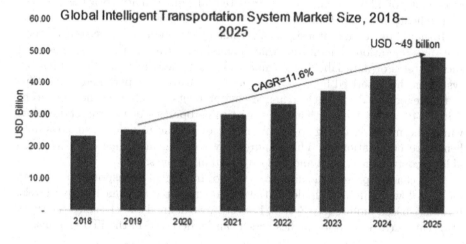

Fig. 1. Glovbal ITS market size (https://marketersmedia.com)

Based on the statistical analysis provide by MarketersMedia[1], it is expected that the market will reach US 42.6 billion in 2025. The leading players are Efkon AG[2] (Austria), Hitachi Ltd.[3] (Japan), Thales S.A.[4] (France), Roper Industries,

[1] https://marketersmedia.com/.
[2] https://www.efkon.com/.
[3] https://www.hitachi.com/.
[4] https://www.thalesgroup.com/.

Inc.[5] (U.S), Xerox Corporation[6] (U.S.), Q–Free ASA[7] (Norway), Kapsch AG[8] (Austria), Siemens AG[9] (Germany), Garmin Ltd.[10] (Switzerland) and TomTom International BV[11] (Netherlands).

Managing transportation systems, especially in highly urbanized environments, is a highly complex problem of optimization and decision making. Simplified mathematical models cannot always accurately capture the high complexity and dynamics of transport systems. For this reason, the use of computer networks, complex data and information transmission and processing systems, and computer simulations have enabled comprehensive analysis, and characterization of traffic flows on a given road network.

Despite the benefits of implementing today's numerous computer models to support transportation management, modern ITS systems must cope with the secure processing of streaming time-series data, induced by the connected real-time data sources. Examples of such streaming datasources include sensors in transportation systems and in intelligent cars. The collected data can be preprocessed locally using the resources and IT infrastructure of the institution (customer) directly responsible for transport management in a given area. Often, however, the data and metadata, along with initial analysis results, are sent to external systems (e.g., cloud computing) that can analyze the data more closely and send back alerts on potential threats and anomalies. All this indicates the complexity of ITS systems and their potential vulnerability to attacks at the local (client) and global levels.

It should be noted that a significant challenge for modern ITS systems is their real-time operation. This means that manual adjustment of the parameters of such systems or data labelling is impossible, and the whole modelled transport system is characterized by high dynamics of changes in its parameters and thus in the generated data. Such dynamic environments are often prone to concept drifts [44], which means that the statistical properties of the target variable, which the model is trying to learn, change over time in unforeseen ways, and hence are non-stationary. This requires any learning intelligent systems to be able to continuously learn and adapt to system changes.

This chapter presents a simple overview of Intelligent Transportation System models, flow traffic models defined at the microscopic and macroscopic levels, business -based models (see Sect. 2. In Sect. 3, we defined and classified the types of threats, attacks and anomalies which can be detected in the ITS systems.

---

[5] https://www.ropertech.com/.

[6] https://www.xerox.com/.

[7] https://www.q-free.com/.

[8] https://www.kapsch.net.

[9] https://www.siemens.com/.

[10] https://www.garmin.com/.

[11] https://www.tomtom.com/.

ITS systems are usually a part of the wider "smart" or "intelligent cities" projects. The futuristic vision of such city is presented in Fig. 2.

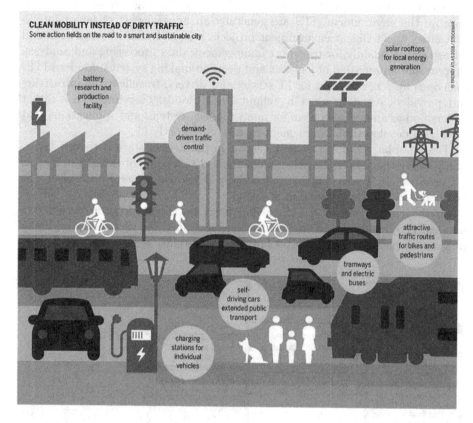

Fig. 2. "Clean mobility instead of dirty traffic" - smart city and sustainable transport conceptual model (https://en.wikipedia.org/wiki/Sustainable_transport)

We present in Sec.4 a real example of such smart city project implemented in the city of Wolfburg (Germany) with a special focus on the Wolfburg ITS system. Such system has been recently integrated with the prototype of the GUARD platform developed as the H2020 GUARD project[12]. The Wolfburg ITS system was implemnted for the 'smart transport' case study in this project.

Simple conclusions are drawn in Sect. 5.

---

[12] A cybersecurity framework to GUArantee Reliability and trust for Digital service chains (GUARD)): https://guard-project.eu/.

2   Intelligent Transportation Models

Modern ITSs are designed to improve the efficiency and safety of conventional transport systems, optimize transport costs, fuel and energy consumption, and improve the environment. ITS are generally an integral part of larger intelligent cities or intelligent environment projects using advanced IT methods and infrastructure, mainly for transport management, data processing and analysis, support and automation of logistics and decision-making systems. Modern ITSs thus open up a new market for IT services for drivers, travellers and infrastructure providers, e.g. as services in computational clouds. Therefore, ITS is rather understood as an umbrella term for many models, systems and applications that have been developed and implemented, not only strictly IT.

Despite a large number of publications in the field of state-of-the-art transportation systems, no exhaustive, multi-faceted taxonomy of these systems has yet emerged. It is also difficult to precisely define the general criteria of this taxonomy without overextending it.

In the early 1990s, the U.S. Department for Transportation accepted a national ITS standard. ITS architecture has identified the variable speed limits as a service package, which consists of two subsystems, as shown in Fig. 3.

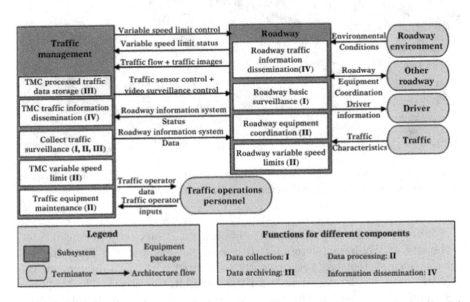

Fig. 3. Variable speed limits service package (http://www.iteris.com/itsarch/html/mp/mpatms22.htm)

In this model, the traffic management subsystem supports monitoring and controlling roadway traffic and exchanges the data with the roadway subsystem. Based on it, the following two criteria can be considered for the classification of the ITS systems:

- intelligent infrastructure and
- intelligent vehicles.

This simple classification is very general. Intelligent vehicles are equipped with devices and information systems that support the driver. These include satellite navigation systems, intelligent speed adaptation (ISA), adaptive cruise control (ACC), forward collision warning (FCW), pedestrian detection systems (PDS), and lane departure warning (LDW). Therefore, there is a need also to classify the ITC models, methods and infrastructure, which may span both of the above criteria. For example, transportation *traffic flow* analysis is the basis of many established technologies for evaluating and improving transportation systems, including analytical methods, ICT methods and techniques and simulation software packages for planning and design, traffic control, traffic safety analysis, and demand management. In addition, business aspects significantly influence both the implementation and design of ITS models and their management.

The following subsections show examples of ITS flow traffic models, ITS models supporting flow traffic models, and business aspects.

In the rest of this section.

2.1 Examples of the Traffic Flow ITS Models

Morrison Hershfield Limited[13] has developed a comprehensive analysis of traffic in the vicinity of a quarry located in Dufferin County, Ontario, Canada, and the impact of that traffic on service levels capacity and operation of the surrounding roadways based on the traffic forecasts performed for the region. This analysis was performed for different scenarios developed based on the number of vehicles (trucks) entering the quarry area and moving in the opposite direction. The results of this analysis were used to optimize the ITS model by, for example, adding offset passing lanes, adding a left-turn lane at an intersection, and adding a new right-turn route at a crossroads[14].

The objective of the project developed by Baby and Al–Sahrawi and presented in [3] is to analyze the traffic impact of residential redevelopment in Kuwait City. The analysis was conducted for thirteen planned locations of new roads, and the potential effect of road infrastructure development on fuel consumption was investigated. Models were developed for changes (balanced growth) in fuel consumption, but also emissions of carbon monoxide (CO), nitrogen oxide (NO2) and volatile organic compounds (VOC). The model predicts increases in air pollution and indicates possible methods to offset these increases.

URSC Canada[15] studied the potential traffic impact and management of the proposed construction of a new thermal processing facility located in the Municipality of Clarington. The project indicates a projected increase of 2% - 3% in traffic volumes throughout the municipality and the need for additional

---

[13] www.en.wikipedia.org/wiki/Morrison_Hershfield.
[14] http://highlandcompanies.ca.
[15] https://ursc.ca/.

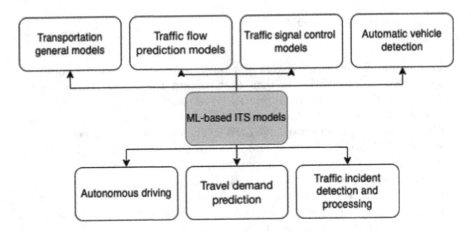

Fig. 4. Classification of ML-based ITS models.

investment in additional traffic signals, widening of certain arterials, intersection improvements and ramp terminals. The infrastructure upgrade project is scheduled to be completed by the end of 2023, which is in sync with Clarington Energy Business Park (CEBP).

Xu et al. in [4] presented a method for effectively adapting a macroscopic urban traffic network model to improve urban planning and urbanization models in general. The developed model also used speed density models to estimate travel time on individual road sections and the CORSIM[16] system to simulate the real traffic. The simulation results obtained with the developed model allowed the development of adequate time forecasts, especially during peak hours and sudden changes in traffic conditions.

The ITS model presented in [5] uses a queuing model of traffic flow in the network. Changes in density in traffic flow at different nodes of the road infrastructure determine different levels of congestion on a given road link. The following criteria are defined in this model: capacity and congestion density, and free-flow speed. The implemented intersection stream functions allow the propagation, initiation and dispersion traffic queues in the road network, which so-called bottlenecks can cause.

2.2 ICT Supporting Models for Traffic Flow

The example ITS models presented in the previous chapter use methods and information systems in forecasting transport flows and decision-making systems and information infrastructure. In general, Machine Learning (ML) methods and artificial intelligence methods are the most commonly used methods in ITS support.

Nguyen et al. in [6] presented in a taxonomy of the ML-based transportation models. Their classification is shown in Fig. 4.

---

[16] https://en.wikipedia.org/wiki/CORSIM.

There are many ML models that span all classes in that taxonomy. Some selected example as of the representatives of each class are presented below.

Li and Lu in [7] presented a new model for highway traffic volume forecasting based on a combined neural network (NN) consisting of a self-organizing feature map (SOM) and an Elman NN. The SOM network was used to classify the traffic condition and the Elman NN identifies the relationships between input and output data to obtain prediction values. As a case study, the performance of this model was evaluated using actual observational data from a highway in Beijing, China.

Ma et al. in [8] developed the transportation network model by defining on-road segments' traffic conditions (links). In this model, traffic congestion for a network with a specified number of links and time intervals is expressed as a two-dimensional matrix. The authors used the recurrent neural network combined with the deep restricted Boltzmann machine model to monitor and predict the traffic flow in the transportation network. The presented model is, however, quite complex, and its main limitation is that the model needs to automatically learn and infer the spatial dependency (e.g. related road segments) from historical data, which may result in low prediction accuracies.

Fouladgar et al. [9] proposed a deep traffic flow model based on a convolutional neural network (CNN) that considered inflow and outflow information in addition to traffic conditions on a road segment. In this model, the features of the processing data are classified into two general groups, namely, Traffic Condition and Incidents. Firstly, past traffic conditions are passed to the first filter of CNN as the training set. Then, the outcome of the first layer is sent to the second convolutional layer.

Huang et al. in [10] introduced a two-level deep learning ITS model, which included a multi-output regression layer at the top and a deep belief network at the bottom for traffic flow prediction. Such a method is executed for a group of road segments. In this case, the related roads should be grouped, as the overall performance is only improved when jointly trained tasks are related.

Effectively eliminating and relieving traffic congestion is a significant challenge in ITS models. This problem can be addressed by expanding road infrastructure, but this approach is generally costly. Another much cheaper method is to improve traffic management systems, which directly impacts road decongestion and vehicle flow optimization.

Genders and Razavi [11] developed a deep artificial neural network synchronized with a multi-agent system (MAS) to build adaptive control of traffic signals. The agents in the MAS were trained using reinforcement learning to develop an optimal control policy. This method was then evaluated in the SUMO traffic micro simulator.

Travel demand forecasting aims to estimate the number of road users or public transport users in the future. It is one of the most fundamental problems in transportation, Liu and Chen in [12] proposed a deep neural network-based model for demand forecasting in Taipei's mass rapid transit system. The model considered various explanatory variables, including historical passenger flows, directional, and holiday factors.

Predicting and managing information about transportation accidents and hazards is another important problem that designers of modern ITSs must face. Chen et al. used a deep denoise autoencoder [13] to model hierarchical feature representation of data collected from passenger and driver mobility monitoring. The goal of the whole model is to generate a traffic incident risk map based on real-time human mobility input data. The experimental analysis results showed that the model could predict the risk of a traffic accident with a relatively small error in simple scenarios. The model should then consider other factors such as land use to be more reliable.

2.3   ITS e-Business Aspects and Models

Most publications present ITS models from the engineering or IT side. Despite standards for ITS developed in some countries such as Japan and the USA, there have been relatively few studies on ITS in a business context and very few publications on business or e-business models in the last 2–3 years.

Osterwalder and Pigneur [1] and then Giannoutakis and Li [2], They defined an e-Business model that contains five main pillars shown in Fig. 5. Each ITS project, to be sustainable, must adequately address these elements.

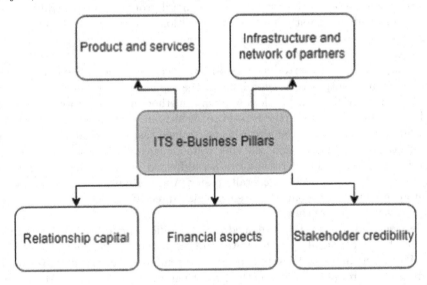

Fig. 5. The main pillars in e-Buisness ITS models.

Products and Services
In ITS models, generating revenue through the sale of products and services occurs at multiple levels. First, ITS system providers build modern infrastructure and provide intelligent vehicles. Then the users of the vehicles (customers)

receive factual information about the potential benefits of the ITS system (e.g. travel safety and travel time reduction) and are willing to pay for it. Therefore, it creates business opportunities for more companies to enter the market as intermediaries and service providers. As a result, the ITS system causes economic development in a given area, but it also influences (through modern technologies) the improvement of life quality and natural environment protection.

Infrastructure and Network of Partners
The operation of ITS systems requires the involvement of many parties and users, e.g. government, funding bodies, transport groups, automotive companies, communications technology companies, the energy sector, road users, etc. In addition, the widespread use of the Internet, including for ITS, provides opportunities for businesses companies to develop e-business models that make minimal use of the physical infrastructure. On the other hand, an ITS infrastructure incompatible with intelligent vehicles will not add value and waste resources. Therefore, intelligent vehicles should be considered as part of the infrastructure when adopting a specific e-Business model.

Relationship Capital
Another essential business aspect, especially for ITS providers, is the relationship with customers and gaining their trust. For ITS companies, the Internet is an ideal marketplace to promote themselves and build a network of trusted customers. The Internet, especially social networks, collects and processes data from and about users.

Financial Aspects
The financial aspects range from adopted product pricing models to methods for efficient use of tangible and intangible assets. In the age of the Internet, the interest of companies is shifting more and more rapidly towards investments in intangible assets (e.g., reputation, supplier network, intellectual property, value information), while tangible or physical assets represent an increasingly smaller percentage of the total enterprise value. This is also the case for ITS vendors. In the age of the Internet, companies' interest is shifting more and more rapidly towards investments in intangible assets (e.g. reputation, a network of suppliers, intellectual property, value information value), while tangible or physical assets represent a decreasing percentage of a company's total value. This in turn also serves to reduce costs and working more efficiently with the same or even fewer resources.

Stakeholder Credibility
The success of the ITS business model and the sustainability and reliability of the system itself depends largely on all stakeholders' support. To achieve such consent, it is necessary to develop a clear plan for the distribution of potential benefits (including financial returns) between the various interest groups and outline the expected more comprehensive societal and economic benefits.

The main challenge for an ITS company, as implied from the analysis above, is to take advantage of the opportunities offered by the internet. There is growing development in the ITS technology, both for transportation infrastructure and vehicles, and several examples of products and services in the ITS industry that could be integrated with, or make use of the internet and digital technologies. Nevertheless, the ITS sector has not taken off and the opportunities offered by the ICTs have remained rather unexplored. In the following, we present a few examples of ITS technologies, where the internet could create business opportunities.

Advanced Traveler Information Systems (ATIS). ATIS are systems that provide customized information to the user, such as on route selection, options about public transport, information about the destination, and warning messages for potential dangers during travelling [14,15]. Many of them are GIS-based, like in–vehicle navigation devices and rely on digital technologies to operate. They offer an excellent opportunity for e–Business model development by providing information on third parties' products (e.g. adverts) or even serving as platforms for added services, such as reporting defects on the road and updating online information about routes. They could also incorporate tourist information for popular destinations, such as sightseeing or online hotel booking suggestions.

Electric Vehicles. With the increasing environmental concerns of the future, there is growing research on electric and hybrid vehicles [16]. Digital technologies could contribute to the establishment of online business for these vehicles, for example, by providing online information about charging posts, or by selling online credit for vehicle charging on a pay–as–you–go with a registered smart-card. Electronic Toll Collection. Electronic Toll Collection (ETC), also known as Electronic Payment and Pricing System, is a topic of growing interest [17,18]. The technology enables the collection of congestion charging automatically by recognizing the vehicle's registration number. Neither have the drivers to stop at toll plazas, nor are cashiers required to collect tolls. Through the internet, public authorities or private companies could enable prepayment of tolls or discounts for frequently used routes by allowing road users to set up online accounts through their websites. ETC could also be a supportive mechanism for tracking down vehicles linked to illegal activities and facilitating law enforcement.

Public Transportation. Public Transportation is one of the areas where ITS have already started to have an impact and to revolutionize public transportation services [19,20]. Widely used examples of ITS are passenger information systems at bus stops or train stations, bus-mounted cameras, online bookings and automatic payment systems. There is room for further developments of internet-based technologies on public Transportation, such as improvements in the integration of traveller information with mobile technology and enforcement of Wi–Fi networks, which could create new business opportunities for third parties.

3 Methods of Detection of Anomalies, Attacks and Threats in ICT Systems

IT infrastructure in ITSs is closely related to the security aspects of integrated ICT systems and IT networks. Anomalies in ICT systems are monitored by dedicated software and may have various causes. They can result from failure, overloading or ineffective management of traffic and transport infrastructure and can also result from external attacks on networks and information systems.

There are various taxonomies and characteristics of the types of threats (attacks). Figure 6 presents threats–attacks classification criteria defined based on the detailed taxonomy presented in [21].

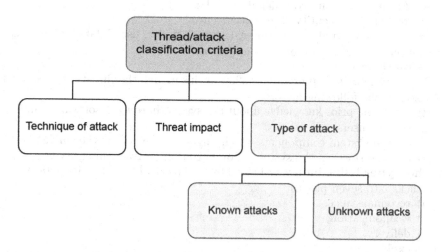

Fig. 6. Criteria of the threats classification in ICT systems

In our taxonomy, we define the following three criteria of categorization of threats in ICT systems:

1. technique of attack,
2. threat impact, and
3. type of attack.

Based on the type, the attacks may be classified into two following groups:

1. known attacks, and
2. unknown attacks (anomalies).

In the rest of this section, we briefly survey the most popular methods which spam the classes of both above-defined classifications.

3.1   Attack Technique and Thread Impact Criteria

Based on the attack techniques criterion, the following popular models may be used for the classification of threats:

- **Three Orthogonal Dimensional Model** was defined by Ruf et al. in[17]. This model decomposes the threat space into sub-spaces according to three orthogonal dimensions (motivation, localization and agent). Threat agent imposes the threat on a specific asset of the system, represented by human, technological, and force majeure. Threat motivation is creating the threat and may be deliberate or accidental. Finally, threat localization is the origin of threats, either internal or external
- **Hybrid C3 Model** was developed by Geric et al. in [22]. In this model, three significant criteria are considered, namely:
  - frequency of security threat occurrence,
  - the area affected by the threat (network nodes, users' data, communication channels, data, operation system)
  - threat's source.
- **Pyramid Model** is presented in [23]. In this model, the threats are classified based on the following factors:
  (i) attackers' prior knowledge about the system hardware, software, employees and users;
  (ii) critical system components which might be affected by the threat; and
  (iii) damage (loss) in the system or organization (privacy, integrity. . .).
- **The Cyber Kill Chain** was defined by Lockheed-Martin [24]. It splits cyberattacks into seven phases:
  (i) reconnaissance,
  (ii) weaponization,
  (iii) delivery,
  (iv) exploitation,
  (v) installation,
  (vi) command and control, and
  (vii) actions and objective.

The following two models have been developed based on analysis of the observed or potential threat impacts:

- **STRIDE Model** [25] developed by Microsoft which allows the characteristics of the known threats according to the goals and purposes of the attacks (or motivation of the attacker). The STRIDE acronym is defined based on the Spoofing identity, Tampering with data, Repudiation, Information disclosure, Denial of service, and Elevation of privilege. It is a goal-based approach, where an attempt is made to get inside the mind of the attacker by rating the threats against.

---

[17] [162] Ruf L, AG C, Thorn A, GmbH A, Christen T, Zurich Financial Services AG, Gruber B, Credit Suisse AG., Portmann R, Luzer H: "Threat Modeling in Security Architecture - The Nature of Threats. ISSS Working Group on Security Architectures", http://www.isss.ch/fileadmin/publ/agsa/ISSS-AG-Security-Architecture-Threat-Modeling_Lukas-Ruf.pdf.

- **ISO Model (ISO 7498-2)**[18] defines five major security threats impacts and services as a reference model: destruction of information and/or other resources, corruption or modification of information, theft, removal or loss of information and/or other resources, disclosure of information, and interruption of services.

3.2 Known and Unknown Attacks

Known Threats

Detection of some threats may be based on prior knowledge of the characteristics of the attack and the potential threat impact. Such threats are referred to as "known" threats because they have been already identified and studied before. Most of the detection methodologies of known threats are signature-based (SD) (sometimes defined as knowledge-based) techniques [26].

The main aim of the signature-based detection methods is to compare the suspicious payload with specific known attacks,i.e., signatures. Depending on the IDS type, the signatures can correspond to different types of data, e.g., byte sequences in network traffic, known malicious instruction sequences used by malware, etc. It is assumed in the SD scheme that patterns can define malware. Signature-based detection is the most popular technique for IDS systems. However, there are several disadvantages of using SD, such as:

- Susceptible to evasion - since the signature byte patterns are derived from known attacks, these byte patterns are also commonly known. Hence they can be evaded by using obfuscation or polymorphic techniques that alter the attack's payload, such that signatures no longer apply. Those methods can be easily used for computer malware, less so in the case of network attacks. Network attacks or exploits usually take advantage of bugs or vulnerabilities found in software and are bounded by specific application protocols.
- Zero–day attacks - since the signature-based IDS systems are constructed based on known attacks, they cannot detect unknown malware or even variants of known malware. Therefore, they cannot effectively detect polymorphic malware [27], which means that SD does not provide zero-day protection. Signature-based detectors use different signatures for each malware variant. Hence, the volume of the database of signatures grows exponentially.

SD methodologies are effective and fast in the detection of known attacks and threats[19]. However, generating new signatures in SD is complex and is usually performed manually by experts. The experts must analyse the attack identify invariant fragments in the involved flows using their understanding of the attacked application and exploited vulnerability. They also construct a signature that fully recognises the threat due to the detailed knowledge. Manual generation of the signatures is a time-consuming process. The provided experiments

[18] ISO. Information Processing Systems-Open Systems Interconnection-Basic Reference Model. Part 2: Security Architecture, ISO 7498-2; 1989.

[19] https://searchsecurity.techtarget.com/tip/IDS-Signature-versus-anomaly-detection.

show that over 90% of vulnerable systems can be "successfully" infected in that time. Therefore, automated signature generation tools are used in IDS systems to limit the propagation of a new threat in an early phase until a manually created signature is available and can be included in the rule sets permanently [28]. These systems work by searching for common features of suspicious flows not seen in regular, benign traffic. Looking for common characteristic traits of different malicious activities is not specific to worm detection - it is a basis of detection systems in other security applications, see, e.g. [29]. The syntax of generated signatures is generally based on the language provided by the system Snort [30]. Several systems for automatic generation of signatures of zero–day polymorphic worms have been developed: Autograph [31], Polygraph [32], Nebula [33], Hamsa [34], Lisabeth [35]. Most of them apply relatively simple (computationally inexpensive) heuristic approaches. Another model is proposed in [36]. The generation of multi–set type signatures is formulated as an optimisation problem. The specialised version of a genetic algorithm (GA) is used to solve it.

Signature-based detection in ITC systems belongs to a broader class of methodologies referred to as Threat Intelligence[20]. Threat intelligence is frequently used in Security Information and Event Management (SIEM), antivirus, and web technologies such as algorithms inspired by the human immune system for detection and prevention of web intrusions [37,38]. In those algorithms, malware samples can be used to create a behavioural model to generate a signature, which is served as an input to a malware detector, acting as the antibodies in the antigen detection process. In the case of malicious botnets, a new trend is to use alternative communication channels, i.e., DNS-tunneling or HTTP, instead of IRC to connect command & control (C&C) servers and infected hosts [39].

Another group of methodologies is Stateful Protocol Analysis (SPA). SPA (specification based) uses predetermined profiles that define benign protocol activity. Occurring events are compared against these profiles to decide if protocols are used correctly or not. IDS based on SPA track the state of network, transport, and application protocols. They use vendor-developed universal profiles and therefore rely on their support [40].

Intruder traps [41] are set for attackers to prevent data or system infection. The pitfalls may include honeypot systems which are often employed to detect, deflect or counteract attempts of unauthorized use of information systems.

Classification Machine Learning (ML) techniques based on supervised learning are successfully used for data classification, considering the unique set of features. Those methodologies may be used to detect known threats using their characteristics for the generation of the validation and testing sets in the learning process. However, together with the other ML techniques, they are much more helpful in detecting anomalies and unknown attacks.

---

[20] "CERT-UK, An Introduction to Threat Intelligence", https://web.archive.org/web/20151003045952/https://www.cert.gov.uk/wp-content/uploads/2015/03/An-introduction-to-threat-intelligence.pdf.

Detection Methods of Unknown Threats and Attacks

All "known threat" detection methodologies defined in the previous section can only detect previously known attack patterns using signatures and rules that describe malicious events and are thus also called black–listing approaches. Known threats can sometimes slip past even the best defensive measures, which is why most security organizations actively look for both known and unknown threats in their environment.

Unknown threats and attacks are not recognized by the IDS based on the collected attack knowledge. One of the possible reasons is that the attacker may use brand new methods or technologies. The "unknown threat" methodologies allow detection of previously unknown attacks, however often with high false positive rate [42].

The core class of the "unknown threats" detection methodologies is anomaly–based detection (AD). AD (behavior based) approaches learn a baseline of normal system behavior, a so–called ground truth. Against this ground truth all occurring events are compared to detect anomalous system behavior. AD techniques permit only normal system behavior, and are therefore also called white-listing approaches. While black-listing approaches are usually easier to deploy, they depend on the support of vendors. They mostly cannot be applied in legacy systems and systems with small market shares; those are often poorly documented and not supported by vendors.

There exist different types of anomalies that can indicate malicious system behavior [43]:

- **Point anomaly** is the simplest form of an anomaly and is often also referred to as outlier, i.e. an anomalous single event. This could be, for example, caused by an anomalous event parameter, such as an unexpected login-name or IP address.
- **Contextual anomaly** is an event that is anomalous in a specific context, but it might be normal in another one. This could, for example, be a system login from an employee outside working hours, which would be normal during normal working time.
- **Collective/frequency anomaly** usually origins in an anomalous frequency of a usually normal single events. In an ICT network this could be a database dump, which could be caused by a SQL–Injection. During a database dump, a large number of log lines that refer to normal SQL–Queries are generated. In this case, the single lines are normal, but their high frequency is anomalous.
- **Sequential anomaly** represents an anomalous sequence of single events usually categorized as normal. In an ICT network a sequential anomaly can be caused for example by violating an access chain. For example, a normal database server access is usually only allowed via a firewall and a Web server. Therefore, it would be malicious, if someone accesses the database server directly, without accessing the Web server.

Anomaly detection methods in distributed ICT systems are based on the analysis of data and information flow monitoring results in these systems. Therefore, they have to adapt to system architecture and configuration changes and analyze large amounts of data and information transmitted and generated by devices integrated with the computer system. The most commonly used methods of detecting anomalies include the following: machine learning methods, methods from the general class of artificial intelligence methods and statistical methods of data analysis:

- **Artificial Neural Networks (ANN)** - Input data activates neurons (nodes) of an artificial network, inspired by the human brain. The nodes of the first layer pass their output to the nodes of the next layer, until the output of the last layer of the artificial network classifies the monitored ICT networks' current state [45]. Bayesian Networks - Bayesian networks define graphical models that encode the probabilistic relationships between variables of interest and can predict the consequences of actions [46].
- **Clustering** – Clustering enables grouping of unlabeled data and is often applied to detect outliers [47]. In particular, clustering can successfully support filtering defence mechanisms in case of DDoS attacks. Robust clustering techniques such as density-based clustering, subspace clustering can be used for evidence accumulation for classifying flow ensembles in traffic classes. One and multi-stage techniques can be investigated. The two-stage algorithm that works on single-link packet-level traffic captured in consecutive time-slots is presented in [48]. In the first stage, the changes in traffic characteristics are observed and at each time–slot, traffic is aggregated using multiple criteria (source and destination IPs, network prefixes, traffic volume measurements, etc.). Flows containing possible attacks are passed for processing to the next stage that employs the clustering techniques and applies them to the suspicious, aggregated flows from stage one.
- **Graph Clustering** – A graph is generated based on a malware data analysis and a graph clustering technique [49] can be used to derive common malware behavior. The method to generate a common behavioral graph representing the execution behavior of a family of malware instances by clustering a set of individual behavioral graphs is proposed in [50]. To speed up the malware data analysis by reduction of sample counts, generic hash functions are applied. The generic hash function for portable executable files that generates a per-binary specific hash value based on structural data found in the file headers and structural information about the executables section data is described in [51].
- **Decision Trees** – Decision trees have a tree-like structure, which comprises paths that lead to a classification based on the values of different features [52].
- **Hidden Markov Models (HMM)** – A Markov chain connects states through transition probabilities. HMM aim at determining hidden (unobservable) parameters from observed parameters [53].
- **Support Vector Machines (SVM)** – SVM construct hyperplanes in a high- or infinite- dimensional space, which can then be used for classification and regression. Thus, similar to clustering, SVM can, for example, be applied for outlier detection [54].

- Ensemble learning - Combination learning based AD (also known as Ensemble methods) combine several methods for their decision. For example, one can include five different classifiers and use majority voting to decide whether a datum should be considered an anomaly [55].
- **Self-learning** – Self-learning systems usually learn a baseline of normal system behavior during a training phase. This baseline serves as ground truth to detect anomalies that expose attacks and especially invaders. Generally, there are three ways how self-learning AD can be realized:
  - Unsupervised - This method does not require any labeled data and is able to learn to distinguish normal from malicious system behavior during the training phase. Based on the findings, it classifies any other given data during the detection phase.
  - Semi-supervised - This method is applied when the training set only contains anomaly–free data and is therefore also called "one-class" classification.
  - Supervised - This method requires a fully labeled training set containing both normal and malicious data.

Self-learning methods do not require active human intervention during the learning process. While unsupervised self-learning is entirely independent from human influence, for the other two methods the user has to ensure that the training data is anomaly free or correctly labeled. However, it might be difficult to provide training data for semi-supervised learning and even harder for supervised approaches.

4   ITS Practical Example – Wobcom Smart City Project with GUARD Support

In this section, we present the example of the real ITS, which is a part of Crown-Castle smart city project[21] implemented in the city of Wolfsburg in Germany. As part of its digital strategy, the city of Wolfsburg is developing and deploying an ICT infrastructure for building intelligent services that help tackle issues like waste management, parking and metering, pollution and transportation. The infrastructure is based on a modern sensor network covering the city and its surroundings, including several Smart Gateways interconnected by a high–speed–low–latency fibre network throughout the whole city (see the left side of Fig. 7).

The Smart Gateway is a slight edge computing installation and consists of 3–5 general-purpose computers. Each gateway has local fast storage, a multi-core multi-tenant CPU, ×4 Ethernet interfaces, and 32 GB RAM per node. Kubernetes acts as the container orchestrator. The first generation of Smart Gateways includes both LoRaWAN and WiFi/LTE interfaces; they implement so-called packet forwarders, protocol/payload decoders, scheduled/recurring (cron type)

---

[21] https://www.commscope.com/globalassets/digizuite/919662-wobcom-cs-115537-en.pdf.

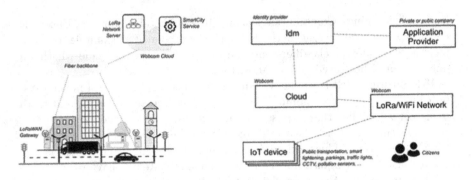

Fig. 7. Smart City project for Wolfsburg

tasks, and other networks functions. The optical backbone connects all Smart Gateways to remote data centres managed by Wobcom, an ICT service provider owned by the municipality.

WobCom already provides free internet access by WiFi (FreeWolfsburg) in the city. Both the edge installations and central data centres can host applications of third parties that create Smart City services.

The right side of Fig. 7 identifies different digital services involved in the Smart City scenario, highlighting the presence of multiple actors (Wobcom, service providers, citizens, owners of the physical infrastructures). Even though most LoraWAN applications are not real-time and tolerate some degree of service interruption, the full range of possible services under the scope of Smart City cannot exclude carrier–grade connectivity that provides reliable and robust quality of service, not to mention the need for trust and high–security guarantees. This is especially critical for the most recent computing paradigms since edge installations do not have enough resources to deploy the same security measures as a normal data centre. Opening access to thousands of devices requires a multi–tenant, self-learning approach. Still, the market for cyber-security tools is currently lacking proper solutions that can be effectively applied in a distributed, heterogeneous, multi-tenancy environment. Monitoring the good and fair behaviour of the different network participants is a tight requirement of the European regulations regarding the usage of open-shared frequencies and properties of LoRaWAN.

The most tangible benefit will be improved service level agreements, including robust security features that each actor can define. While infrastructure providers will be primarily concerned about the availability and integrity of their infrastructures, service providers will care about their operation's reliability, continuity, and trustworthiness, which are essential to delivering high levels of (end) user experience.

4.1 Security Aspects of ITS Integration with the GUARD Project

The main technical challenge for implementing smart city services is the interconnection of heterogeneous components (IoT devices, applications, citizens, processes) in different domains. While a lot of effort has been put in proposing n
web services, middleware, and service-oriented architectures, security concerns
beyond identity management and access control have been largely overlooked.
Indeed, existing tools in the market for complex systems, including cloud, IoT,
and network assets, are often designed and integrated for each specific scenario,
resulting in rigid architectures that cannot be adapted to evolving systems and
partially unknown topologies. The introduction of security capabilities in each
digital component, accessible through standard interfaces and APIs, represents
a ground-breaking evolution in security architectures for smart cities, allowing
the composition of dynamic environments where devices, users, applications,
and processes can be easily plugged or removed in multi-tenancy environments
without requiring the re-design of the cyber–security architecture.

The main aim of the GUARD project[22] is to construct the ICT platform,
described in detail in Chap. 1, allows end-to-end assurance and protection of
business service chains by assessing the level of trustworthiness of the involved
services and tracing data propagation. GUARD platform can be successfully
integrated with the local client infrastructures, such as the Wobcom network,
for enforcement functionalities by leveraging "programmability" to shape the
granularity of context information to the actual needs.

The intelligent local city Wobcom infrastructure has already been integrated
with the ICT GUARD platform. Figure 8 shows the block diagram of the local
system integrated with the GUARD platform.

In considered scenarios, the cloud applications is hosted on the WOBCOM
city infrastructure. The IoT device connects to the IBIS-Bus of the buses to
collect route information, provides positioning and counts the number of wireless
(Wi–Fi) devices in proximity to estimate the passenger count. It also provides
LoRaWAN Network Information and is able to respond to commands sent from
the management application. The data are collected and processed by the system
using the following FIWARE services[23].

Wobcom developed Fleet Management application for the full integration
with the GUARD platform and its security service components. Such application consists of smart devices installed on city bus that collect several data from
the CAN bus, including speed, position, traveling distance, and measures from
the engine. This data is transmitted to a LoRa Gateway, which forwards it to
the remote LoRa Server, deployed in a remote cloud. Data is then consumed by
the Fleet Management application, deployed in the cloud as well, which provides
current position and delay of the bus to the citizens, and is also used for pre-
dictive maintenance of the vehicle fleet. A simplified view of the service chain is
presented in Fig. 9.

---

[22] https://guard-project.eu/.

[23] https://www.fiware.org/about-us/smart-cities/.

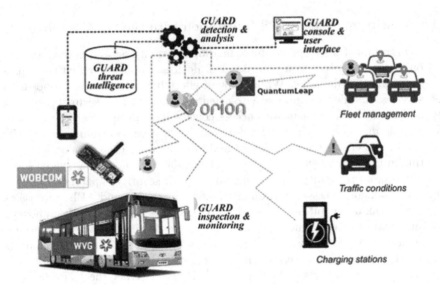

Fig. 8. Smart mobility diagram integrating the GUARD platform

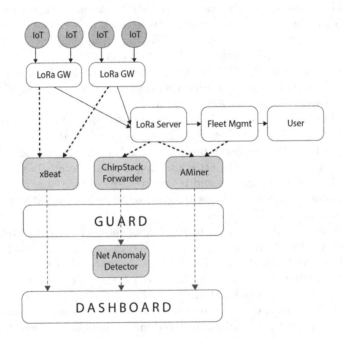

Fig. 9. Architecture of fleet management use case and GUARD SAPs

With GUARD platform, each digital component of the Wobcom system implements internally its own monitoring, inspection, and enforcement tasks; a common interface exposes these capabilities, together with the description of security properties (vendor, release, updates). Local agents deployed in each component report measurements, events, logs to a common central framework, which therefore gains deep visibility over the whole chain to detect and analyse even the weakest correlations in the cyber–security context. Beyond the common interface to security capabilities, the great value of GUARD local agents is their programmability, i.e., a large flexibility in defining the local operations (filtering rules, log aggregation, pre-processing tasks, etc.). For example, the amount of traffic generated by IoT devices could be compared with that received by cloud/edge applications, to detect anomalies and possible ongoing volumetric Denial–of–Service (DoS) attacks. Suspicious end devices and gateways could be selectively monitored at the radio/network level, so to identity incorrect or malicious behaviours, including various kinds of DoS (volumetric, syn flood, amplification), man–in–the middle (e.g., rogue diversion of network traffic), tampering, manipulation or alteration of the device (operating system, libraries, applications, data). It helps detect intrusion especially at the edge, which is one of the weakest links in the chain.

The dichotomy between local and central processing should also be leveraged to improve the resilience of the same framework. As a matter of fact, some "cron types" might not have an "always connected" requirement, and could work locally for a certain period of time. Local GUARD agents are able to apply pre-defined or fallback enforcement rules in case the central framework cannot be reached, so to ensure continuity of service even in case of direct or indirect attack to the framework itself.

Another important feature of the GUARD framework is support for multiple users. A single installation are managed by a trusted security provider, offering interfaces to all users that might be affected by security concerns: Wobcom, the municipality, service providers, infrastructure owners, and citizens. Through the external interface, each user can set up its own security service. For example, infrastructure owners may be interested in detecting if their devices get compromised (to avoid responsibility when they are used for other attacks), Wobcom may be interested in avoiding DoS and amplification attacks that overwhelm its ICT infrastructure, service providers may be interested in the integrity and availability of their applications.

GUARD platform integrated with the Wobcom intelligent infrastructure through the local LoRaWAN network plays a role of cross–layer Intrusion Detection Systems (IDS). In general, cross—ayer IDS aim to maximize the available information, and therefore raise the detection capability to an optimum level and minimize the false alarm rate at the same time. Therefore, various data sources, such as log data and network traffic data, can be used for intrusion detection. Especially lightweight solutions that work resource-efficient are required. A high data throughput is important to enable real time analysis and evaluation of the collected information and thus timely detection of attacks and invaders [56,57].

In the case of GUARD, the anomalies defined in Sect. 3.2, are detected by two secure service modules of the platform, namely (i) Network Anomaly Detection (NAD) module developed by NASK[24] and described in details in Chap. 4, and (ii) AMiner with AECID[25] developed by Austrian Institute of Technology (AIT)[26] and presented in Chap. 5 of this book.

The critical factor ensuring the success of modern ITS systems is highly developed technology and IT infrastructure. It is hard to imagine an intelligent system without IT support. However, it carries the risk of numerous anomalies, and the whole implementation is exposed to hacking attacks, which can result in enormous difficulties in ITS management and can be dangerous for users. Sect. 3 defines the most critical types of threats and presents a brief characterization of selected classes of methods for detecting attacks and anomalies in ITS.

The last part of the chapter contains an example of a real ITS system implemented in the city of Wolfburg, Germany. This system was integrated with the GUARD platform, developed as part of the European H2020 project.

We believe that we have succeeded in drawing the reader's attention in this chapter to the most critical challenges and aspects related to the development of ITS systems, which we will all be using in the near or distant future. The example of the GUARD platform and integrated ITS developed by Wobcom shows that this future does not have to be very far away.

5   Conclusions

This chapter introduced the complexity of modelling intelligent transportation systems, especially in highly urbanized areas. Although there are many projects concerning smart cities and smart infrastructures in general, these projects have been implemented in practice only in a few cases. The reasons for these difficulties are manifold: from economic and technological barriers to increasingly restrictive environmental regulations and financial constraints. The most critical problems and challenges faced by ITS systems developers were discussed in Sect. 2.

Acknowledgements. The works of Joanna Kolodziej, Cornelio Hopfmann and Giovanni Coppa were supported in part by the GUARD European Commission project under Grant Agreement no. 833456.

References

1. Osterwalder, A., Pigneur, Y.: An e-business model ontology for modelling e-business. In: Bled 2002 Proceedings, Paper 2: Bled, Slovenia (2002)
2. Giannoutakis, K., Li, F.: Developing sustainable e-business models for intelligent transportation systems (ITS). In: Proceedings of the 11th Conference on e-Business, e-Services, and e-Society (I3E), Kaunas, Lithuani, pp. 200–211 (2011)

---

[24] https://www.nask.pl/.
[25] https://aecid.ait.ac.at//.
[26] https://www.ait.ac.at/.

3. Baby, S., Al-Sarawi, M.A.: Traffic environmental assessment studies for township re-development: present status and future prediction. In: Proceedings of the International Conference on Biology, Environment and Chemistry, vol. 1, IACSIT Press, Singapore (2011)

4. Xu, Y., Kong, Q. J., Lin, S., Liu, Y.: Urban traffic flow prediction based on road network model. In: Proceedings of the 9th IEEE International Conference on Networking, Sensing and Control (ICNSC), pp. 334–339 (2012)

5. Jin, W.L.: A link queue model of network traffic (2012)

6. Nguyen, H., Kieu, L.M., Wen, T., Cai, C.: Deep learning methods in transportation domain: a review. IET Intell. Transp. Syst. **12**(9), 998–1004 (2018)

7. Li, R., Lu, H.: Combined neural network approach for short-term urban freeway traffic flow prediction. In: Advances in Neural Networks-ISNN, pp. 1017–1025 (2009)

8. Ma, X., et al.: Large-scale transportation network congestion evolution prediction using deep learning theory. PLoS ONE **10**(3), e0119044 (2015)

9. Fouladgar, M., et al.: Scalable deep traffic flow neural networks for urban traffic congestion prediction. arXiv preprint arXiv:1703.01006 (2017)

10. Huang, W., et al.: Deep architecture for traffic flow prediction: deep belief networks with multitask learning. IEEE Trans. Intell. Transp. Syst. **15**(5), 2191–2201 (2014)

11. Genders, W., Razavi, S.: Using a deep reinforcement learning agent for traffic signal control. arXiv preprint arXiv:1611.01142 (2016)

12. Liu, L., Chen, R.C.: A MRT daily passenger flow prediction model with different combinations of influential factors. In: Proceedings of the 31st International Conference Advanced Information Networking and Applications Workshops (WAINA), Taipei, Taiwan, pp. 601–605 (2017)

13. Bengio, Y.: Learning deep architectures for AI. Trends Mach. Learn. **2**(1), 1–27 (2009)

14. Singh, V., Kumar, P.: Web-based advanced traveler information system for developing countries. J. Transp. Eng. ASCE **136**(9), 836–845 (2010)

15. Yang, H., Huang, H.-J.: Modeling user adoption of advanced traveler information systems: a control theoretic approach for optimal endogenous growth. Transp. Res. Part C: Emerg. Technol. **12**(3–4), 193–207 (2004)

16. Yang, C.J.: Launching strategy for electric vehicles: lessons from China and Taiwan. Technol. Forecast. Soc. Change **77**(5), 831–834 (2010)

17. Chen, C.D., Fan, Y.W., Farn, C.K.: Predicting electronic toll collection service adoption: an integration of the technology acceptance model and the theory of planned behavior. Transp. Res. Part C Emerg. Technol. **15**, 300–311 (2007)

18. Lee, W.H., Tseng, S.S., Wang, C.H.: Design and implementation of electronic toll collection system based on vehicle positioning system techniques. Comput. Commun. **31**(12), 2925–2933 (2008)

19. Velastin, S.A., Boghossian, B.A., Lo, B.P.L., Sun, J., Vicencio-Silva, M.A.: PRISMATICA: toward ambient intelligence in public transport environments. IEEE Trans. Syst. Man Cybern. Part A Syst. Humans. **35**(1), 164–182 (2005)

20. Vanajakshi, L., Subramanian, S.C., Sivanandan, R.: travel time prediction under heterogeneous traffic conditions using global positioning system data from buses. IET Intell. Transp. Syst. **3**(1), 1–9 (2009)

21. Pawar, M., Anuradha, J.: Network security and types of attacks in network. In: Proceedings of the International Conference on Computer, Communication and Convergence (ICCC 2015), Procedia Computer Science, vol. 48, pp. 503–506 (2015)

22. Geric, S., Hutinski, Z.: Information system security threats classifications. J. Inf. Organ. Sci. **31**, 51–61 (2007)

23. Alhabeeb, M., Almuhaideb, A., Le, P., Srinivasan, B.: Information security threats classification pyramid. In: Proceedings of the 24th IEEE International Conference on Advanced Information Networking and Applications, pp. 208–213 (2010)
24. Hutchins, E.M., Cloppert, M.J., Amin, R.M.: Intelligence-driven computer network defense informed by analysis of adversary campaigns and intrusion kill chains. Lead. Issues Inf. Warf. Secur. Res. **1**(1), 80 (2011)
25. Meier, J., Mackman, A., Vasireddy, S., Dunner, M., Escamilla, R., Murukan, A.: Improving the application security: threats and counter measures. Microsoft Corporation, Satyam Computer Services (2003)
26. Liao, H.-J., Lin, C.-H.R., Lin, Y.-C., Tung, K.-Y.: Intrusion detection system: a comprehensive review. J. Netw. Comput. App. **36**(1), 19–24 (2013)
27. Sounak, P., Mishra, B.K.: Survey of polymorphic worm signatures. Int. J. u-Serv. e- Serv. Sci. Technol. **7**, 129–150 (2014)
28. Uddin, M., Rehman, A.A., Uddin, N., Memon, J., Alsaqour, R., Kazi, S.: Signature-based multi-layer distributed intrusion detection system using mobile agents. Int. J. Netw. Secur. **15**, 97–105 (2016)
29. Branitskiy, J., Kotenko, A.: Hybridization of computational intelligence methods for attack detection in computer networks. J. Comput. Sci. **23**, 145–156 (2016)
30. Roesch, M.: Snort - lightweight intrusion detection for networks. In: Proceedings of the 13th Conference on Systems Administration, pp. 229–238, Seattle, WA (1999)
31. Kim, H.-A., Karp, B.: Autograph: toward automated, distributed worm signature detection. In: Proceedings of the 13th conference on USENIX Security Symposium (SSYM 2004), vol. 13. USENIX Association, Berkeley, CA, USA (2004)
32. Newsome, J., Karp, B., Song, D.: Polygraph: automatically generating signatures for polymorphic worms. In: Proceeding of the IEEE Symposium on Security and Privacy (S&P 2005), pp. 226–241. IEEE Computer Society, Los Alamitos, US (2005)
33. Werner, T., Fuchs, C., Gerhards-Padilla, E., Martini, P.: Nebula - generating syntactical network intrusion signatures. In: Proceedings of the 4th International Conference on Malicious and Unwanted Software (MALWARE), pp. 31–38 (2009)
34. Li, Z., Sanghi, M., Chen, Y., Kao, M., Chavez, B.: HAMSA: fast signature generation for zero-day polymorphic worms with provable attack resilience. In: Proceedings of the IEEE Symposium on Security and Privacy (S&P 2006) (2006)
35. Cavallaro, L., Lanzi, A., Mayer, L., Monga, M.: LISABETH: automated content-based signature generator for zero-day polymorphic worms. In: Proceedings of the 4th International Workshop on Software Engineering for Secure Systems SESS 2008, pp. 41–48 (2008)
36. Szynkiewicz, P., Kozakiewicz, A.: Design and evaluation of a system for network threat signatures generation. J. Comput. Sci. **22**, 187–197 (2017)
37. Forrest, S., et al.: Self-nonself discrimination in a computer. In: Proceedings of Computer Society Symposium on Security and Privacy, Oakland, CA, USA, vol. 10, pp. 311–324 (1994)
38. de Oliveira, I.L., Grégio, A.R.A., Cansian, A.M.: A malware detection system inspired on the human immune system. In: Murgante, B., et al. (eds.) ICCSA 2012. LNCS, vol. 7336, pp. 286–301. Springer, Heidelberg (2012). https://doi.org/10.1007/978-3-642-31128-4_21
39. Stalmans, E., Irwin, B.: A framework for DNS based detection and mitigation of malware infections on a network. In: Proceedings of 10th Annual Information Security South Africa Conference ISSA 2011, Johannesburg, South Africa (2011)
40. Scarfone, K., Mell, P.: Guide to Intrusion Detection and Prevention Systems (IDPS), vol. 800. NIST Special Publication, US (2007)

41. Lakshmi, S.D., Arunkumar, G., Viswanatham, V.M.: Network security enhancement through honeypot based systems. Int. J. Eng. Technol. **7**(1), 290–293 (2015)
42. Garcia-Teodoro, P., Diaz-Verdejo, J., Macia-Fernandez, G., Vazquez, E.: Anomaly-based network intrusion detection: techniques, systems and challenges. Comput. Secur. **28**(1), 18–28 (2009)
43. Chandola, V., Arindam, B., Vipin, K.: Anomaly detection: a survey. ACM Comput. Surv. (CSUR) **41**(3), 15 (2009)
44. Subutai, A., Lavin, A., Purdy, S., Agha, Z.: Unsupervised real-time anomaly detection for streaming data. Neurocomputing **262**, 134–147 (2017)
45. Cannady, J.: Artificial neural networks for misuse detection. In: National Information Systems Security Conference, pp. 368–381 (1998)
46. Heckerman, D., et al.: A tutorial on learning with Bayesian networks. Nato ASI Ser. D Behav. Soc. Sci. **89**, 301–354 (1998)
47. Xu, R., Wunsch, D.: Survey of clustering algorithms. IEEE Trans. Neural Netw. **16**(3), 645–678 (2005)
48. Kalkan, K., Gur, G., Alagoz, F.: Filtering-based defense mechanisms against DDoS attacks: a survey. IEEE Syst. J. **11**(4), 2761–2773 (2017)
49. Shaeffer, S.E.: Graph clustering. Comput. Sci. Rev. **1**, 27–64 (2010)
50. Mulukutla, V., Sundaravel, B., Park, Y., Reeves, D.: Fast malware classification by automated behavioral graph matching. In: Proceedings of the Sixth Annual Workshop on Cyber Security and Information Intelligence Research, pp. 1–4 (2010)
51. Wicherski, G.: A novel approach to fast malware clustering. In: Proceedings of LEET 2009 -The 2nd USENIX Conference on Large-Scale Exploits and Emergent Threats: Botnets, Spyware, Worms, and More, pp. 1–8 (2009)
52. Safavian, S.R., Landgrebe, D.: A survey of decision tree classifier methodology. IEEE Trans. Syst. Man Cybern. **21**(3), 660–674 (1991)
53. Baum, L.E., Eagon, J.A.: An inequality with applications to statistical estimation for probabilistic functions of Markov processes and to a model for ecology. Bull. Am. Math. Soc. **73**(3), 360–363 (1967)
54. Steinwart, I., Christmann, A.: Support Vector Machines. Springer Science & Business Media, Cham (2009). https://doi.org/10.1007/978-0-387-77242-4
55. Tsai, C.-F., et al.: Intrusion detection by machine learning: a review. Expert Syst. App. **36**(10), 11994–12000 (2009)
56. Skopik, F.: Collaborative Cyber Threat Intelligence: Detecting and Responding to Advanced Cyber Attacks at the National Level, 416p., 1st edn. ISBN-10:1138031828, ISBN-13:978-1138031821, Taylor & Francis, CRC Press (2007)
57. Michael, W., Herbert, M.: Principles of Information Security. Cengage Learning, Boston (2011)

NAD: Machine Learning Based Component for Unknown Attack Detection in Network Traffic

Mateusz Krzysztoń$^{(\boxtimes)}$, Marcin Lew, and Michał Marks

Research and Academic Computer Network (NASK),
Kolska 12, 01-045 Warszawa, Poland
mateuszkr@nask.pl

Abstract. Detection of unknown attacks is challenging due to the lack of exemplary attack vectors. However, previously unknown attacks are a significant danger for systems due to a lack of tools for protecting systems against them, especially in fast-evolving Internet of Things (IoT) technology. The most widely used approach for malicious behaviour of the monitored system is detecting anomalies. The vicious behaviour might result from an attack (both known and unknown) or accidental breakdown. We present a Net Anomaly Detector (NAD) system that uses one-class classification Machine Learning techniques to detect anomalies in the network traffic. The highly modular architecture allows the system to be expanded with adapters for various types of networks. We propose and discuss multiple approaches for increasing detection quality and easing the component deployment in unknown networks by known attacks emulation, exhaustive feature extraction, hyperparameter tuning, detection threshold adaptation and ensemble models strategies. Furthermore, we present both centralized and decentralized deployment schemes and present preliminary results of experiments for the TCP/IP network traffic conducted on the CIC-IDS2017 dataset.

Keywords: Anomaly detection · Machine learning · One-class classification · IoT networks · LoRaWAN security

1 Introduction

According to the current report [1] attacks against corporate networks increases each year. Only in 2021 did the annual number of such attacks rise by 50%. The rapid development of IoT systems is conducive to new unknown attacks. Those unknown attacks are a significant danger for systems due to standard signature-based intrusion detection systems' ineffectiveness for protecting systems against them. Thus, anomaly detection is a commonly used solution to detect malicious behaviour in network traffic [4]. The anomaly in network traffic might result from an attack (both known and unknown) or accidental breakdown.

Distinguishing between normal and abnormal behaviour is difficult due to irregularity of users and external systems behaviour (e.g. different frequency of

J. Kołodziej et al. (Eds.): Cybersecurity of Digital Service Chains, LNCS 13300, pp. 83–102, 2022.
https://doi.org/10.1007/978-3-031-04036-8_4

visiting websites depending on the time of day and marketing campaigns). As a result, detecting anomalies is usually a trade-off between accepting significant irregularities that might result from attack (false-negative errors) and frequent reporting of alarms in situations where the system is working correctly (false-positive errors).

Applying machine learning (ML) to detect anomalies in extensive data set is a well-established approach [18]. At the same time, according to the recent review on anomaly detection [21], cybersecurity is currently one of the most popular fields for applying anomaly detection. When considering anomaly detection, the two types of tasks must be distinguished—outlier detection [10] and novelty detection [23]. In the outlier detection task, the anomaly (i.e. outlier—an object that differs much from the others) is included in the training data. The task objective is to find the most deviant objects in the set. The outlier detection is unsupervised learning due to the lack of labels in the training set. In novelty detection, the training set contains normal (correct, benign) objects only. The task objective is to find anomalies (i.e. novelties—the objects that differ much from those observed before) in the new data. Anomaly detection is considered a semi-supervised learning task as the elements in the training set contain labelled data, but there are no outliers. In the context of ML algorithms applicable for both tasks, the main difference is related to data distribution. In the outlier detection, abnormal objects do not form a dense group (otherwise, those objects are not considered outliers). In contrast, in novelty detection, abnormal objects can form such groups (e.g. samples recorded based on the network traffic during one specific attack).

In this work, we present Net Anomaly Detector (NAD) – the component designed to detect unknown attacks by recognising the network traffic novelties. The NAD module records regular traffic of the system and creates multiple models of normal traffic in the system using ML algorithms. Then module selects the model with the best performance according to the given criteria or combines models with one of the proposed strategies (i.e. ensemble model) and detect anomalies in network traffic using the selected model. The selected base approach is well established and widely used. Thus, we focused on the several features to increase robustness and ease both the deployment of the component in unknown networks and extending the module in the future—known attacks emulation, exhaustive features extraction, hyperparameter tuning, an adaptation of detection threshold and ensemble models strategies. The highly modular architecture allows the system to be expanded with adapters for various types of networks. Additionally, we propose three different component deployment schemes that differ in the level of decentralisation. One of the schemes was used in the actual testbed deployment within GUARD project[1].

---

[1] GUARD is a project co-funded within Horizon 2020 Funding Programme. The project aims to provide a cybersecurity framework to guarantee reliability and trust for digital service chains. More information can be found on the project website: https://guard-project.eu/.

The chapter is organized as follows. First, we discuss the application of machine learning for novelty detection within the NAD component. Then modular architecture of the NAD component is presented—main modules, variants of component deployment scheme and an exemplary deployment within the GUARD project. Finally, selected results of the experiments conducted on the CIC-IDS2017 dataset are presented.

2   Anomaly Detection with Machine Learning

The main aim of using the NAD component is to define the characteristics of the monitored network traffic, which should allow traffic anomalies detection with reasonably high quality (i.e. both low false-positive (FP) and false-negative (FN) rates). Machine learning is used to create a model of benign network traffic. The result of the learning phase is a model of initial network traffic. The model is used to validate new traffic in real-time—NAD checks whether online traffic fits the created model (i.e. if the traffic does not deviate from benign traffic too much). NAD activates anomaly alert if an outlier in traffic characteristic is detected.

2.1   Machine Learning Methods

The network traffic monitored in a specified location can be defined as a set of consecutive network messages recorded at that point. Timestamp of creation or registering can be assigned to each message. The set of messages can be divided into separate subsets according to some criteria (e.g. into time windows or by address of the sending device). The raw traffic needs to be converted into numeric vectors (a features extraction phase), each one representing a single set of messages. Vectors representing sets of messages recorded during regular (normal, benign, not malformed) system operation are used to create a model of the regular network traffic. The traffic (converted to numeric vectors) that does not match the network model is recognised as an anomaly.

As pointed out, the anomaly detection considered in this work is of the novelty detection type. Thus to train the model, only benign traffic is required. However, in our approach, abnormal traffic samples are also needed to validate models. If abnormal traffic is not available or cannot be produced in the monitored network, the NAD emulation module can be used to generate such traffic.

Training model with samples of one class only is known as One-Class Classification (OOC) [20]. The following ML-based classifiers have been implemented in NAD for solving OOC problems:

- One-Class SVM [30]—version of Support Vector Machine method [13], which builds a hyperplane that separates all or most input data points (representing regular traffic) from the origin (instead of the second class).
- Autoencoder [12]—the type of artificial neural network that can encode input vector and then decode the encoded input vector to get the original value. The autoencoder is built on data points representing regular traffic only.

Hence, only such data points can be encoded and decoded correctly. Other data points representing abnormal traffic after encoding and decoding are not similar to the original values.

– Variational Autoencoder [6]—the type of autoencoder which, instead of constructing latent space explicitly, first learns how to generate distribution depending on input sample (encoder part). The distribution is used to sample latent variable that is then used to reconstruct the input sample (decoder part).

– Local Outlier Factor [11]—to detect anomaly density of training samples around the evaluated sample is calculated and compared with the density of the given number of neighbours. If the density of the evaluated sample is significantly lower than the one of neighbours, then the sample is considered an anomaly.

– Clustering [5]—the input data are divided into one or more clusters (e.g. if network traffic varies at a different time of day). Each cluster is described with mean and radius. If a new data point does not belong to any cluster, it is identified as an anomaly. In most cases, the number of clusters that input data should be divided is unknown. Hence, using clustering methods that do not require an expected number of clusters as an input (e.g. model-based clustering based on finite Gaussian mixture modelling) or simple clustering (e.g. k-means) combined with the elbow method for the best number of cluster detection should be used.

The features selection in OCC problems is challenging due to lack of malicious samples in the training set—it is hard to predict which features will infer the presence of an anomaly. The optimal features set for detecting an attack may depend strongly on the attack type. Hence, the feature selection phase can be omitted in the case of machine learning methods that cope well with high dimensional data. However, this is not the case for all methods, e.g. One-Class SVM. Hence, the following methods were implemented in the NAD for extraction:

– Principal component analysis (PCA) [22]—a dimensionality reduction method, which performs orthogonal linear transformation to transform a set of features to a set of new features. The objective of the change is to keep the maximum possible variance of data while reducing the cardinality of the features set.

– Simple measures selection—a bunch of simple statistical measures are used to rank all features, and the defined number of best features is selected. The following measures were considered: kurtosis, Laplacian score [16], variance, Spectral score [19], the mean distance between points and centroid, inter-cluster distance, inter-quartile range. Following rank aggregation methods for combining rankings acquired by each measure were examined: average, Borda [29] and Dowdall [24].

– Static selection—features are filtered based on a predefined list of feature names to include or exclude.

– Pipeline—the features selection methods proposed above can be combined to create a pipeline, i.e. features set is reduced by each method, and the result is forwarded as the input to the consecutive method.

It could be argued that since malformed traffic is available during the training phase, the problem of attack detection could be considered as the outlier detection problem. However, the malicious traffic samples potentially form dense areas (e.g. traffic originating from one specific type of attack). Additionally, in practice, the traffic recorded in the network that is not under attack may contain contamination forming sparse areas. Such elements may result from, i.a. untypical user behaviour (but not malicious). We would call them *semi-outliers* since they are outliers from the perspective of the machine learning methods, but on the other hand, they are benign from the perspective of network security. However, in the case of binary classification, due to the infrequency and irregularity of those samples, they could be marked as anomalies with a greater probability than emulated malformed traffic injected into the training set.

Semi-outliers cause problems in novelty detection as well. ML algorithms tend to mark those samples as anomalies. Thus, reducing the high false-positive errors rate is one of the biggest challenges in anomaly detection in network traffic. The trade-off between false positive and false negative rates can be controlled with the decision threshold parameter.

2.2 Attack Emulation

Lack of malicious data in the training dataset causes problems with models evaluation and comparison, as detection quality for malicious samples cannot be evaluated. Thus, to overcome those problems, we used simulation techniques to implement attacks emulation. The attack emulation module is responsible for the artificial malformation of the network traffic. The result of the emulation is abnormal traffic that is further used to:

– Tune models hyperparameters,
– Adjust the detection threshold value,
– Compare models.

It needs to be highlighted that applying emulated malicious traffic has drawbacks as well—if the unknown attack is not similar to the ones emulated, it still can be missed by the anomaly detector. Thus emulation attacks should be diverse and representative.

2.3 Adjusting Detection Threshold

The OCC methods create a model of benign traffic. This model is then used to evaluate how well the newly monitored traffic fits the model. The evaluation result can be binary (does or does not fit) or numeric (i.e. score value). The score interpretation differs depending on algorithm type, but generally, it can be interpreted as the indicator of how much the evaluated sample differs from the normal sample. Binary decision mode is the default behaviour and is based on the threshold. The OCC method calculates the threshold value based on the training data. However, in the case of novelty detection, the OCC method has to guess what threshold will be optimal for detecting anomalies caused by future cyberattacks. In practice, the OCC method calculates some statistical measures for training data to decide how much of that data is abnormal. Such an approach is justified as training data may contain anomalies originating from other sources (more or less similar to the anomalies created by attacks). However, data with anomalies originating from some cyberattacks (real or emulated) within the NAD system is available. Even though such anomalies are mostly not identical to those caused by unknown attacks, still they are potentially more similar than anomalies caused by other sources. Thus those data can be used to support the decision-making process. We decided to implement a mechanism that makes it possible to use malicious data to adjust the classifier threshold value instead of the default one. The benign and malicious traffic samples are scored using the model in the adjusting threshold phase. For calculation of the optimal threshold value of Youden's J statistic [9] or f_β-score is used.

2.4   Ensemble Learning

When malicious traffic is available, the comparison of various algorithms and parameters is possible. However, the quality of unknown attacks detection cannot be predicted with high certainty. Moreover, models that proved to be of lower quality during the validation phase may outperform better models when new attacks occur. Therefore, we implemented in the NAD component several ensemble techniques that increase the stability of detection quality for various attacks. Ensemble learning is a technique to combine multiple models in one compound detector [14]. Thus, in NAD, the outcome of building an anomaly detector can be a bunch of base detectors—one detector for each user-defined configuration space. With each base detector, the weight value is assigned. The weight value is equal to the quality of the detector on the validation set, normalised for all detectors. The creation of an ensemble detector can increase the robustness of the detection. Four basic ensemble strategies were implemented in NAD:

- Non-weighted voting (SV)—each base detector votes if the sample represents an anomaly. The resulting score of the ensemble detector is the number of positive votes divided by a number of base detectors.
- Weighted voting (WV)—each base detector votes if the sample represents an anomaly. The resulting score of the ensemble detector is the sum of weights of base detectors that voted for the anomaly existence.
- Non-weighted scoring (AS)—each base detector scores the sample. The resulting score of the ensemble detector is the average score of all scores.
- Weighted scoring (WS)—each base detector scores the sample. The resulting score of the ensemble detector is a weighted average of all scores.

The important aspect of the two last strategies was to ensure that each base detector uses the same range of scores. Additionally, if two detectors assess the possibility that the sample is an anomaly on a similar level, they should score the sample with a similar value. Each base detector scores the samples with a value from 0 to 1. The scaling factor is learned on the training set. The detection threshold value is adjusted for each ensemble detector as for the base detector.

3   The NAD Architecture

The NAD component was designed as highly modular software. The architectural model of NAD is presented in Fig. 1. High modularity eases maintaining software and cross-team development in potential future applications of the NAD component. Adding a new feature, e.g. new ML algorithm for building models, requires only implementation of the specific interface and does not require any knowledge about NAD. Additionally, in the process of component deployment, the user's role should be limited as much as possible, mainly to set system properties, which depend on the user's preferences (e.g. sensitivity of the detection algorithms) and to ensure normal behaviour of the monitored network and system during the learning phase. This section briefly describes the main modules of the component and possible deployment schemes.

3.1   Modules

According to the data flow within the component, the consecutively modules are as follow:

Features Extraction. Feature extraction is an essential part of the learning process. It transfers as many traffic characteristics as possible from raw traffic logs to numerical vectors (features values). On the other hand, the NAD development's main goal was to automate the component deployment from the user perspective, so feature extraction should be as a general process as possible. The NAD component contains a special tool (i.e. extensive features extractor) that makes implementing adaptors for any network type much more effortless.

The general concept of the feature extraction process is as follows. Let us assume that there is a set of messages. Each message has some message attributes (payload length, source IP address, gateway id, timestamp etc.). The list of attributes depends on the network type. We define **grouping operation** as dividing a set of messages into disjunctive groups by some criteria— grouping attributes (e.g. session-id divides traffic into TCP/IP flows, grouping by timestamp range divides traffic into time windows). Grouping operation can be hierarchical—set can be divided first by one grouping attribute (e.g. time)

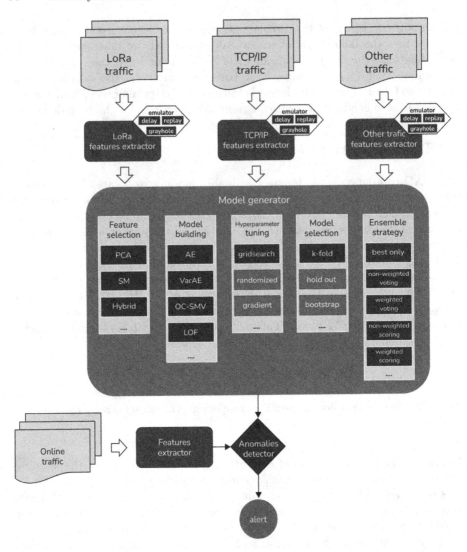

Fig. 1. The NAD modular architecture.

and then, e.g. into flows to obtain subgroups. When messages are grouped, each group can be characterised by a set of **group attributes**. The group attribute is a vector of values representing that group, e.g. intervals between consecutive messages in the group or payload length of each message. If the group attribute is not one of the message attributes (requires additional computation, e.g. intervals mentioned above), such attribute is called **derived attribute**.

As a result, each group is described with a set of vectors of different sizes, which is, in most cases, inconvenient for effective traffic modelling with ML. Hence, **aggregation functions** (e.g. sum, mean, max, min, skewness, etc.) are introduced to reduce the size of data. Each attribute can be aggregated with one or more functions. As a result of each aggregation, one value, called **feature value**, is obtained. If more than one grouping operation was applied, more aggregation operations also need to be involved (e.g. mean of means is calculated). Summing up, a **feature** is defined as a tuple of one or more grouping operations, one attribute and aggregation functions (number of aggregating functions is equal to the number of grouping operations). An exemplary feature definition is (time, source IP address, payload length, mean, mean). All computed features values create a vector that describes a set of messages used in further analysis.

Within the NAD component, versatile feature extraction [32] was implemented. The core idea of such feature extraction is to generate as many features as possible using many simple statistical measures as aggregation functions. The solution proved to be successful in domains with little domain knowledge. Little knowledge is also the case of unknown attack detection since it cannot be predicted which statistical measure will best reflect anomaly in network traffic during the specific attack. In NAD following aggregation functions were introduced:

- The mean value
- The maximal value
- The minimal value
- The range (difference between the maximal and minimal values)
- The sum of squared values (mean power)
- The standard deviation
- Skewness
- Kurtosis
- The 5th central moment
- The maximal difference between two consecutive measurements
- Autocorrelation taken at $t = 1, 2, 5, 20$ and 50
- Count of the given value (e.g. TCP in case protocol field)

Attack Emulation. The traffic is malformed within the feature extractor module: between raw traffic to standard format conversion and features extraction. The attack emulator contains a library of attacks (the current list includes DDoS, grayhole, replay, delay) and can be included in the new feature extractor "as it is". Each attack is configurable, e.g. intensity of the attack can be adjusted— performing the same type of attack with various configuration increases the quality of the abnormal dataset. Extending the library of attacks is possible if the specific attack for the given network type should be implemented.

Model Generator is the core component of NAD. The input data used in the model generator is defined as a set of samples—each sample (e.g. the flow in TCP/IP or traffic recorded in a time window) is represented by one vector. Within the model generator few submodules exist:

- Features selection—submodule responsible for selecting the most promising features of the network traffic (see Sect. 2.1).
- Model building—submodule responsible for building a model of the benign network traffic, mainly with the use of Machine Learning (see Sect. 2.1).
- Hyperparameters tuning—within the NAD platform, the space of hyperparameters values can be defined by the user. There exists several strategies for searching optimal set of hyperparameters values, e.g. grid search [26], randomized [8] and gradient [7].
- Model selection—various techniques can be used to validate the model quality and compare models to choose the most promising one. The exemplary of commonly used techniques are k-fold, bootstrap and hold out [17]. It should be stressed that in the NAD component, those techniques were modified due to introducing abnormal samples only to the validation set.
- Ensemble strategies—submodule responsible for combining multiple models into one to increase detection reliability (see Sect. 2.4).

Each submodule is easily extensible with new approaches.

Anomalies Detection. The model obtained from the model generator module examines traffic in the monitored network. Before the examination, the traffic is proceeded by the features extraction module mentioned above.

3.2 Deployment schemes

The high modularity of the architecture creates an opportunity to consider a few possible schemes of component deployment. In this section, we discuss three approaches (Fig. 2), but other variations are also possible.

Central Deployment (Fig. 2a). Network traffic is gathered in the edge device (e.g. router or gateway) and sent to the central system, where all modules of the NAD component are deployed. In this variant, resources of an edge device are barely used, but network load between edge and central nodes can be high, depending on the monitored network size and load.

Quasi-Central Deployment (Fig. 2b). The edge device is responsible not only for gathering traffic but also for feature extraction. The feature vectors are sent to the central node, and they're used there to train the model and examine new traffic. The network load is significantly lower than in the case of central deployment, whereas computation performed by edge devices does not require many resources. However, in the case of some resource-constrained devices, the burden of performing feature extraction can be significant.

Distributed Deployment (Fig. 2c). The edge device sends extracted features vectors to the central system in the training phase. Then the central system computes a model of the benign traffic and sends the model to the edge device. Then an edge device can examine network traffic without sending any network data outside of the system, which increases data safety. In this variant, the most resource-demanding computations are performed in the central system. Checking network traffic against the model of benign network traffic requires little computation. The drawback of this scheme is a potentially higher vulnerability for attacks, which use Adversarial Machine Learning techniques [15] due to a more accessible model of the benign traffic model for the attacker.

The choice of deployment scheme depends on the type of monitored network, resources available on the edge device, sensitivity of network data and risk of attacks based on adversarial machine learning.

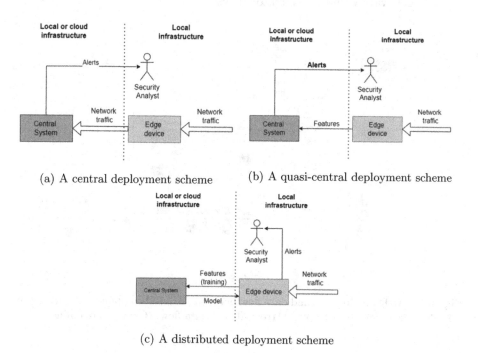

(a) A central deployment scheme   (b) A quasi-central deployment scheme

(c) A distributed deployment scheme

Fig. 2. Data flows in various schemes of the NAD component deployment. The thickness of the lines indicates the size of the data.

3.3   Integration with the Real Network Infrastructure

The NAD component was integrated and successfully deployed within the GUARD project as one of the Security Services. GUARD is a cybersecurity framework to guarantee reliability and trust for digital service chains. One of the main goals of the GUARD structure is to improve the detection of attacks and the identification of new threats, which the NAD component fits into. Two use cases were proposed as part of the project, and the appropriate testbeds were implemented. The NAD component was used to monitor LoRaWAN [28] network traffic within the use case related to the smart city [2]. In this use case, the NAD component was successfully integrated with the testbed and the real network deployed in Wolfsburg.

The GUARD framework architecture is presented in Fig. 3. The *GUARD agents* are deployed in monitored system infrastructure. Their responsibility is to gather security-related data from the monitored system and forward them to the core platform. There multiple *security services* are deployed. One of them is the NAD component. Due to GUARD framework architecture [3], the centralized variant of NAD deployment was chosen (Fig. 3). The component consumes network traffic from the ChirpStack Forwarder agent, which collects traffic from all LoRa gateways within the monitored system.

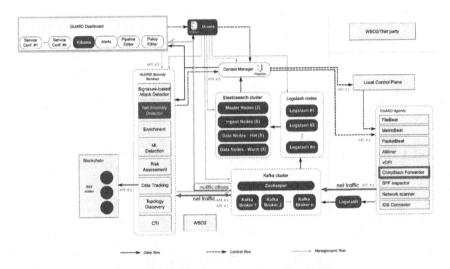

Fig. 3. GUARD architecture and data flow between GUARD components. With green color NAD component is marked. Arrows depict data flow. (Color figure online)

4   Experiments

In this work to conduct experiments on unknown attacks detection, the NAD component and the CIC-IDS2017 dataset [25] were used. This dataset contains TCP/IP traffic represented as a set of flows. Each flow is labelled according to the source—if it comes from a benign source or results from a malicious connection. In this experiment, three types of DDoS attacks are included in the validation set: DoS slowloris, DoS Slowhttptest and DoS Hulk. Only one attack, DoS Goldeneye, was included in the test dataset. In the case of flows analysis, anomaly detection aims not only to detect that the monitored network is under attack (which in the case of DDoS attack is an easy task) but also to label flows responsible for the attack. As the model quality indicator and to tune hyperparameters values, the area under the precision-recall curve (AUC-PR) [27] measure was used. In the process of decision threshold adjustment, $f_{0.5}$ score was used to provide higher weight to the precision of the model over recall (in anomaly detection problems, the high false-positive rate is usually highly undesirable)

4.1 Repeatability

The main goal of the NAD component is to select the best configuration according to some given measure (AUC-PR in the case of experiments described in this section). In this process, all checked configurations are ranked. The ranking process needs to be characterised with high repeatability—the configurations should be ranked in the same or very similar order each time the process is repeated, independently on random factors (e.g. splitting the dataset into training, validation and testing sets). In this experiment k-fold approach, which is widely used in the ML area to compare decision models, is examined. The k-fold is slightly modified in our system as validation data is extended with abnormal traffic, which is not included in training data. Thus, some preliminary test of repeatability was performed on the exemplary dataset—we checked how much the ranking of configurations is similar within each configuration space. We selected five configuration spaces:

- Static feature selection + Autoencoder (AE, 9 configurations)
- Static feature selection + Variantional Autoencoder (VarAE, 9 configurations)
- PCA + SVM (PCA-SVM, 7 configurations)
- PCA + LOF (PCA-LOF, 42 configurations)
- Simple measures based feature selection + SVM (SM-SVM, 10 configurations)

The ranking method was applied three times on the same dataset (the learning and validation sets varied due to random split). Rank-biased Overlap (RBO) [31] measure was used to check the similarity of rankings. RBO measure can be parametrised with $p \in \langle 0, 1 \rangle$ to determine the weight of the top ranks for the value of the similarity measure—$p = 1$ means that all ranks have equal weight, the smaller value of p the highest contribution of top ranks is. In the case of our approach, the most important is the repeatability of choosing a few top configurations (the best ones can be dropped due to instability; thus, the order of the following configurations is also important). In Table 1 RBO for $p = 1$ and $p = 0.5$ as well as standard deviation of APR AUC that determines the ranking are presented.

Table 1. Rank-biased Overlap of rankings obtained in three runs of the experiments and standard deviation of APR AUC of all configurations in the given space.

Configuration space	RBO ($p = 1$)	RBO ($p = 0.5$)	SD_{AUPRC}
AE	0.61	0.38	0.004
VarAE	0.85	0.64	0.006
PCA-SVM	0.86	0.58	0.001
PCA-LOF	0.93	0.97	0.115
SM-SVM	0.95	0.99	0.057

Table 2. The confusion matrix for SM-SVM detector (results for one run only).

		Predicted value	
		Negative	Positive
Actual value	Negative	0.64	0.006
	Positive	0.58	0.001

In the case of PCA-LOF and SM-SVM, the repeatability is high. For the rest configurations spaces, the repeatability of the process seemingly looks insufficient. However, the reason for low repeatability is a slight variance of the APR AUC within each space—the quality of all configurations is comparable: thus, even significant changes in ranking those configurations is irrelevant.

4.2   Unknown DoS Detection

The obtained base detectors (one for each configuration space) were examined against the test set (benign traffic and DoS Goldeneye, which was not seen previously by the system). The experiment was repeated three times as before. The $f_{0.5}$-score value obtained by each base detector on the validation set (known attacks) and the test set (unknown attack) is shown in Fig. 4. Firstly, it can be observed that the quality of detection for the test set is lower (except SM-SVM). The high standard deviation of PCA-SVM was caused by choosing another configuration in one of three experiment runs. As expected, that configuration performed well on the validation set ($f_{0.5}$-score equal to 0.92), similarly to all other configurations in this configuration space (see Table 1). However, surprisingly it was significantly weaker on the test set ($f_{0.5}$-score equal to 0.59).

The confusion matrix for the first run of the experiment for the SM-SVM detector (the best detector according to the mean score) is presented in Table 2. The frequency of raised alarms during the attack is much higher than when the system operates in normal conditions, making detection that the monitored system is under attack easy. Additionally, as intended, the FPR is relatively low. However, in case of mitigation of the attack (e.g. by dropping the suspicious traffic), the number of dropped benign connections may be unacceptable.

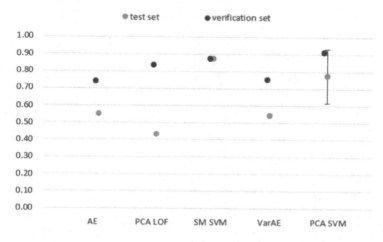

Fig. 4. Average $f_{0.5}$-score and standard deviation obtained by base detection models for the validation set (in blue) and the test set (in orange). (Color figure online)

4.3   Ensemble Models

The weight of each base detector was calculated based on the value of the APR AUC measure (see Table 3) obtained on the validation set. In each experiment run, the PCA-SVM detector was recognized as the best detector (the highest value of APR AUC on the validation set). The quality of all ensemble detectors for the testing set is shown in Fig. 5. It can be observed that the high standard deviation of the most significant detector (PCA-SVM) propagates on ensemble detectors, except for the case of weighted voting strategy. In the case of all assemble detectors, the standard deviation of the results is smaller than for the PCA-SVM base detector. In this scenario, the weighted voting strategy proved to be insensitive to the instability of base detectors, increasing the robustness of the approach.

Table 3. Quality (APR AUC) and weight of base detectors obtained on the validation set.

Base detector	APR AUC		Weight
	Mean	Standard deviation	
AE	0.82	0.001	0.19
VarAE	0.81	0.002	0.19
PCA-SVM	0.92	0.007	0.22
PCA-LOF	0.80	0.007	0.19
SM-SVM	0.91	0.003	0.21

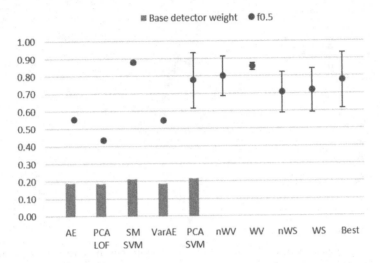

Fig. 5. Base detectors weights (marked with orange), the mean and standard deviation of base and ensemble detectors (marked with blue). (Color figure online)

4.4 Threshold Adjustment

The performance of each detector depends on how well the model evaluates the anomaly level of the sample (scoring) and on the detection threshold value—the minimal score value to assess the sample as an anomaly. The threshold in NAD is calculated based on the validation set that contains initial traffic and exemplary malicious traffic (originated from known attacks), which may be much different from the malicious traffic in the test set (derived from unknown attacks). The experiment aimed to check how much optimal threshold value acquired with the validation set differs from the one calculated for the test set and how this difference influences the model quality.

In our experiment, $f_{0.5}$-score measure is used to calculate the optimal value of the threshold. In Figs. 6 and 7, the precision-recall curves for the weighted votes detector and Autoencoder detector for the test set are presented, respectively. In both figures, green dots denote the optimal threshold values calculated for the validation set, while red dots denote the optimal threshold values calculated for the test set. Although the curves differ, their area is similar—the WV detector performs better if a small recall is preferable, the AE in the opposite situation. In the case of the WV detector, the value of the threshold obtained with the validation set is close to the optimal value for the test set, which is a highly desirable situation. In the case of the Autoencoder detector, the optimal value of the threshold obtained with the validation set does not perform well in the case of the test set. The AE model quality makes it possible to obtain $f_{0.5}$-score equal to 0.8 (if optimal threshold value could be calculated on the test set). Thus, it may be concluded that the quality of the threshold adjustment is mainly responsible for the poor detector performance on the test set ($f_{0.5}$-score equal to 0.55). On the other hand, the threshold adjustment mechanism performs well for the WV detector and other ensemble detectors.

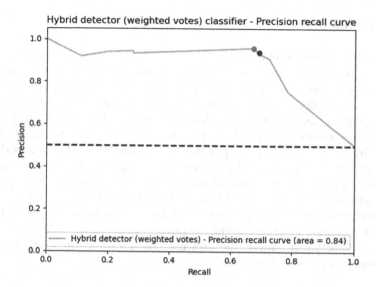

Fig. 6. Precision recall curve for Weighted Votes detector for test set. Green dot denotes the optimal threshold value calculated for the validation set, while red dote denotes the optimal threshold value calculated for the test set. (Color figure online)

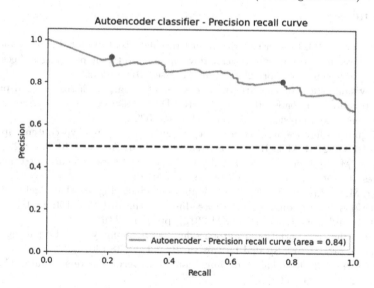

Fig. 7. Precision recall curve for Autoencoder detector for test set. Green dot denotes the optimal threshold value calculated for the validation set, while red dote denotes the optimal threshold value calculated for the test set. (Color figure online)

5   Conclusions

In this chapter, we presented the Net Anomaly Detector component, which is designed to detect anomalies in network traffic of various types using ML. The component incorporates several mechanisms for increasing the quality of unknown attack detection, i.e. known attacks emulation, exhaustive feature extraction, hyperparameter tuning, detection threshold adaptation and ensemble models strategies. The architecture of the component, its potential deployment variances and exemplary deployment within the GUARD framework were presented. We showed that: the proposed hyperparameter tuning and modified k-fold are characterised with acceptable repeatability; adjusting hyperparameters values and detection threshold values with the use of dataset with samples malformed with known attacks allows to detect of unknown attacks with high quality; application of some ensemble strategies increase the robustness of the anomalies detection. However, the presented results are preliminary and more experiments on heterogeneous datasets are required.

Acknowledgement. This work was supported in part by the European Commission under Grant Agreement no. 833456 (GUARD).

References

1. Check point's 2021 cyber security report reveals extent of global cyber pandemic, and shows how organizations can develop immunity. https://pages.checkpoint.com/cyber-security-report-2021.html. Accessed 10 Jan 2022
2. D2.1 vision, state of the art and requirements analysis. https://guard-project.eu/wp-content/uploads/2019/11/GUARD_D2.1_Vision-State-of-the-Art-and-Requirements-Analysis.pdf. Accessed 10 Jan 2022
3. D2.2 guard reference architecture. https://guard-project.eu/wp-content/uploads/2020/04/D2.2_GUARD-Reference-Architecture.pdf. Accessed 10 Jan 2022
4. Ahmed, M., Mahmood, A.N., Hu, J.: A survey of network anomaly detection techniques. J. Netw. Comput. Appl. **60**, 19–31 (2016)
5. Amer, M., Goldstein, M.: Nearest-neighbor and clustering based anomaly detection algorithms for rapidminer. In: Proceedings of the 3rd RapidMiner Community Meeting and Conference (RCOMM 2012), pp. 1–12 (2012)
6. An, J., Cho, S.: Variational autoencoder based anomaly detection using reconstruction probability. Special Lecture on IE **2**(1), 1–18 (2015)
7. Bengio, Y.: Gradient-based optimization of hyperparameters. Neural Comput. **12**(8), 1889–1900 (2000)
8. Bergstra, J., Bengio, Y.: Random search for hyper-parameter optimization. J. Mach. Learn. Res. **13**(2), 281–305 (2012)
9. Bewick, V., Cheek, L., Ball, J.: Statistics review 13: receiver operating characteristic curves. Critic. Care **8**(6), 1–5 (2004)
10. Bhatti, M.A., Riaz, R., Rizvi, S.S., Shokat, S., Riaz, F., Kwon, S.J.: Outlier detection in indoor localization and internet of things (IoT) using machine learning. J. Commun. Netw. **22**(3), 236–243 (2020)

11. Breunig, M.M., Kriegel, H.P., Ng, R.T., Sander, J.: LOF: identifying density-based local outliers. In: Proceedings of the 2000 ACM SIGMOD international conference on Management of data, pp. 93–104 (2000)
12. Chen, Z., Yeo, C.K., Lee, B.S., Lau, C.T.: Autoencoder-based network anomaly detection. In: 2018 Wireless Telecommunications Symposium (WTS), pp. 1–5. IEEE (2018)
13. Cortes, C., Vapnik, V.: Support-vector networks. Mach. Learn. **20**(3), 273–297 (1995)
14. Dietterich, T.G., et al.: Ensemble learning. The handbook of brain theory and neural networks. Arbib MA **2**(1), 110–125 (2002)
15. Grieco, G., Grinblat, G.L., Uzal, L., Rawat, S., Feist, J., Mounier, L.: Toward large-scale vulnerability discovery using machine learning. In: Proceedings of the Sixth ACM Conference on Data and Application Security and Privacy, pp. 85–96 (2016)
16. He, X., Cai, D., Niyogi, P.: Laplacian score for feature selection. In: Weiss, Y., Schölkopf, B., Platt, J. (eds.) Advances in Neural Information Processing Systems, vol. 18. MIT Press (2006). https://proceedings.neurips.cc/paper/2005/file/b5b03f06271f8917685d14cea7c6c50a-Paper.pdf
17. Kim, J.H.: Estimating classification error rate: repeated cross-validation, repeated hold-out and bootstrap. Comput. Stat. Data Anal. **53**(11), 3735–3745 (2009)
18. Lane, T., Brodley, C.E.: An application of machine learning to anomaly detection. In: Proceedings of the 20th National Information Systems Security Conference, vol. 377, pp. 366–380. Baltimore, USA (1997)
19. Lorena, L.H., Carvalho, A.C., Lorena, A.C.: Filter feature selection for one-class classification. J. Intell. Robot. Syst. **80**(1), 227–243 (2015)
20. Moya, M.M., Hush, D.R.: Network constraints and multi-objective optimization for one-class classification. Neural Netw. **9**(3), 463–474 (1996)
21. Nassif, A.B., Talib, M.A., Nasir, Q., Dakalbab, F.M.: Machine learning for anomaly detection: a systematic review. IEEE Access **9**, 78658–78700 (2021)
22. Partridge, M., Calvo, R.A.: Fast dimensionality reduction and simple PCA. Intell. Data Anal. **2**(3), 203–214 (1998)
23. Pimentel, M.A., Clifton, D.A., Clifton, L., Tarassenko, L.: A review of novelty detection. Signal Process. **99**, 215–249 (2014)
24. Reilly, B.: Social choice in the south seas: electoral innovation and the borda count in the pacific island countries. Int. Politic. Sci. Rev. **23**(4), 355–372 (2002)
25. Sharafaldin, I., Lashkari, A.H., Ghorbani, A.A.: Toward generating a new intrusion detection dataset and intrusion traffic characterization. ICISSP **1**, 108–116 (2018)
26. Shekar, B.H., Dagnew, G.: Grid search-based hyperparameter tuning and classification of microarray cancer data. In: 2019 Second International Conference on Advanced Computational and Communication Paradigms (ICACCP), pp. 1–8 (2019). https://doi.org/10.1109/ICACCP.2019.8882943
27. Sofaer, H.R., Hoeting, J.A., Jarnevich, C.S.: The area under the precision-recall curve as a performance metric for rare binary events. Method. Ecol. Evol. **10**(4), 565–577 (2019)
28. Sornin, N., Yegin, A.: Lorawan^{TM} 1.1 specification (2017). https://lora-alliance.org/wp-content/uploads/2020/11/lorawantm_specification_-v1.1.pdf. Accessed 10 Jan 2022
29. Tang, Y., Tong, Q.: Bordarank: A ranking aggregation based approach to collaborative filtering. In: 2016 IEEE/ACIS 15th International Conference on Computer and Information Science (ICIS), pp. 1–6 (2016). https://doi.org/10.1109/ICIS.2016.7550761

30. Wang, Y., Wong, J., Miner, A.: Anomaly intrusion detection using one class SVM. In: Proceedings from the Fifth Annual IEEE SMC Information Assurance Workshop, pp. 358–364 (2004). https://doi.org/10.1109/IAW.2004.1437839
31. Webber, W., Moffat, A., Zobel, J.: A similarity measure for indefinite rankings. ACM Trans. Inf. Syst. **28**(4), 1–38 (2010). https://doi.org/10.1145/1852102.1852106
32. Zagorecki, A.: A versatile approach to classification of multivariate time series data. In: 2015 Federated Conference on Computer Science and Information Systems (FedCSIS), pp. 407–410. IEEE (2015)

Detecting Unknown Cyber Security Attacks Through System Behavior Analysis

Florian Skopik[(✉)] [iD], Markus Wurzenberger[iD], and Max Landauer[iD]

AIT Austrian Institute of Technology, Vienna, Austria
{florian.skopik,markus.wurzenberger,max.landauer}@ait.ac.at

Abstract. For many years signature-based intrusion detection has been applied to discover known malware and attack vectors. However, with the advent of malware toolboxes, obfuscation techniques and the rapid discovery of new vulnerabilities, novel approaches for intrusion detection are required. System behavior analysis is a cornerstone to recognizing adversarial actions on endpoints in computer networks that are not known in advance. Logs are incrementally produced textual data that reflect events and their impact on technical systems. Their efficient analysis is key for operational cyber security. We investigate approaches beyond applying simple regular expressions, and provide insights into novel machine learning mechanisms for parsing and analyzing log data for online anomaly detection. The AMiner is an open source implementation of a pipeline that implements many machine learning algorithms that are feasible for deeper analysis of system behavior, recognizing deviations from learned models and thus spotting a wide variety of even unknown attacks.

Keywords: Cyber security · Anomaly detection · Unknown attacks · Log data analysis · System behavior monitoring · Intrusion detection · Machine learning · Artificial intelligence

1 Introduction

Log files capture information about almost all events that take place in a system. Depending on the set log level, the deployed logging infrastructure automatically collects, aggregates and stores the logs that are continuously produced by many components and devices, e.g., web servers, databases, or firewalls. The textual log messages are usually human-readable and attached to a timestamp that specifies the point in time when the log entry was generated. Especially for large organizations and enterprises, the benefits of having access to long-term log data are manifold: Historic logs enable forensic analysis of past events. Most prominently applied after faults occurred in the system, forensic analysis gives system administrators the possibility to trace back the roots of observed problems. Moreover, the logs may help to recover the system to a non-faulty state, reset incorrect

---

An adapted version of this article has been published in [11].

J. Kołodziej et al. (Eds.): Cybersecurity of Digital Service Chains, LNCS 13300, pp. 103–119, 2022.
https://doi.org/10.1007/978-3-031-04036-8_5

transactions, restore data, prevent losses of information, and replicate scenarios that lead to erroneous states during testing. Finally, logs also allow administrators to validate the performance of processes and discover design bottlenecks. In addition to these functional advantages, storing logs is typically inexpensive since log files can effectively be compressed due to a high number of repeating lines. Consequently, capturing and storing logs is rather straight forward compared to their analysis. Eventually, we do not face a big data problem, but rather a big analysis problem.

A major issue with forensic log analysis is that problems are only detected in hindsight. Furthermore, it is a time- and resource-consuming task that requires domain knowledge about the system at hand. For these reasons, modern approaches in cyber security shift from a purely forensic to a proactive analysis [6]. Thereby, real-time fault detection is enabled by constantly monitoring system logs in an online manner, i.e., as soon as they are generated. This allows timely responses and in turn reduces the costs caused by incidents and cyber attacks [10]. On top of that, indicators for upcoming erroneous system behavior can frequently be observed in advance. Detecting such indicators early enough and initiating appropriate countermeasures can help to prevent certain faults altogether.

Unfortunately, this task is hardly possible for humans since log data is generated in immense volumes and fast rates. When considering large enterprise systems, it is not uncommon that the number of daily produced log lines is up in the millions, for example, publicly available Hadoop Distributed File System (HDFS) logs comprise more than 4 million log lines per day [17] and small organizations are expected to deal with peaks of 22,000 events per second [2]. Clearly, this makes manual analysis impossible and it thus stands to reason to employ machine learning algorithms that automatically process the lines and recognize interesting patterns that are then presented to system operators in a condensed form. Literally hundreds of different machine learning approaches have been proposed over the last decades. However, when it comes to processing log data online (i.e., when they are generated), it becomes quite tricky to pick (and possibly adapt) them to the specific requirements of this application area. The reasons for that are manifold:

- Single log lines cannot easily be categorized as good or bad, but their classification often relies on the surrounding context.
- Most machine learning approaches were designed for numerical data, e.g., sensor readings, not complex text-based data.
- Log data possess unknown grammar, which means their style, format, and meaning is usually not fully documented and understood by those analyzing them.
- For intrusion detection near real-time use is preferred, this means approaches must be able to process data online, i.e., when they are produced. As a consequence, approaches need to work in a "single pass" manner and process data in streams in an efficient way.

– Since the monitored environment may change rapidly, the usually separated training- and detection-phases of machine learning approaches may overlap and disturb each other. It is not acceptable that a single change triggers the need to learn a complex model from scratch, but models should be rather adaptable.

Bearing these challenges in mind, in recent years, we have worked on several concepts to extend the State of the Art, specifically to move from token-based to character-based parsing and analysis and enable much more fine-grained analysis at comparable speed. To accomplish this, we went away from linear lists of search patterns to tree-based parsers which at the same time tremendously simplify structured access to unstructured log data. Eventually, this is an important prerequisite for advanced analysis, such as time series analysis, correlation analysis or sequence analysis.

The Open Source Software AMiner [1] implements these concepts. We take a closer look into challenges of log data analysis for security purposes, the design methodology of a modern machine learning based solution, and provide insights into its application with some practical examples.

2 Log Data Analysis for Security Purposes

A wide variety of security solutions have been proposed in recent years to cope with increasing security challenges. While some solutions could effectively address upcoming cyber security problems, research on intrusion detection systems is still one of the main topics of computer security science. Signature-based approaches (using blocklists) are still the de-facto standard applied today for some good reasons: they are simple to configure, can be centrally managed, i.e., do not need much customization for specific networks, yield an efficient, robust and reliable detection and provide low false positive rates. While these are significant benefits for their application in today's enterprise environments, there are, nevertheless, solid arguments to work on more sophisticated anomaly-based detection mechanisms.

For instance, technical zero-day vulnerabilities are not detectable by blocklisting approaches; in fact, there are no signatures to describe the indicators of an unknown exploit. Furthermore, attackers can easily circumvent conventional intrusion detection, once indicators are widely distributed. Re-compiling a malware with small modifications will change hash sums, names, IP addresses of command and control servers, rendering previous indicators useless. The interconnection of previously isolated infrastructures entails new entrance points to ICT infrastructures. Especially in infrastructures comprising legacy systems and devices with small market shares, signature-based approaches are mostly inapplicable, because of their lack of (long-term) vendor support and often poor documentation. Eventually, sophisticated attacks use social engineering as an initial intrusion vector. Here, no technical vulnerabilities are exploited, hence, no concise blocklist indicators for the protocol level can appropriately describe erratic and malicious behavior.

Especially the latter aspect requires smart anomaly detection approaches to reliably discover deviations from a desired or previously observed system's behavior because of an unusual utilization through an illegitimate user. This is the usual case when an adversary manages to steal user credentials, e.g., by phishing, and uses these legitimate credentials to illegitimately access a system. However, an attacker will eventually utilize the system differently from the legitimate user, for instance running scans, searching shared directories and trying to extend their presence to surrounding systems. These activities will be executed at either unusual speed, or at unusual times, taking unusual routes in the network, issuing actions with unusual frequency, or causing unusual data transfers at unusual bandwidth. This will generate a series of events, visible in log data and identifiable by anomaly-based detection approaches.

Blocklisting approaches can be effective in some of these cases. For instance, detecting access attempts outside business hours is a standard case, which every well-configured IDS can handle. Nevertheless, using blocklisting only, the security personnel must think upfront of all the potential attack cases, and how they could manifest in the network. This is not only a cumbersome and tedious task, but also extremely error-prone. In contrast to that, the application of anomaly-based approaches seems promising: one needs to describe the "normal and desired system behavior" (this means to create an allowlist of what is known good) and everything that differs from this description is classified as potentially hostile. The effort is comparatively lower, and remarkably demonstrates the advantage of an anomaly-based approach [4]. However, these advantages come with a price. While signature-based approaches tend to generate false negatives, i.e., not detected attacks, anomaly-based approaches usually are prone to high false positive rates. Complex behavior models and potentially error-prone training phases are just some of the drawbacks to consider. Deploying, configuring and effectively operating an anomaly detection system that ingests log data, is a complicated task. We employ the setting described in Example 1.1 as a guiding scenario for the step-wise introduction of our log data analysis solution.

Example: An internal web server hosts numerous services and sensitive resources. Legitimate users may retrieve these resources and modify them via Web-based forms. The security operators collect access logs, using client IP, user agent, requested resource name, and request method to build a system model, consisting of expected event types and values, used as a baseline for anomaly detection. The log data look like this:

```
[...]
10.0.0.130 - - [04/Mar/2021:06:55:35] "GET /projX/doc1 HTTP/1.1" 200 3844 "http://doc.
    acme.com/projX/" "Mozilla/5.0"
10.0.0.139 - - [04/Mar/2021:06:55:45] "GET /projX/doc2 HTTP/1.1" 200 2845 "http://doc.
    acme.com/projX/" "Mozilla/5.0"
10.0.0.139 - - [04/Mar/2021:06:55:45] "GET /projX/doc2p1 HTTP/1.1" 200 849 "http://doc.
    acme.com/projX/" "Mozilla/5.0"
10.0.0.121 - - [04/Mar/2021:06:55:47] "GET /projX/doc1 HTTP/1.1" 200 3844 "http://doc.
    acme.com/projX/" "Mozilla/5.0"
10.1.0.137 - - [04/Mar/2021:06:55:48] "GET /projY/xls7 HTTP/1.1" 200 3574 "http://doc.
    acme.com/projY/" "Mozilla/5.0"
```

```
10.0.0.130 - - [04/Mar/2021:06:55:54] "POST /edit/doc2 HTTP/1.1" 200 3243 "http://doc.
    acme.com/projX/edit.php?page=doc2" "Mozilla/5.0"
10.0.0.130 - - [04/Mar/2021:06:55:55] "GET /projX/doc2 HTTP/1.1" 200 3243 "http://doc.
    acme.com/projX/" "Mozilla/5.0"
10.0.0.130 - - [04/Mar/2021:06:55:55] "GET /projX/doc2p1 HTTP/1.1" 200 849 "http://doc.
    acme.com/projX/" "Mozilla/5.0"
10.0.0.130 - - [04/Mar/2021:06:55:56] "GET /projX/doc1 HTTP/1.1" 200 3844 "http://doc.
    acme.com/projX/" "Mozilla/5.0"
10.0.0.130 - - [04/Mar/2021:06:56:34] "POST /edit/doc1 HTTP/1.1" 200 4341 "http://doc.
    acme.com/projX/edit.php?page=doc1" "Mozilla/5.0"
10.0.0.130 - - [04/Mar/2021:06:56:36] "GET /projX/doc1 HTTP/1.1" 200 3844 "http://doc.
    acme.com/projX/" "Mozilla/5.0"
[...]
```

Looking into this rather short and simplified snippet, we can already observe a number of properties feasible for model building. For instance, we can observe different client IPs accessing different types of Web resources, although not all IPs access the same resources. We can observe similarities in paths (there is projectX and projectY), we can see that only one user 10.0.0.130 edits documents (using HTTP POST requests), while the others mainly retrieve data (using GET). We learn that all users utilize the same user agent, presumably the browser of the companys software standard. Looking closer, we observe even certain sequences per IP address, for instance, whenever there is a POST request, the same client retrieves the changed document again via a consecutive GET request. Furthermore, doc2 consists of two parts, which are both always retrieved together, assuming doc2 includes doc2p1 the browser automatically fetches both in two consecutive requests. These are all behavioral properties of using the Web based systems which can be observed and captured using machine learning.

Example 1.1. Illustrative scenario

3   Incremental Character-Based Event Processing

Every analysis starts with dissecting the input data to make it fit for further processing. Commonly, predefined parsers are used to break up log data according to known event structures. This is also the right phase in the analysis process to get rid of excessive raw data and keep only those parts with high entropy, i.e., that contribute most knowledge in the further analysis process. For instance, an access event on a web server, as illustrated in Example 1.1, could be associated with a representative event class id and enriched with the most important parameters (e.g., client IP, user agent and accessed resource name), while the raw log text could be dumped. This way, fixed parts of log lines that add little to the further analysis and variable parts that carry the interesting information can be distinguished. Moreover, progressing from word-based tokenizing to the character level and considering similarities between words at specific positions within a log line, e.g., similarities of IP addresses, resource names and file paths, adds additional value and simplifies the construction of a baseline. Character-based event processing and templating aims to achieve exactly that.

Clustering is an effective technique to describe the computer system and network behavior by grouping similar log lines in clusters [7]. Furthermore, it allows to periodically review rare events (outliers) and checking frequent events by comparing cluster sizes over time (e.g., trends in the number of requests to certain resources) [8]. Hence, clustering supports organizations to have a thorough understanding about what is going on in their network infrastructures, to review log data and to find anomalous events in log data. Existing tools are not fully suitable to cover all these requirements, as they still show some essential deficits. Most of them, such as SLCT [13] implement token-based matching of log entries, i.e., they split up log lines at whitespaces or other defined delimiters. They treat terms and words with multiple spellings or differences in one character, such as "php-admin" and "phpadmin", or similar URLs, as entirely different. This motivated our research on character-based matching algorithms with comparable runtime performance to token-based matching. Furthermore, existing traditional tools applied for log line clustering are usually not able to process log data with high throughput and therefore are only applicable for forensic analysis, but not for online anomaly detection.

Our incremental clustering approach [16] that implements density and character-based clustering, applies a single pass clustering algorithm that processes data in streams or line by line, instead of batches. This enables online anomaly detection, i.e., log lines are processed at the time they are generated. Clustering approaches that are applied for online anomaly detection have to fulfill some essential requirements: (i) process data timely, i.e., when it is generated, (ii) adopt the cluster map promptly (Notice, cluster map refers to the structure of the clustering, i.e., the clusters and their identifiers, which can be, for example, a template or a representative for each cluster.), and (iii) deal with large amounts of data. Nevertheless, existing clustering approaches that usually process all data at once, such as SLCT [13], suffer from three major drawbacks, which make them unsuitable for online anomaly detection in log data: (i) Static cluster maps: Adapting/updating a cluster map is time consuming and computationally expensive. If new data points occur that account for new clusters, the whole cluster map has to be recalculated. (ii) Memory expensive: Distance-based clustering approaches are limited by the available memory, because large distance matrices have to be stored – depending on the applied distance, n^2 or $n^2/2$ elements have to be stored. (iii) Computationally expensive: Log data is stored as text data. Therefore, string metrics are applied to calculate the distance (similarity) between log lines. Their computation is usually expensive and time consuming.

In order to overcome these challenges, we introduced an incremental clustering approach that processes log data sequentially in streams to enable online anomaly detection in ICT networks. We proposed a concept, applied in Example 1.2, that comprises a number of novel features [16] as follows:

– The processing time of incremental clustering grows linearly with the rate of input log lines, and there is no re-arrangement of the cluster map required. The distances between log lines do not need to be stored.

- Fast filters reduce the number of distance computations that have to be carried out. A semi-supervised approach based on self-learning reduces the configuration and maintenance effort for a system administrator.
- The modularity of our approach allows the application of different existing metrics to build the cluster map and carry out anomaly detection.
- Our approach enables detection of point anomalies, i.e., single anomalous log lines, by outlier detection. Collective anomalies, i.e., anomalous number of occurrences of normal log lines that represent a change in the system behavior, are detected through time series analysis.

Example: Applying the introduced incremental clustering to the log data of Example 1.1, the following clusters emerge (assuming we blind out the timestamp from the similarity calculations). Naturally, the two POST requests are different from all the GET requests, furthermore the two requests for doc2p1 are longer and look a bit different from the others. Also, the one request to /projY is different from all the others in at least two spots and the IP address differs too from all the others. In this simple example, the advantage of character-level templates becomes already visible: We can account for similarities in paths and IP addresses (e.g., distinguish IP address from different subnets without the need to specify the same).

```
[Cluster 1]
10.0.0.130 - - [04/Mar/2021:06:55:35] "GET /projX/doc1 HTTP/1.1" 200 3844 "http://doc.
    acme.com/projX/" "Mozilla/5.0"
10.0.0.139 - - [04/Mar/2021:06:55:45] "GET /projX/doc2 HTTP/1.1" 200 2845 "http://doc.
    acme.com/projX/" "Mozilla/5.0"
10.0.0.121 - - [04/Mar/2021:06:55:47] "GET /projX/doc1 HTTP/1.1" 200 3844 "http://doc.
    acme.com/projX/" "Mozilla/5.0"
10.0.0.130 - - [04/Mar/2021:06:55:55] "GET /projX/doc2 HTTP/1.1" 200 3243 "http://doc.
    acme.com/projX/" "Mozilla/5.0"
10.0.0.130 - - [04/Mar/2021:06:55:56] "GET /projX/doc1 HTTP/1.1" 200 3844 "http://doc.
    acme.com/projX/" "Mozilla/5.0"
10.0.0.130 - - [04/Mar/2021:06:56:36] "GET /projX/doc1 HTTP/1.1" 200 3844 "http://doc.
    acme.com/projX/" "Mozilla/5.0"

[Cluster 2]
10.1.0.137 - - [04/Mar/2021:06:55:48] "GET /projY/xls7 HTTP/1.1" 200 3574 "http://doc.
    acme.com/projY/" "Mozilla/5.0"

[Cluster 3]
10.0.0.139 - - [04/Mar/2021:06:55:45] "GET /projX/doc2p1 HTTP/1.1" 200 849 "http://doc.
    acme.com/projX/" "Mozilla/5.0"
10.0.0.130 - - [04/Mar/2021:06:55:55] "GET /projX/doc2p1 HTTP/1.1" 200 849 "http://doc.
    acme.com/projX/" "Mozilla/5.0"

[Cluster 4]
10.0.0.130 - - [04/Mar/2021:06:55:54] "POST /edit/doc2 HTTP/1.1" 200 3243 "http://doc.
    acme.com/projX/edit.php?page=doc2" "Mozilla/5.0"
10.0.0.130 - - [04/Mar/2021:06:56:34] "POST /edit/doc1 HTTP/1.1" 200 4341 "http://doc.
    acme.com/projX/edit.php?page=doc1" "Mozilla/5.0"
```

Example 1.2. Clustered log lines

4 Creating Cluster Templates

Most clustering algorithms [7], when applied to our problem scope, provide no or only inaccurate and insufficient information on the content of a log line cluster.

Specifically, tokens that differ in only single characters are seen as entirely different; furthermore, optional tokens in a log line disturb the sequence of tokens and lead to wrong comparisons. Thus, we developed template generators [14] that create meaningful cluster descriptions, a prerequisite for feature selection used by machine learning solutions as well as generating log parsers [15]. Furthermore, templates can be applied for log classification in general, for log reduction through filtering, and for event counting. A template is basically a string that consists of substrings which occur in every log line of a cluster in a similar location. Those substrings are referred to as static parts of the log lines of the cluster. They are separated by wildcards, which represent variable parts of the log lines, such as usernames, IP addresses, and identifiers (IDs). Furthermore, a template matches all log lines of the corresponding cluster.

A sequence alignment is the result of an algorithm that arranges two strings, so that the least number of operations (i.e., insertions, deletions, or replacements of characters) is required to transform one string into the other one, i.e., it assumes the highest possible similarity. We solved the problem of generating a sequence alignment for more than two log lines on a character level [16], i.e., generating a multi-line alignment [9]. In contrast to token-based template generators, character-based approaches do not rely on predefined building blocks in the form of tokens. These approaches recognize static and variable parts of log lines independently from predefined delimiters. Example 1.3 provides an example of generated templates.

There exist many efficient algorithms and string metrics, such as the Levenshtein distance and the Needleman-Wunsch algorithm, to achieve an alignment for two character sequences. Furthermore, there are algorithms for genetic or biologic sequences to calculate pair-wise and multi-line alignments, which however require knowledge about the evolution of nucleotides and are therefore not suitable for log data [9]. Algorithms to align multiple sequences of any characters with no genetic context are challenging. The main reason is the difficulty to overcome the high computational complexity of this problem, which is at least $O(n^m)$, where n is the length of the shortest log line and m is the number of lines in a cluster. We proposed a character-based cluster template generator that incrementally processes the lines of a log line cluster and reduces the computational complexity $O(n^m)$ to $O(mn^2)$. The algorithm processes log lines sequentially and thus follows an incremental approach, which needs to handle each line only once. The resulting template (cf. Example 1.3) has a high similarity to the optimal template on pre-clustered data [14].

Example: Based on the four clusters of Example 1.2, our template generation approach would come up with the following four templates. Notice, we use only a very limited amount of log lines to demonstrate the approach. In a productive setting, we would record access logs over several days, if not weeks, and create the templates out of a much larger number, resulting in much more generic templates. We further skipped the processing of the timestamp and manually set it to be variable, reflected by an asterisk symbol.

```
[Cluster 1]: 10.0.0.1* - - [*] "GET /projX/doc* HTTP/1.1" 200 * "http://doc.acme.com/
      projX/" "Mozilla/5.0"
[Cluster 2]: 10.1.0.137 - - [*] "GET /projY/xls7 HTTP/1.1" 200 3574 "http://doc.acme.com
      /projY/" "Mozilla/5.0"
[Cluster 3]: 10.0.0.13* - - [*] "GET /projX/doc2p1 HTTP/1.1" 200 849 "http://doc.acme.
      com/projX/" "Mozilla/5.0"
[Cluster 4]: 10.0.0.130 - - [*] "POST /edit/doc* HTTP/1.1" 200 * "http://doc.acme.com/
      projX/edit.php?page=doc*" "Mozilla/5.0"
```

Example 1.3. Log line templates

Eventually, we have now a method to dissect single log lines, analyze their content character-wise, and identify regions of similarities. These are all prerequisites to learn data structures and automatically create parsers.

5 Learning Data Structures and Creating Tree-Based Parsers

Advanced data analysis does much more than clustering and outlier detection. To enable further analysis of e.g., trends, correlations or value distributions, a first step is to make the single parts of a log line (i.e., the features of log data) easily accessible and to identify which parts carry important information (i.e., help us to characterize the type of event and its unique parameters). Log parsers enable us to do that.

Currently, most log parsers simply apply a set of regular expressions to process log data. The set describes all possible log events and log messages, when the monitored system or service runs in a normal state. Each regular expression looks for static and variable parts that are usually separated by whitespaces, and describes one type of log event or log message. Regular expressions applied in parsers can be depicted as templates. For example, in the template "Connection from * to *", "Connection", "from" and "to" are static and "*" are variable. Those templates are generated applying clustering and template generator, as just discussed. Subsequently, to parse log data, all of these regular expressions are applied in the same order to each log line separately until the line matches a regular expression. This procedure is inefficient, with a complexity of $O(n)$ per log line, where n is the number of regular expressions.

A tree-based parser approach [15] aims at reducing the complexity of parsing and therefore increasing the performance. Since there are no commonly accepted standards that dictate the overall log syntax, developers may freely choose the structure of log lines produced by their services or applications. For example, the syslog standard defines that each log line has to start with a timestamp followed by the host name. However, the remainder of the syntax can be chosen without any restrictions.

Applying standards, such as syslog, causes log lines produced by the same service or application to be similar in the beginning but differ more towards the end of the lines. Consequently, modeling a parser as a tree, leads to a parser tree that comprises a common trunk and branches towards the leaves, see Example 1.5. The parser tree represents a graph theoretical rooted out-tree. This means, during parsing, it processes log lines token-wise from left to right and only parts of the parser tree that are relevant for the log line at hand are reached. Hence, this type of parser avoids parsing over the same log line more than once as it would be done when applying distinct regular expressions. As a result, the complexity for parsing reduces from $O(n)$ to $O(\log(n))$. Eventually, each log line relates to one path, i.e., branch, of the parser tree.

Example 1.4 visualizes a part of a parser tree for Web server access logs. This example demonstrates that the tree-based parser consists of three main building blocks. The nodes with bold lines represent tokens with static text patterns. This means that in all corresponding log lines, a token with this text pattern has to occur at the position of the node in the tree. Oval nodes represent nodes that allow variable text until the next separator or static pattern along the path in the tree occurs. The third building block is a branch element. The parser tree branches, when in a certain position only a small number of different tokens with static text occur.

In a nutshell, applying a tree-like parser model provides the following advantages, regarding performance and quality of log analysis:

- In opposite to an approach that applies distinct regular expressions, a tree-based parser avoids to parse over the same data entity more than once, because it follows for each log line one path of the parser tree, in the graph-theoretical tree that represents the parser, and leaves out irrelevant model parts.
- Because of the tree-like structure, the parser model could be seen as a single, very large regular expression that models a system's log data. Therefore, the computational complexity for log line parsing is more like $O(\log(n))$ than $O(n)$ when handling data with separate regular expressions.
- The tree-like structure allows to reference all the single tokens with an exact path; e.g., "/accesslog/hostip" enables access to the requesting client's IP address. Thus, parsed log line parts are quickly accessible so that rule checks can just pick out the data they need without searching the tree again. Furthermore, it allows to quickly apply anomaly detection algorithms to the different tokens and to correlate the information of different tokens within a single line and across lines.

Example: Using the generated templates given in Example 1.3, we steer the creation of a tree-like parser by applying the described parser generation methodology. Notice that the resulting tree may differ depending on the selected configuration parameters that influence whether different values result in a variable node, denoted by a circle below, or a branching point. For instance, the request size would naturally be considered a variable value, however, if only two or three different sizes are recorded in the log data, it could also be modeled as three parallel branches each consisting of a static but different value.

Taking the cluster templates above, a resulting parser tree might look like this, whereas the blue bubbles reflect a variable node that may assume any value.

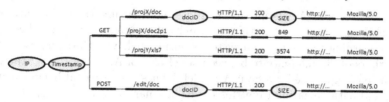

Eventually, we gain a tree structure where each node is referenced by a unique path to retrieve its value. Further generalizing this view, e.g., introducing variable nodes for response code, url path, and user agent, the model becomes generally applicable. The table below shows the first log line of our example dissected according to the generalized parser model. In the analysis phase, the different tokens are referenced with the paths given below.

```
10.0.0.130 - - [04/Mar/2021:06:55:35] "GET /projX/doc1 HTTP/1.1" 200 3844 "http://doc.
    acme.com/projX/" "Mozilla/5.0"
```

Node (parser path)	Token value
/accesslog/hostip	10.0.0.130
/accesslog/time_model	04/Mar/2021:06:55:35
/accesslog/time_model/time	1614837335
/accesslog/time_model/timezone	0
/accesslog/method	GET
/accesslog/request	/projX/doc1
/accesslog/protocol	HTTP
/accesslog/version	1.1
/accesslog/status	200
/accesslog/size	3844
/accesslog/referrer	http://doc.acme.com/projX/
/accesslog/useragent	Mozilla/5.0

Example 1.4. Log line parsers

With the tree-like parser, we have now the means to match incoming log lines to observed structures and can thus categorize events. Furthermore, we are able to distinguish static from variable parts – a vital means of feature selection for the machine learning algorithms applied on top of log data. Regardless of whether domain-specific and customized algorithms or general purpose algorithms are employed (such as neural networks, principal component analysis, long short-term memory), feature selection is a mandatory prerequisite for analysis and anomaly detection.

6   System Behavior Modeling and ML-Based Anomaly Detection

Anomaly detection (AD) approaches [4] are more flexible than signature-based approaches and can detect novel and previously unknown attacks. They apply machine learning to determine a system's normal behavior through observation. The authors of [3] differentiate between six classes of AD algorithms. Statistical AD is a semi-supervised method: A model defines the expected behavior of the system and data deviating from this model are marked as anomalies. Statistical AD uses simple algorithm that may be challenged by complex attacks. In Classification based AD a classifier is trained on two or more categories of data, typically on benign and attack samples. Optionally, attacks could be sub-categorized, e.g., DoS attacks, intrusion and malicious software infections. In production mode the system signals samples categorized other than benign. Classification is supervised, depending on correct categorization of all training samples. Clustering based AD is an unsupervised anomaly detection method. Clustering is the process of assigning samples with common or similar properties – the so-called features – to distinct clusters. We discussed clustering earlier in this paper. Main challenges for clustering include the identification of anomalous clusters, as well as the definition of their bounds (i.e., finding the optimum boundary between benign samples and anomalous samples). Knowledge based AD is included for the sake of completeness. It utilizes a list of known attacks and for each data sample it compares whether it matches a known attack pattern. This can be done using regular expression on log data. Combination learning based AD (also known as ensemble methods) combine several methods for their decision. For example, one can include five different classifiers and use majority voting to decide whether a datum should be considered an anomaly. Although [12] lists Machine learning based AD as a distinct category, we argue that ML denotes an ensemble of methods and technologies that are typically used for classification and clustering.

Most "classic" machine learning approaches suffer from several drawbacks when applied for anomaly detection on log data as discussed in the introduction. Specifically, complex "monolithic" models are of limited use in an environment that undergoes frequent changes, such as triggered by updates in computer systems. Fine-granular, explainable models that may be adapted to new situations are required.

The AMiner [1] implements a wide variety of machine learning based anomaly detection approaches, ranging from rather simple (outlier) detection mechanisms that signal new types of events or new values at certain paths, to more complex sequence violation and time-series analysis. Figure 1 depicts the whole AMiner pipeline that provides interfaces to ingest and parse log data with the mechanisms described in this article, forwards the pre-processed data to the analysis components and enables output on various channels, including console, message queues, syslog and e-mail. For the sake of brevity, we do not describe all mechanisms here in detail, but highlight the results of their application main in context of the example that we started earlier in this article.

Example 1.5 provides insights on the capabilities of some machine learning approaches in the area of simple detection, time series analysis, correlation analysis, and sequence detection. With these few approaches it becomes already rather hard for an attacker to mount a successful attack unnoticed. For more details on the concrete algorithms, we refer the reader to the scientific literature [7,14–16]; regarding the AMiner specifically to [12].

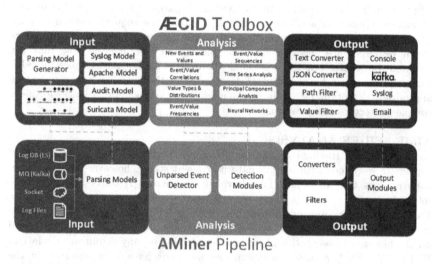

Fig. 1. The AMiner pipeline implements a wide variety of anomaly detection approaches applicable to log data.

Attack scenario: The attacker Mallory has gained remote access to local client 10.0.0.130 and tries to collect as many resources as possible from the web server for later exfiltration.

SIMPLE DETECTORS:

Detection of new values: Mallory simply uses wget to crawl (parts of) the Web server and leaves traces in logs similar to that below. Here, specifically the user agent can easily be detected as the new value "Wget/1.20.3 (linux-gnu")" in the path "/accesslog/useragent", because until analyzing this event the only observed user agent was "Mozilla/5.0".

```
10.0.0.130 - - [14/May/2021:06:06:18] "GET /projX/doc1 HTTP/1.1" 200 4569 "-" "Wget
    /1.20.3 (linux-gnu)"
```

Detection of new value combinations: Mallory changes the user agent to the legitimate standard user agent "Mozilla/5.0" and thus evades detection in the first place. She, however, attempts to access a resource from a directory which was never retrieved by the client that she owns, e.g. "GET /projY/xls7". Since the IP "10.0.0.130" only occurred with resources "/projX/doc1", "/edit/doc2", "/projX/doc2", "/projX/doc2p1", and "/edit/doc1" up to this point, this triggers a new value combination of values at paths "/accesslog/hostip" and "/accesslog/request" that was never observed before. Notice, here the advantage of character-based templates comes into play. If a huge amount of documents reside within "/projX/" we could generally consider accesses to documents therein as normal, but may still alert on access to any documents in "/projY/". In addition, it would be possible to use even more paths to increase the granularity of value combination analysis. Specifically, adding the request method at path "/accesslog/method" to aforementioned paths does not only allow to analyze which resources are accessed by which users, but also include how they are accessed. Be aware that there is usually a limit to adding paths, since all value combinations must be observed at least once in the training phase to enable appropriate detection, i.e., training the models takes considerably longer for more complex detector configurations.

TIME SERIES ANALYSIS:

Improved attack: Having learned from previous experiences, Mallory accesses only legitimate resources with a legitimate user agent string, however since she is in a hurry does that in bursts, i.e., downloads numerous resources in short time intervals.

Detection of frequency anomalies: The SARIMA [5] model predicts how many events of a specific type or of a certain source are considered normal, based on the history of observations, and enables alerting on any significant deviation. If, let's say 10-20 requests of documents per hour have been observed in the past few observation cycles for user 10.0.0.130, Mallory's attempt to retrieve documents in bulks (say, 100 requests made in one hour) will be detected.

CORRELATION ANALYSIS:

Advanced attack: Mallory again changes her behavior to evade detection and carries out a much slower moving attack, e.g., she downloads only a couple of resources per hour, to evade detection using the SARIMA model.

Detection of divergent correlations: Going back to what we consider normal behavior, the log data listing shows that 10.0.0.130 triggered 7 HTTP request, specifically 5 GET and 2 POST requests. After observing requests for a longer time span, a certain ratio of GET/POST requests will emerge, depending on the user's typical activities. If Mallory polls the Web server for new documents, she will issue over time lots of GET request, but no POST request and therefore disturbs this established ratio. The Variable Correlation Detector aims to establish a baseline (i.e., an expected value that is considered normal) and alerts on any significant deviations from that. For example, using aforementioned data the learned model could describe that a reasonably sized sample of events have IP "10.0.0.130" occur with a GET request in 70% and a POST request in 30% of all cases, while for all other IP addresses this ratio is around 95% and 5%. Any deviations reported by statistical tests on sufficiently large sections of the data, e.g., an increase of GET requests made by "10.0.0.130" to 90%, are then detected and reported as anomalies.

SEQUENCE DETECTION:
Stealthy attack: Mallory expanded remote access to several internal clients, not just 10.0.0.130, and is now able to collect only small portions of the resources from each single client she owns. As a consequence, there are no request bursts from single IPs, nor does the correlation of client IPs to request methods change significantly. This way, Mallory hopes to evade detection once and for all.

Detection of breaking sequences: Usually a GET request to a single html site triggers a set of sub requests to fetch linked content (we assume here that caching is disabled on client side to make this example easier comprehensible, i.e., all linked resources are fetched every time a resource is requested). In the example, whenever doc2 is fetched, doc2p1 is fetched too – the detector thus learns the sequence "/projX/doc2" followed by "/projX/doc2p1" as normal behavior. Since Mallory attempts to crawl the page with a command line tool and not the browser, she fetches linked content only once and leaves out e.g., linked images, such as a site logo, which is embedded on every page. For the aforementioned example, this means that any new pair of subsequently requested resources is detected as an anomaly, e.g., the sequence "/projY/xls7" followed by "/projX/doc2". Also, session management might break, depending on the deployed Web technology stacks. This breaks previously observed and learned sequences, which is easily detected. Note that detection complexity here mainly depends on the lengths of the analyzed sequences, i.e., a sequence length of two as in the example above allows efficient learning, but has lower model granularity than larger sequence lengths that require long training phases and tend to overfit the data more easily.

Example 1.5. Application of log anomaly detection methods

7   Conclusion

Log data analysis and anomaly detection in computer networks need to cope with some significant challenges, such as frequent changes of the observed systems (which is not the case for other machine learning domains), a certain degree of adaptability of learned models (which is not the case for most classic machine learning approaches) and a high amount of produced complex data that need to be processed as streams (in contrast to offline multi-pass analysis). A multitude of approaches are available, from rather simple detectors to much more complex analysis solutions that account for the interdependencies of log events, including sequence and time series analysis.

Keep in mind, the more complex detectors we apply, the more likely we are able to discover malicious behavior. The disadvantage of using complex detectors however are that (i) they are much more complex to configure and maintain, (ii) it takes longer for them to learn, and (iii) they are prone to high false positive rates. The art is to find the sweet spot between detecting enough to act in time and not drowning in false alerts.

The concepts for anomaly detection described in this chapter are deployed in the GUARD[1] cybersecurity framework. The GUARD framework specifically makes use of the tree-like parser approach and the light-weight AMiner agent that enables log-based online anomaly detection on host and service level.

For a more comprehensive view on the material covered in this article, please refer to [12].

Acknowledgements. This work was supported in part by the European Union H2020 project GUARD under grant 833456.

References

1. Aminer project on github. https://github.com/ait-aecid/logdata-anomaly-miner
2. Allen, R., Richardson, B.: Neural network, that's the tech; to free your staff from, bad regex (2019)
3. Bhuyan, M.H., Bhattacharyya, D.K., Kalita, J.K.: Network anomaly detection: methods, systems and tools. IEEE Commun. Surv. Tutor. **16**(1), 303–336 (2013)
4. Chandola, V., Banerjee, A., Kumar, V.: Anomaly detection: a survey. ACM Comput. Surv. (CSUR) **41**(3), 1–58 (2009)
5. Cryer, J.D.: Time Series Analysis, vol. 286. Springer, Heidelberg (1986)
6. He, P., Zhu, J., Zheng, Z., Lyu, M.R.: Drain: an online log parsing approach with fixed depth tree. In: 2017 IEEE International Conference on Web Services (ICWS), pp. 33–40. IEEE (2017)
7. Landauer, M., Skopik, F., Wurzenberger, M., Rauber, A.: System log clustering approaches for cyber security applications: a survey. Comput. Secur. **92**, 101739 (2020)
8. Landauer, M., Wurzenberger, M., Skopik, F., Settanni, G., Filzmoser, P.: Dynamic log file analysis: an unsupervised cluster evolution approach for anomaly detection. Comput. Secur. **79**, 94–116 (2018)
9. Notredame, C.: Recent evolutions of multiple sequence alignment algorithms. PLoS Comput. Biol. **3**(8), e123 (2007)
10. Skopik, F.: Collaborative Cyber Threat Intelligence: Detecting and Responding to Advanced Cyber Attacks at the National Level. CRC Press, Boca Raton (2017)
11. Skopik, F., Landauer, M., Wurzenberger, M.: Online log data analysis with efficient machine learning: a review. IEEE Secur. Priv. https://doi.org/10.1109/MSEC. 2021.3113275. https://www.computer.org/csdl/magazine/sp/5555/01/09563044/ 1xvtlDhkcz6
12. Skopik, F., Wurzenberger, M., Landauer, M.: Smart Log Data Analytics: Techniques for Advanced Security Analysis. Springer, Cham (2021). https://doi.org/ 10.1007/978-3-030-74450-2

---

[1] GUARD is a project co-funded within Horizon 2020 Funding Programme (833456). The project aims to provide a cybersecurity framework to guarantee reliability and trust for digital service chains. More information can be found on the project website: https://guard-project.eu/.

13. Vaarandi, R.: A data clustering algorithm for mining patterns from event logs. In: Proceedings of the 3rd IEEE Workshop on IP Operations & Management (IPOM 2003) (IEEE Cat. No. 03EX764), pp. 119–126. IEEE (2003)
14. Wurzenberger, M., Höld, G., Landauer, M., Skopik, F., Kastner, W.: Creating character-based templates for log data to enable security event classification. In: Proceedings of the 15th ACM Asia Conference on Computer and Communications Security, pp. 141–152 (2020)
15. Wurzenberger, M., Landauer, M., Skopik, F., Kastner, W.: AECID-PG: a tree-based log parser generator to enable log analysis. In: 2019 IFIP/IEEE Symposium on Integrated Network and Service Management (IM), pp. 7–12. IEEE (2019)
16. Wurzenberger, M., Skopik, F., Landauer, M., Greitbauer, P., Fiedler, R., Kastner, W.: Incremental clustering for semi-supervised anomaly detection applied on log data. In: Proceedings of the 12th International Conference on Availability, Reliability and Security, pp. 1–6 (2017)
17. Xu, W., Huang, L., Fox, A., Patterson, D., Jordan, M.I.: Detecting large-scale system problems by mining console logs. In: Proceedings of the ACM SIGOPS 22nd Symposium on Operating Systems Principles, pp. 117–132 (2009)

Signature-Based Detection of Botnet DDoS Attacks

Paweł Szynkiewicz[✉] [iD]

Research and Academic Computer Network (NASK),
ul. Kolska 12, 01-045 Warsaw, Poland
pawel.szynkiewicz@nask.pl
http://www.nask.pl

Abstract. The distributed denial of service (DDoS) attack is an attempt to disrupt the proper availability of a targeted server, service or network. The attack is achieved by corrupting or overwhelming the target's communications with a flood of malicious network traffic. In the current era of mass connectivity DDoS attacks emerge as one of the biggest threats, staidly causing greater collateral damage and heaving a negate impacting on the integral Internet Infrastructure. DDoS attacks come in a variety of types and schemes, they continue to evolve, steadily becoming more sophisticated and larger at scale. A close investigation of attack vectors and refining current security measures is required to efficiently mitigate new DDoS threats. The solution described in this article concerns a less explored variation of signature-based techniques for DDoS mitigation. The approach exploits one of the traits of modern DDoS attacks, the utilization of Packet generation algorithms (PGA) in the attack execution. Proposed method performs a fast, protocol-level detection of DDoS network packets and can easily be employed to provide an effective, supplementary protection against DDoS attacks.

Keywords: Network security · DDoS · Signatures · Detection · PGA · eBPF

1 Introduction

The detection of distributed denial-of-service (DDoS) attacks is a process that involves distinguishing malicious and normal network traffic in order to perform effective attack mitigation. The primary goal of a DDoS attack is to either limit or totally block the access to an application or network service, thereby denying legitimate users access to the service. Nowadays, an array of DDoS attack vectors has been recognized and studied [5,14,17]. Nonetheless, the principal of operation stays predominately the same i.e. to overwhelm targeted network resources with traffic coming from a mass of different sources. A seemingly simple problem of identifying and blocking specific malicious IP address proves to be a non-trivial task. Mainly due to the sheer distribution of attacking sources, which

© The Author(s) 2022
J. Kołodziej et al. (Eds.): Cybersecurity of Digital Service Chains, LNCS 13300, pp. 120–135, 2022.
https://doi.org/10.1007/978-3-031-04036-8_6

makes distinguishing the legitimate user traffic from attack traffic increasingly difficult, when spread across so many points of origin.

Consequently, original and more advanced DDoS mitigation techniques are being investigated. Solutions inspired by the control theory [7] or machine learning [3,4,12] that are able to recognize attack patterns in captured network traffic or aggregated traffic statistics are considered a next step in successful DDoS prevention. However, such methods have their limitations. Putting aside the costs and complexities of proper learning and tuning stages, for the pattern in network traffic to be recognized some amount of malicious traffic must pass through the protected network. In other words, DDoS can be detected only when the attack reaches proper scale inside the network. Solution described in this paper adopts the signature-based approach of DDoS detection. While this method lacks the self-learning aspect, signature-based DDoS detection methods can provide a effective, supplementary protection against DDoS attacks. Their main advantage being the ability to detect and block malicious network packets as soon as they arrive at the edge of protected network, practically mitigating the attack in its tracks.

In this paper we present our novel approach to signature-based detection of cyperthreats. PGA Filter is a prototype of a self-contained IDS system targeting botnet originating denial-of-service attacks by employing botnet fingerprinting techniques; packet generation algorithm (PGA) signatures. To our knowledge, this is the only complete ecosystem of this kind providing a full IDS experience. Our contribution includes definition of a new signature paradigm and description of a signature generation process. The core of the solution consists of the module responsible for the translation of signatures into packet filtering rules, and applying those rules to network traffic. The implantation leverages the enhanced Berkeley Packet Filter (eBPF) Linux kernel technology (since kernel ver. 4.9) that enables the augmentation of kernel logic with custom procedures. eBPF is currently considered a state-of-the-art for all packet processing requirements of networking solutions due to it's high efficiency and programmability. Our proof of concept study is finalized by the integration and tests of PGA Filter as a part of GUARD[1] cypersecurity framework.

The rest of the paper is organized as follows. In Sect. 2 the concept of PGA signatures is explained. We provide a brief understanding of the context required i.e. the principle of operation for network telescopes, the characteristics of botnets and botnet denial-of-service attacks and how we are able to identify them. Next, in Sect. 3 we describe the PGA Filter, its implementation and technologies employed. Finally, we give our conclusion in Sect. 4, which includes the overview of future plans.

2   PGA Signatures

Successful signature-based detection of DDoS attacks requires a source of specialized, high quality, up to date network traffic signatures. The proposed solution

---

[1] https://guard-project.eu/, Guarantee Reliability and trust for Digital service chains (GUARD).

integrates with the infrastructure built around the Network telescope (dark-net) [2] developed under the SISSDEN project[2]. Network telescope provides the access to valuable and hard to come by data about ongoing mass-scale cyber-attack campaigns. By analyzing said data we are able to extract and generate specific, network packet level, DDoS attack signatures. The above-mentioned signatures, dubbed as PGA signatures advance a novel approach of depicting the patterns in malicious network packet headers. The idea of PGA signatures was previously investigated in SISSDEN project. The solution described in this paper builds on this knowledge to offer a prototype concept of PGA signatures defined by an explicit signature syntax.

2.1 Network Telescope

Network telescope (known also as a black hole, an Internet sink, darkspace, or a darknet) is an unused space of IP addresses that are used solely for the purpose of passive monitoring [2, 16]. Unused IP addresses should receive no legitimate network traffic. In practice, however many packets are observed arriving at this IP space. This continuous view of anomalous unsolicited traffic is by definition classified as suspicious. This observed traffic is a result of a wide range of events, such as backscatter from randomly spoofed source denial-of-service attacks, scan-ning of address space by attackers or malware looking for vulnerable targets, the automated spread of Internet worms and viruses and various misconfigurations (e.g. mistyping an IP address or deprecated DNS records). In general, mali-cious activities observed in a form of victims' echo responses in darknet fall into following categories:

- backscatters from denial-of-service attacks,
- scanning activities,
- exploitation attempts.

Network telescopes are a valuable source of information about ongoing events in the whole Internet Infrastructure. However, access to this data is rather restricted. First of all, network telescopes are usually managed by the institu-tion responsible for the administering of IP addresses for the given regions of the world. The list of unused IP addresses is a closely guarded secret, which should remain undisclosed to cyber-criminals. Also, there are serious privacy and secu-rity concerns associated with network telescope datasets. Viruses and worms may involve the installation of backdoors which provide unfettered access to infected computers. Therefore telescope data may inadvertently advertise these vulnerable machines. Additionally, while the source of some types of telescope traffic, including denial-of-service attacks and worms, is readily apparent, a sig-nificant volume of traffic is of unknown origin. Without identifying the causes of this traffic, the security and privacy impact of releasing these data cannot be categorically assessed.

---

[2] https://sissden.eu, Secure Information Sharing Sensor Delivery Event Network (SISSDEN).

For our purposes the access to network telescope data is granted thanks to the fact that NASK, as an institution governing the Polish IP address space, has established a darknet infrastructure. Network telescope at NASK is a time-tested, working system integrated with security incident exchange platforms (n6[3]) and actively used by Polish CERT. It passively observes and analyzes network traffic that reaches NASK sinkhole, which consists of over 250 thousands IPv4 addresses. Network telescopes at NASK is used internally by many cybersecurity teams and sends reports to external organizations, including Shadowserver[4]. All of the traffic reaching NASK darknet (around 10 000 network packets per second) is being captured and analyzed. On the basis of this data, it is possible to:

- collect intelligence regarding new threats and trends (also DDoS)
- detect both large-scale and targeted attacks,
- fingerprint actors responsible for those events.

2.2   DDoS Seen Through Network Telescope

Despite medium resolution of NASK's network telescope (resolution corresponds to the number of IP addresses the telescope monitors), it is "precise" enough to serve its purpose in our scenario, that is to monitor the spread of random-source distributed denial-of-service attacks.

To make it difficult for the attack target (and the target's ISPs) to block an incoming attack, the attacker may use a fake source IP address (similarly to a fake return address in traditional mail) in each network packet sent to the victim 1 as shown in Fig. 1.

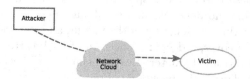

Fig. 1. The attacker sends packets with spoofed source addresses to the denial-of-service attack victim

This technique is known as IP spoofing in the trade. Because the victim of the denial-of-service attack can't distinguish between incoming requests from an attacker and legitimate inbound traffic, the victim tries to respond to every received request (see Fig. 2).

When the attacker spoofs a source address monitored by network telescope, we observe a response destined for a host that doesn't exist (and therefore could not sent the initial query), this effect is also know as a backscatter and is shown in Fig. 3.

---

[3] https://n6.cert.pl/en/.

[4] https://shadowserver.org.

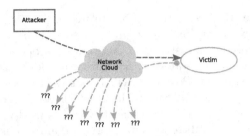

Fig. 2. The denial-of-service attack victim cannot differentiate between legitimate traffic and the attack packets, so the victim responds to as many of the attack packets as possible.

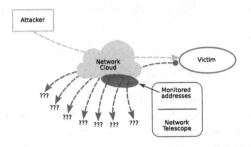

Fig. 3. Because the NASK's network telescope composes of 250 000 IPv4 addresses there is a chance that some of the responses to spoofed packets generated by the denial-of-service attack victim will be received.

By following these unsolicited responses, researchers can identify denial-of-service attack victims and infer information about the volume of the attack, the bandwidth of the victim, the location of the victim, and the types of services the attacker targets. Moreover, a deeper inspection of backscatter packets can lead to the discovery of certain characteristics and similarities between the values in the packet headers. This is the backbone of our approach.

2.3 Botnets

During recent years, traffic destined to darknet has been gradually evolving due to the growing numbers of rapidly expanding bot networks (botnets). The considerable impact of their operations is clearly mirrored by the network telescope observations; firstly through the presence of longer-duration, low-intensity events intended to establish and maintain botnets; secondly, by the dominating aftermath effects of well orchestrated, large-scale DDoS attacks.

Botnet [15,18,21] are collections of devices infected with a bot program which allows an attacker to control them. They range in size from only a few hundreds to millions of infected devices. Attackers typically use the collective resources of the botnet to perform various disruptive or criminal activities, such as sending vast amounts of spam emails, distributing malware and launching denial-of-Service attacks [6]. Botnets are considered one of the biggest threats to the Internet Infrastructure. The growing number of smart and connected but weakly secured and easy to compromise devices [9] (smartphones, IoT, etc....) indicates that this threat will remain significant.

Network telescope proves a valuable asset in monitoring and disabling botnets [1,13,20]. Tracking of botnet activities is made possible through the process of fingerprinting. As described in the next section, the information required to identify (fingerprint) specific botnet packets can be extracted by analyzing network telescope data.

2.4   Packet Generation Algorithm

As mentioned in previous sections, botnets are mainly used by attackers to perform denial-of-service and scanning attacks. When the command is issued infected bots start to generate network traffic directed at the attack victims. The logic of the attack itself is usually an integral part of the bot malware. Malicious packets are constructed depending on the kind of attack performed. Often some additional logic is employed to speed up this process. The procedure behind packet generation is know as packet generation algorithm (PGA). Every PGA has some unique characteristics, packet generation rules are attack specific. Most relevant is also the fact that PGA are typically botnet specific, hence they can be used to identify the entity behind the attack (fingerprinting).

The malicious packets of botnet generated attacks usually include fixed patterns. Patterns occur when a single or multiple bytes of particular protocol specific parameters (e.g. TCP sequence number or IP destination address) are deterministically dependent on each other. A simple example of a fixed pattern is an equality of TCP sequence number and destination IP address, which is often observed during port scanning. In this case the PGA copies bytes from the address into the sequence number instead of generating a random one. The motivation behind this additional operations is to optimize computation complexity and memory usage of the algorithm. Botnet malware often targets devices with limited computing power (legacy PCs, IoT, etc....), also botnet attack capabilities scale with the number of infected devices. Therefore every small improvement in packet generation speed greatly impacts the attack effectiveness.

Presented example of PGA for scanning purposes is of course a simple form of optimization. The authors of malicious software may include more sophisticated rules using logical shift, negations, incrementation, decrementation, bytes swapping etc. It all comes to a trade-off between computational simplicity and amount of effort required to detect a pattern.

2.5   Generating PGA Signatures

With the data provided by the darknet infrastructure, the main aim of the PGA analysis is the detection of packet generation rules in traffic generated by botnets and other malware. During online analysis of malicious network traffic the detection and documentation of packet generation rules used during particular network activity (e.g. TCP SYN scan or flood) is performed. The practical aspects of PGA signatures are described in [11, 19]. Methods for extraction of PGA signatures candidates vary in nature. From the simplest, like deterministic conditions on header fields - PGA headers often defy RFCs guidelines, which makes resulting traffic stand out from legitimate one, to more sophisticated ones based on statistical, hierarchical analysis and machine learning. Constant monitoring of the incoming traffic by the network telescope helps maintain situational awareness with the proper collection of details about current threats and signatures for botnet fingerprinting.

The process of extracting PGA signatures from suspicious traffic involves reverse engineering of packet generation algorithm by analyzing the headers of packets arriving at darknet. First, packets sharing the same source and close arrival times are grouped together to establish a backscatter of possible DDoS attack (victims response to packets with spoofed source address). By inspecting such packets we are able to partially recreate the original DDoS packet that was sent to the victim (see Sect. 2.2). Finally, the most challenging part is determining whether recreated packets could be generated by the same packet generation algorithm, and if so, what are the steps and operations performed by said algorithm.

An example TCP/IP packet which could be a part of a DDoS backscatter observed by network telescope is shown in the Fig. 4. To recreate the original DDoS packet the following operations are performed:

1. Swap source and destination fields:
   IP: Source IP Address $\longleftrightarrow$ Destination IP Address
   TCP: Source TCP port number $\longleftrightarrow$ Destination TCP port number
2. Set the value of TCP Sequence Number to decremented TCP Acknowledgment Number

The result of those operations is presented in the Fig. 5, limited to only the key header fields. The A, B and C denote some specific byte values, in case of A and B a 4-byte value, and C a 1-byte value. It would be plausible that this example packet is a result of a packet generation algorithm. Such algorithm would reuse the first two bytes of source IP address, and copy it over to first two bytes of TCP sequence number. Next, the last two bytes of destination IP address would be copied over to the last two bytes of TCP sequence number. The signature of such PGA would state:

"The first two bytes (0, 1) of Source IP Address are equal to the first two bytes of TCP Sequence Number and the last two bytes (2, 3) of Destination IP Address are equal to the last two bytes of TCP Sequence Number"

or in our less verbose signature naming syntax:

```
ip-src:0:1_is_tcp-seq:0:1_and_ip-dst:2:3_is_tcp-seq:2:3
```

Presented principle of operation is part of semi-automated service running as a part of NASK's network telescope system. The algorithms are still being refined new reverse engineering methods are research. Currently supported internet protocols are: Ethernet, IPv4, IPv6, UDP, TCP, ICMP.

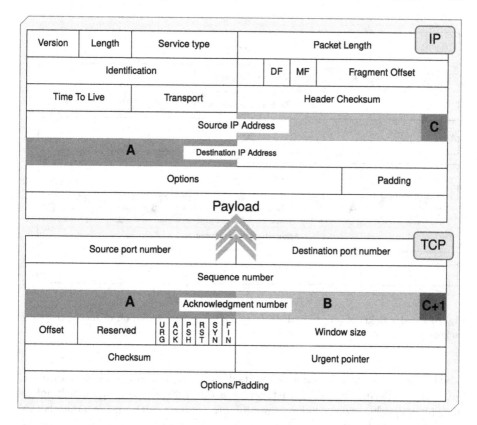

Fig. 4. *TCP/IP* packet observed by darknet.

3 PGA Filter

The main challenge is the implementation of mechanisms able to interpret said data to translate it into system-comprehendible set of rules, which in turn, can be deployed in client's network security infrastructure. Since the standard signature IDS/IPS solutions (Snort, Suricata, etc.) focus on analyzing the patterns in the payload data, rather than the dependencies between values in protocol headers, new solutions have to be developed.

3.1 Extended Barkeley Packet Filter

Proposed implementation makes use of eBPF (extended Berkeley Packet Filter), a robust, highly flexible and efficient virtual machine-like construct that allows for extending standard kernel in Unix-like systems with custom functionality by executing bytecode at various hook points in a safe manner. It is applicable in a number of Linux kernel subsystems, most prominently networking, tracing and security.

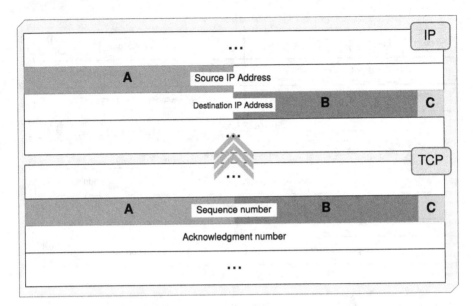

Fig. 5. Header fields of an original *TCP/IP* DDoS packet based on observed response packet.

BPF, as a concept, does not define itself by only providing its instruction set, but also by offering further infrastructure around it such as maps which act as efficient key/value stores, helper functions to interact with and leverage kernel functionality, tail calls for calling into other BPF programs, security hardening primitives, a pseudo file system for pinning objects (maps, programs), and infrastructure for allowing BPF to be offloaded, for example, to a network card.

The kernel subsystems making use of BPF are part of BPF's infrastructure. The subsystem utilized for the purposes of PGA signature rule-based detection is XDP (eXpress Data Path). XDP is a framework that makes it possible to perform high-speed packet processing within BPF applications. To enable faster response to network operations, XDP runs a BPF program as soon as possible, usually immediately as a packet is received by the network interface. However, since this processing occurs so early, full network stack is yet to be established, the packets' metadata extracted and parsed (Fig. 6).

BPF is a general purpose RISC instruction set and was originally designed for the purpose of writing programs in a subset of C which can be compiled into BPF instructions through a compiler back end (e.g. LLVM), so that the kernel can later on map them through an in-kernel JIT compiler into native opcodes for optimal execution performance inside the kernel. Among other use-cases, BPF as a technology, is a perfect candidate for the implementation of DDoS mitigation software. It provides the compromise between the efficiency of execution - inside the kernel, and the extensibility and programmability - subset of C programming language. Until recently similar results were possible only with custom compiled

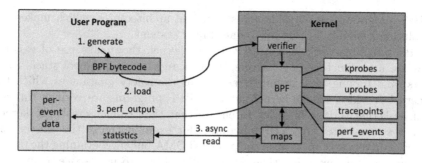

Fig. 6. *(e)BPF* lifecycle (https://www.brendangregg.com/).

kernels. Preparing a custom kernel is a cumbersome process, which requires a great deal of attention, as a simple mistakes can make the target system unstable. Understandably, such solutions are adopted with great deal of restraint and are rather unwelcome in third-party software. However, in contrast to custom kernel approach, BPF gives guarantees for safety and predictability of execution, also can easily be loaded and unloaded from the target system. By employing BPF as a main technology in our signature-based DDoS mitigation solution we are able to directly translate DDoS signatures in to sets of instructions executed inside system's network stack. The advantages for pushing these instructions directly into the kernel include[5]:

1. Making the kernel programmable without having to cross kernel/user space boundaries. For example, BPF programs related to networking, can implement flexible networking policies (firewall), load balancing and other means without having to move packets to user space and back into the kernel. State between BPF programs and kernel/user space can still be shared through maps whenever needed.
2. Given the flexibility of a programmable data path, programs can be heavily optimized for performance also by compiling out features that are not required for the use cases the program solves. For example program can support only required set of network protocols: TCP/IP, UDP, ICMP, etc.
3. In case of networking (e.g. XDP), BPF programs can be updated atomically without having to restart the kernel, system services or containers, and without traffic interruptions. Furthermore, any program state can also be maintained throughout updates via BPF maps. That means that programs logic (e.g. traffic filtering rule-set) can be modified on the go and hot-deployed without stopping the service.
4. BPF provides a stable ABI towards user space, and does not require any third party kernel modules. BPF is a core part of the Linux kernel that is shipped everywhere, and guarantees that existing BPF programs keep running with newer kernel versions. This guarantee is the same guarantee that the kernel provides for system calls with regard to user space applications. Moreover,

---

[5] Cilium project documentation (https://cilium.io/).

BPF programs are portable across different architectures, which makes our solution available for any up-to-date Linux systems.

5. BPF programs work in concert with the kernel, they make use of existing kernel infrastructure (e.g. drivers, netdevices, tunnels, protocol stack, sockets) and tooling (e.g. iproute2) as well as the safety guarantees which the kernel provides. Unlike kernel modules, BPF programs are verified through an in-kernel verifier in order to ensure that they cannot crash the kernel, always terminate, etc. XDP programs, for example, reuse the existing in-kernel drivers and operate on the provided DMA buffers containing the packet frames without exposing them or an entire driver to user space as in other models. Moreover, XDP programs reuse the existing stack instead of bypassing it. BPF can be considered a generic "glue code" to kernel facilities for crafting programs to solve specific use cases.

3.2   PGA Filter Architecture

PGA filter runs as a system daemon. The tasks performed by this daemon are:

– parsing configuration and rules,
– generating BPF bytecode based on configuration and rules,
– loading or unloading BPF bytecode to kernel,
– accumulating and sending packet statistics to Kafka.

The architecture of PGA Filter is presented in the Fig. 7. The whole implementation resides in *pgafitler.py* Python script responsible for parsing configuration, generating and loading of BPF code, gathering and sending results. The configuration is split between two files in YAML format: *rules.yml* and *config.yml* for convenience. The *rules.yml* file is dedicated for the declaration of available PGA signatures. It can be edited by hand by the administrator or downloaded from the signature sharing service. The general configuration resides in *config.yml* file. Besides the standard configuration parameters, i.e., the name of the inspected network interface or the desired logging level, this file contains the list of currently enabled PGA signatures from the *rules.yml* file.

The most crucial operation is translating chosen PGA signatures into valid BPF code. Generated BPF program performs packet inspection operations and gathers data regarding signature matches. The moment a new PGA filter configuration is applied, updated BPF program is generated and swapped with the previous one. During the update phrase, the BPF infrastructure ensures the atomic operation of swapping BPF code (unloading the previous program code and loading the new one). The inspection of network packets is performed continuously and without delay through the whole process.

Below, in Listings 1 and 2 two examples of configuration rules (in YAML format) corresponding to PGA signatures are presented. Each rule can be identified by a unique name (e.g. ``tcp-sport_is_tcp-seq:0:1``) or numerical id (*sid* – signature id). Each rule also has a revision number (*rev*) which should be incremented every time said rule is modified. The *content* filed contains the

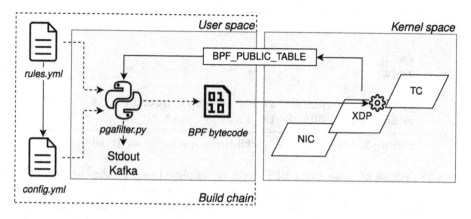

Fig. 7. Architecture of the PGA Filter framework.

representation of the PGA signature itself. In order to allow for high degree of flexibility, signatures are represented in valid C programming language syntax. Code can span across multiple lines of code separated by the semicolon (';'), but the last line must always evaluate to boolean (true or false) value. Standard syntax is extended with some helpful macros and function described bellow. The *args* filed declared which protocol headers should be passed to signature function. Multiple headers can be passed, each header corresponds to protocols supported by PGA filter, i.e.: ethhdr, iphdr, ip6hdr, udphdr, tcphdr, icmphdr. Headers are in fact structures defined in Linux Kernel User API source code [8,10].

```
1  "tcp-sport_is_tcp-seq:0:1":
2      sid: 1003
3      rev: 1
4      args:
5          - tcphdr
6      content: "tcphdr->source == pga_2_byte32(tcphdr->
           seq, 0, 1)"
7      comment: "TCP SOURCE PORT is equal to TCP SEQ
           bytes 0:1"
```

Listing 1. Simple PGA signature for TCP

```
1  ip1:
2      sid: 1
3      rev: 2
4      args:
5          - iphdr
6      content: "iphdr->saddr == bpf_htonl(16843009)"
7      comment: "SOURCE IP is 1.1.1.1"
```

Listing 2. PGA signature blacklisting a specific source IP address

The process of generating BPF code is simplified due to the architectural decision to represent signatures in C programming language code. An example of the conditional function generated based on a signature is presented in listing 3. The function is executed for every packet arriving TCP packet, and evaluates to "true" if given packet matches signature.

```
1  static __always_inline int tcp-sport_is_tcp-seq_0_1(
2      struct tcphdr *tcphdr)
3  {
4      /* some additional operations are possible */
5      return tcphdr->source ==
6              pga_2_byte32(tcphdr->seq, 0, 1);
7  }
```

Listing 3. PGA signature translated into code for BPF compiler

All helper BPF functions and macros are available for use in signature representation, e.g.:`bpf_htons`, `bpf_htonl`, `bpf_ntohs`, `bpf_ntohl` macros which translate short and long integers to network byte representation and back to host representation. Additionally, dedicated macros that allow for more comprehensive translation of signatures to C code are provided, i.e. `pga_1_byte16`, `pga_2_byte16`, `pga_1_byte32`, `pga_2_byte32` are used for extracting specific byte values from integers. Library of convenient helper functions and macros can easily be extended.

3.3 PGA Filter Integration in the GUARD Framework

PGA filter, as one of GUARD's Agents, is deployed inside use-case owner infrastructure, preferably at the edge of the local network. Agent is listening on the network interface at which all the incoming network traffic should be arriving. Each packet is analyzed and validated against the set of loaded DDoS signatures. If no signature is detected no actions are taken. However if packet matches one or more signatures, information about the possible malicious packet is recorded, i.e., source/destination IP address, source/destination port, timestamp, etc... and sent to the Kafka bus.

Data is placed in two channels: Results channel for GUARD Dashboard to visualize the information, and Network-Data channel that any GUARD Security

Service can subscribe to. Data is also dumped to Elasticsearch and can possible be used for detecting attack correlation and attack campaigns. Set of currently enabled signatures is a part of PGA filter configuration and can be modified on the go without letting a single packet through. Set of available PGA signatures is also a part of agent's configuration. Signature set is periodically updated by Security Controller service, which inquires NASK's database about newly generated PGA signatures. PGA signature database is semi-automatically (requires human input) updated with new signatures based on information coming from darknet traffic analysis (Fig. 8).

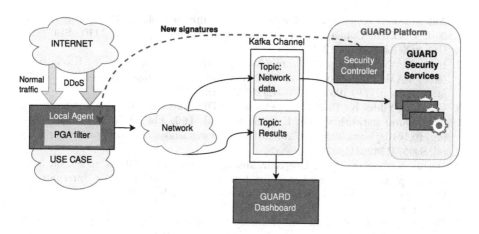

Fig. 8. Integration of PGA filter in the GUARD framework.

4   Conclusion

In conclusion, this work contributes to existing knowledge of denial-of-service prevention. It is our hope that presented approach will prove useful in developing new security solutions in the face of the growing threat posed by botnets. Although the concept of PGA signatures requires further development, this prototype shows the potential behind converting botnet fingerprints into rules for network traffic filtration. Based on the results achieved, levering the eBPF technology is a step in the right direction. Indeed, this solution provides a lightweight and portable approach, yet extensible enough for our use case while still allowing to operate on network packet at the lowest possible level in operating system. Improvements in the implementation of our module are however necessary to unlock the full potential of eBPF and XDP (cross-compiling, modularity). Future development should consider improving the overall experience and availability of our solution. Well-known, full-fledged IDS/IPS solutions like Snort[6] Suricata[7]

---

[6] https://www.snort.org/.

[7] https://suricata.io/.

should be taken as a point of reference to make our system more applicable in practice. Possibly, a way for integrating our concepts with above-mentioned platforms should be considered. Extending proved solutions seems like the most suitable way to integrate our approach in a common security ecosystem.

Acknowledgment. This work was supported in part by the European Commission under Grant Agreement no. 786922 (ASTRID) and no. 833456 (GUARD).

References

1. Antonakakis, M., et al.: Understanding the mirai botnet. In: Proceedings of the 26th USENIX Conference on Security Symposium. pp. 1093–1110. SEC2017, USENIX Association (2017)
2. Brownlee, N.: One-way traffic monitoring with `iatmon`. In: Taft, N., Ricciato, F. (eds.) PAM 2012. LNCS, vol. 7192, pp. 179–188. Springer, Heidelberg (2012). https://doi.org/10.1007/978-3-642-28537-0_18
3. Cil, A.E., Yildiz, K., Buldu, A.: Detection of DDoS attacks with feed forward based deep neural network model. Exp. Syst. Appl. **169**, 114520 (2021). https://doi.org/10.1016/j.eswa.2020.114520, https://www.sciencedirect.com/science/article/pii/S0957417420311647
4. Deepa, V., Sudar, K.M., Deepalakshmi, P.: Detection of DDoS attack on SDN control plane using hybrid machine learning techniques. In: 2018 International Conference on Smart Systems and Inventive Technology (ICSSIT). pp. 299–303 (2018). https://doi.org/10.1109/ICSSIT.2018.8748836
5. Dong, S., Abbas, K., Jain, R.: A survey on distributed denial of service (DDoS) attacks in SDN and cloud computing environments. IEEE Access **7**, 80813–80828 (2019). https://doi.org/10.1109/ACCESS.2019.2922196
6. Hoque, N., Bhattacharyya, D.K., Kalita, J.K.: Botnet in DDoS attacks: trends and challenges. IEEE Commun. Surv. Tutor. **17**(4), 2242–2270 (2015). https://doi.org/10.1109/COMST.2015.2457491
7. Karpowicz, M.P.: Adaptive tuning of network traffic policing mechanisms for DDoS attack mitigation systems. Eur. J. Control **61**, 101–118 (2021). https://doi.org/10.1016/j.ejcon.2021.07.001, https://www.sciencedirect.com/science/article/pii/S0947358021000935
8. Kerrisk, M.: The UAPI header file split. https://lwn.net/Articles/507794/ (2012). Accessed 9 Feb 2022
9. Kolias, C., Kambourakis, G., Stavrou, A., Voas, J.: DDoS in the IoT: Mirai and other botnets. Computer **50**, 80–84 (2017). https://doi.org/10.1109/MC.2017.201
10. Linux Kernel Community Contributors: L.T.: Linux kernel source code (2022). https://github.com/torvalds/linux. Accessed 9 Feb 2022
11. Liu, Y.: Improve DDoS botnet tracking with honeypots. https://www.botconf.eu/wp-content/uploads/2016/11/PR10-Improve-DDoS-Botnet-Tracking-With-Honeypots-LIU.pdf (2017). Accessed 9 Feb 2022
12. Makuvaza, A., Jat, D.S., Gamundani, A.M.: Deep neural network (DNN) solution for real-time detection of distributed denial of service (DDoS) attacks in software defined networks (SDNs). SN Comput. Sci. **2**(2), 1–10 (2021). https://doi.org/10.1007/s42979-021-00467-1
13. Malécot, E.L., Inoue, D.: The Carna botnet through the lens of a network telescope. In: FPS (2013)

14. Mallikarjunan, K.N., Muthupriya, K., Shalinie, S.M.: A survey of distributed denial of service attack. In: 2016 10th International Conference on Intelligent Systems and Control (ISCO), pp. 1–6 (2016). https://doi.org/10.1109/ISCO.2016.7727096

15. Mansfield-Devine, S.: DDoS goes mainstream: how headline–grabbing attacks could make this threat an organisation's biggest nightmare. Netw. Secur. **2016**(11), 7–13 (2016). https://doi.org/10.1016/S1353-4858(16)30104-0, https://www.sciencedirect.com/science/article/pii/S1353485816301040

16. Moore, D., Shannon, C., Voelker, G., Savage, S.: Network telescopes: Technical report (2004–07)

17. Sharafaldin, I., Lashkari, A.H., Hakak, S., Ghorbani, A.A.: Developing realistic distributed denial of service (DDoS) attack dataset and taxonomy. In: 2019 International Carnahan Conference on Security Technology (ICCST), pp. 1–8 (2019). https://doi.org/10.1109/CCST.2019.8888419

18. Silva, S.S., Silva, R.M., Pinto, R.C., Salles, R.M.: Botnets: a survey. botnet Activity: Analysis, Detection and Shutdown. Comput. Netw. **57**(2), 378–403 (2013). https://doi.org/10.1016/j.comnet.2012.07.021, https://www.sciencedirect.com/science/article/pii/S1389128612003568

19. SISSDEN Contributors NASK, USAAR, EXYS, DTAG, CYBE, MI: Deliverable d5.3: Final data analysis results (2019), https://sissden.eu/download/SISSDEN-D5.3-Final_Data_Analysis_Results.pdf Accessed 9 Feb 2022

20. Torabi, S., Bou-Harb, E., Assi, C., Karbab, E.B., Boukhtouta, A., Debbabi, M.: Inferring and investigating IoT-generated scanning campaigns targeting a large network telescope. IEEE Trans. Depend. Secur. Comput. **19**(1), 402–418 (2022). https://doi.org/10.1109/TDSC.2020.2979183

21. Zhang, X., Upton, O., Beebe, N.L., Choo, K.K.R.: IoT botnet forensics: a comprehensive digital forensic case study on Mirai botnet servers. Forensic Sci. Int.: Digit. Invest. **32**, 300926 (2020). https://doi.org/10.1016/j.fsidi.2020.300926, https://www.sciencedirect.com/science/article/pii/S2666281720300214

Automatic Attack Pattern Mining for Generating Actionable CTI Applying Alert Aggregation

Markus Wurzenberger$^{(\boxtimes)}$ ⓘ, Max Landauer ⓘ, Agron Bajraktari ⓘ, and Florian Skopik ⓘ

AIT Austrian Institute of Technology, Vienna, Austria
{markus.wurzenberger,max.landauer,agron.bajraktari,
florian.skopik}@ait.ac.at

Abstract. Intrusion Detection Systems (IDSs) monitor all kinds of IT infrastructures to automatically detect malicious activities related to cyber attacks. Unfortunately, especially anomaly-based IDS are known to produce large numbers of alerts, including false positives, that often become overwhelming for manual analysis. However, due to a fast changing threat landscape, quickly evolving attack techniques, and ever growing number of vulnerabilities, novel anomaly detection systems that enable detection of unknown attacks are indispensable. Therefore, to reduce the number of alerts that have to be reviewed by security analysts, aggregation methods have been developed for filtering, grouping, and correlating alerts. Yet, existing techniques either rely on manually defined attack scenarios or require specific alert formats, such as IDMEF that includes IP addresses. This makes the application of existing aggregation methods infeasible for alerts from host-based or anomaly-based IDSs that frequently lack such network-related data. In this chapter, we present a domain-independent alert aggregation technique that enables automatic attack pattern mining and generation of actionable CTI. The chapter describes the concept of the proposed alert aggregation process as well as a dashboard that enables visualization and filtering of the results. Finally, the chapter demonstrates all features in course of an application example.

Keywords: Alert aggregation · Attack pattern mining · Actionable CTI

1 Introduction

Cyber attacks pose a constant threat for IT infrastructures. As a consequence, Intrusion Detection Systems (IDSs) have been developed to monitor a wide range of activities within systems and analyze system events and interactions for suspicious and possibly malicious behavior, in which case they generate alerts that are subsequently reported to administrators or Security Information and Event

---

An adapted version of this article has been published in [8].

J. Kołodziej et al. (Eds.): Cybersecurity of Digital Service Chains, LNCS 13300, pp. 136–161, 2022.
https://doi.org/10.1007/978-3-031-04036-8_7

Management (SIEM) systems. The main advantage of IDSs is that they are capable of processing massive amounts of data in largely autonomous operation and are therefore usually deployed as network-based IDSs that analyze network traffic or host-based IDSs that also analyze system logs.

One of the main issues with IDSs is that they often produce large amounts of alerts that easily become overwhelming for analysts, a situation that is commonly referred to as alert flooding [5]. The number of produced alerts depends on the deployed IDSs as well as the type of attack, for example, attacks that result in many alerts include denial-of-service attacks that access machines with high intensity, brute-force attacks that repeatedly attempt to log into accounts with random passwords, and automatic scripts that search for vulnerabilities [4]. These attacks produce high loads on the network and consequently cause the generation of many events in the monitored logs, of which a large part is reported by signature-based IDSs that search for patterns corresponding to such common attacks. On the other hand, anomaly-based IDSs that learn a baseline of normal system behavior and report alerts for statistical deviations are known to suffer from high false positive rates, i.e., they frequently report alerts during normal operation. Independent from their origin, alerts that occur in large frequencies are problematic, because they are difficult to categorize and may cause that analysts oversee other relevant alerts that occur less frequently [2,5]. To alleviate this issue, alerts should be filtered or aggregated before being presented to human analysts.

Alert aggregation techniques usually rely on automatic correlation or manual linking of alert attributes [11]. However, organizations frequently deploy heterogeneous IDSs to enable broad ·and comprehensive protection against a wide variety of threats, causing that generated alerts have different formats and thus require normalization [13]. Most commonly, attributes of alerts are thereby reduced to timestamps, source and destination IP addresses and ports, and IDS-specific classifications, which are considered the most relevant features of alerts [1]. Unfortunately, alerts from host-based IDSs do not necessarily contain network information and alerts from anomaly-based IDSs do not involve alert types, which renders them unsuitable for existing aggregation techniques. In their survey, Navarro et al. [11] therefore recommend to develop alert aggregation techniques that operate on general events rather than well-formatted alerts to avoid loss of context information. The authors also found that most existing approaches rely on predefined knowledge for linking alerts, which impedes detection of unknown attack scenarios. In addition, modern infrastructures consist of decentralized networks and container-based virtualization that prevent IP-based correlation [4]. Hence, there is a need for an automatic and domain-independent alert aggregation technique that operates on arbitrary formatted alerts and is capable of generating representative attack patterns independent from any pre-existing knowledge about attack scenarios.

IDSs generate streams of individual alerts. Aggregating these alerts means to group them so that all alerts in each group are related to the same root cause, i.e., a specific malicious action or attack. Unfortunately, finding such a mapping between alerts and attacks is difficult for a number of reasons.

First, attack executions usually trigger the generation of multiple alerts [12], because IDSs are set up to monitor various parts of a system and any malicious activity frequently affects multiple monitored services at the same time. This implies that it is necessary to map a set of alerts to a specific attack execution, not just a single alert instance. Second, it is possible that the same or similar alerts are generated as part of multiple different attacks, which implies that there is no unique mapping from alerts to attacks. This is caused by the fact that IDSs are usually configured for a very broad detection and do not only consist of precise rules that are specific to particular attacks. Third, repeated executions of the same attack do not necessarily manifest themselves in the same way, but rather involve different amounts of alerts and changes of their attributes. This effect is even more drastic when parameters of the attack are varied, their executions take place on different system environments, or alerts are obtained from differently configured IDSs. Fourth, randomly occurring false positives that make up a considerable part of all alerts [5] as well as interleaving attacks complicate a correct separation of alerts that relate to the same root cause.

In addition, alert sequences should be aggregated to higher-level alert patterns to enable the classification of other alerts relating to the same root cause. In the following, we refer to these patterns as *meta-alerts*. The aforementioned problems are insufficiently solved by existing approaches, which usually rely on models built on pre-existing domain knowledge, manually crafted links between alerts, and exploitation of well-structured alert formats.

The development of alert aggregation techniques is usually motivated by specific problems at hand. Accordingly, existing approaches base on different assumptions regarding available data, tolerated manual effort, etc. With respect to the previously issues outlined, we derive the following list of requirements for domain-independent alert aggregation techniques:

(1) **Automatic.** Manually crafting attack scenarios is time-consuming and subject to human errors [11]. Therefore, unsupervised methods should be employed that enable the generation of patterns and meta-alerts relating to unknown attacks without manual interference.

(2) **Grouping.** Attacks should be represented by more than a single alert. This grouping is usually based on timing (T), common attributes (A), or a combination of both (C).

(3) **Format-independent.** Alerts occur in diverse formats [11]. Methods should utilize all available information and not require specific attributes, such as IP addresses.

(4) **Incremental.** IDSs generate alerts in streams. Alert aggregation methods should therefore be designed to derive attack scenarios and classify alerts in incremental operation.

(5) **Meta-alerts.** Aggregated alerts should be expressed by human-understandable meta-alerts that also enable automatic detection [2]. Thereby, generated patterns are usually based on single events (E), sequences (S), or a combination (C) of both.

This chapter thus presents a framework for automatic and domain-independent alert aggregation that meets the requirements listed above. The approach consists of an algorithm that groups alerts by their occurrence times, clusters these groups by similarity, and extracts commonalities to model meta-alerts. This is achieved without merging all considered alerts into a single common format. Our implementations as well as data used for evaluation are available online[1,2]. We summarize our contributions as follows:

- An approach for the incremental generation of meta-alerts from heterogeneous IDS alerts.
- Similarity-metrics for semi-structured alerts and groups of such alerts.
- Aggregation mechanisms for semi-structured alerts and groups of such alerts.
- A dashboard that visualizes alert aggregation results.
- An application example that demonstrates the alert aggregation approach.

The remainder of the chapter structures as follows: Section 2 outlines important concepts of our approach, including alerts, alert groups, and meta-alerts. In Sect. 3 we provide an application example to demonstrate the alert aggregation approach and introduce a dashboard to visualize and access actionable CTI. Finally, Sect. 4 concludes the chapter.

2   Entities and Operations

This section presents relevant concepts of our alert aggregation approach. We first provide an overview of the entities and their relationships. We then discuss our notion of alerts, outline how alerts are clustered into groups, and introduce a meta-alert model based on aggregated alert groups. A detailed description of the implementation and evaluation results are provided in [8]. The implementation is available as open source via Github (see Footnote 1).

2.1   Overview

Our approach transforms alerts generated by IDSs into higher-level meta-alerts that represent specific attack patterns. Figure 1 shows an overview of the involved concepts. The top of the figure represents alerts occurring as sequences of events on two timelines, which represent different IDSs deployed in the same network infrastructure or even separate system environments. Another possibility is that events are retrieved from historic alert logs and used for forensic attack analysis. Alert occurrences are marked with symbols and colors that represent their types. Thereby, two alerts could be of the same type if they share the same structure, were generated by the same rule in the IDS, or have coinciding classifications. We differentiate between square ($\square$), triangle ($\triangle, \triangledown, \triangleleft, \triangleright$), circle ($\circ$),

---

[1] https://github.com/ait-aecid/aecid-alert-aggregation.
[2] https://github.com/ait-aecid/alert-aggregation-dashboard.

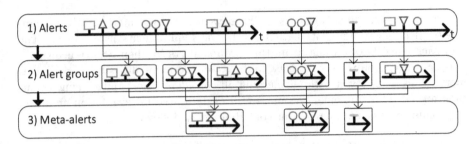

Fig. 1. Overview of the relationships between concepts. Alerts (top) occurring on time-lines (t) are grouped by temporal proximity (center) and then aggregated to meta-alerts by similarity (bottom).

and dash (−) symbols, which are marked blue, red, green, and yellow respectively. For the examples presented throughout this paper, we consider alerts represented by one of $\{\triangle, \triangledown, \triangleleft, \triangleright\}$ as variations of the same alert type, i.e., these alerts have sufficiently many commonalities such as matching attributes and are thus similar to each other. In general, each alert represents a unique event that occurs only at one specific point in time. However, alerts of the same type, e.g., alerts that are generated by the same violation of a predefined rule or alerts reported by the same IDS, may occur multiple times. We mark these alerts accordingly with the same color.

As outlined in Sect. 1, automatic mapping of alerts to higher-level meta-alerts is non-trivial. In the simple example shown in Fig. 1, it is easy to see that the alert sequence $(\square, \triangle, \circ)$ and the similar sequence $(\square, \triangledown, \circ)$ occur a total of three times, and that the pattern $(\circ, \circ, \triangledown)$ occurs two times over the two timelines. This is intuitively visible, because these alerts occur close together. Accordingly, it is reasonable to allocate alerts to groups that reflect this characteristic.

The center part of the figure shows groups of alerts based on their respective positions on the timelines. Note that grouping by alert type instead of temporal proximity would result in a loss of information, because alerts would be allocated to groups independent of their contexts, i.e., other alerts that are generated by the same root cause. For example, grouping all alerts of type $\circ$ would have neglected the fact that this type actually occurs in the patterns $(\square, \triangle, \circ)$ as well as $(\circ, \circ, \triangledown)$ and may thus not be a good indicator for a particular attack execution on its own.

Computing similarities between groups means measuring the differences of orders, frequencies, and attributes of their contained alerts. Alert groups that yield a high similarity are likely related to the same root cause and should thus be aggregated into a condensed form that reflects a typical instance of that group, i.e., a meta-alert. The bottom of the figure shows the generation of meta-alerts from similar groups. Thereby, orders, frequencies, and attributes of meta-alerts are created in a way to represent all allocated alert groups as accurate as possible. The figure shows that this is accomplished by merging the second alert in the patterns $(\square, \triangle, \circ)$ and $(\square, \triangledown, \circ)$ into alert χ, which combines attributes and values of $\triangle$ and $\triangledown$ so that both are adequately represented. In practice, this could mean that two different values of the same attribute in both alerts are combined into a set.

The second meta-alert with alert sequence $(\circ, \circ, \triangledown)$ is formed from two identical groups and thus does not involve changes to merged alerts. If meta-alert generation was based on similarity of alerts rather than groups, all occurrences of similar alerts $\triangle$ and $\triangledown$ would be replaced with $\mathbb{X}$, thereby decreasing the specificity of the second meta-alert. This suggests that forming groups of logically related alerts is an essential step for meta-alert generation. Finally, the third meta-alert contains a single alert that only occurred once and is the only alert in its group. Since alerts form the basis of the presented approach, the following section will discuss their compositions in more detail.

2.2   Alerts

IDSs are designed to transmit as much useful information as possible to the person or system that receives, interprets, and acts upon the generated alerts. This includes data derived from the event that triggered the alert, e.g., IP addresses present in the monitored data, as well as information on the context of detection, e.g., detection rule identifiers. As outlined in [8], most approaches omit a lot of this information and only focus on specific predefined attributes. Our approach, however, utilizes all available data to generate meta-alerts without imposing any domain-specific restrictions.

To organize all data conveyed with each alert in an intuitive form, alerts are frequently represented as semi-structured objects, e.g., XML-formatted alerts as defined by the IDMEF[3] or JSON-formatted alerts generated by Wazuh[4] IDS. Even though such standards exist, different IDSs produce alerts with data fields specific to their detection techniques. For example, a signature-based detection approach usually provides information on the rule that triggered the alert, while anomaly-based IDSs only indicate suspicious event occurrences without any semantic interpretation of the observed activity. In addition, some IDSs do not provide all attributes required by standards such as IDMEF, e.g., host-based IDSs analyze system logs that do not necessarily contain network and IP information.

Figure 2 shows such an alert that was caused by a failed user login attempt generated by Wazuh. Note that it does not support IP-based correlation, since only "srcip" that points to localhost is available. The alert contains semi-structured elements, i.e., key-value pairs (e.g., "timestamp"), lists (e.g., "groups"), and nested objects (e.g., "rule"). In alignment with this observation, we model alerts as abstract objects with arbitrary numbers of attributes. Formally, given a set of alerts $\mathcal{A}$, an alert $a \in \mathcal{A}$ holds one or more attributes κ_a, where each attribute $a.k$ is defined as in Eq. 1.

---

[3] Intrusion Detection Message Exchange Format (IDMEF) is defined in IETF RFC 4765 (https://tools.ietf.org/html/rfc4765).

[4] https://wazuh.com/.

$$a.k = v_1, v_2, ..., v_n \quad \forall k \in \kappa_a, n \in \mathbb{N} \tag{1}$$

Note that Eq. 1 also holds for nested attributes, i.e., $a.k.j, \forall j \in \kappa_{a.k}$, and that v_i is an arbitrary value, such as a number or character sequence. In the following we assume that the timestamp of the alert is stored in key $t \in \kappa_a, \forall a \in \mathcal{A}$, e.g., $a.t = 1$ for alert a that occurs at time step 1. These alert attributes are suitable to compare alerts and measure their similarities, e.g., alerts that share a high number of keys and additionally have many coinciding values for each common key should yield a high similarity, because they are likely related to the same suspicious event. This also means that values such as IPs are not ignored, but matched by common keys like all other attributes. We define a function $alert\_sim$ in Eq. 2 that computes the similarity of alerts $a, b \in \mathcal{A}$.

$$alert\_sim : a, b \in \mathcal{A} \to [0, 1] \tag{2}$$

Thereby, the similarity between any non-empty alert and itself is 1 and the similarity to an empty object is 0. Furthermore, the function is symmetric, which is intuitively reasonable when comparing alerts on the same level of abstraction. On the other hand, the function implicitly computes how well one alert is represented by another more abstract aler. We summarize the properties of the function in Eq. 3–5.

$$alert\_sim(a, a) = 1 \tag{3}$$
$$alert\_sim(a, \emptyset) = 0, \quad a \neq \emptyset \tag{4}$$
$$alert\_sim(a, b) = alert\_sim(b, a) \tag{5}$$

As mentioned, we do not make any restrictions on the attributes of alerts and only consider the timestamp $a.t$ of alert a as mandatory, which is not a limitation since the time of detection is always known by the IDS or can be extracted from the monitored data. In the next section, this timestamp will be used to allocate alerts that occur in close temporal proximity to groups.

2.3   Alert Groups

Alerts generated by an arbitrary number of deployed IDSs result in a sequence of heterogeneous events. Since attacks typically manifest themselves in multiple mutually dependent alerts rather than singular events, it is beneficial to find groups of alerts that were generated by the same root cause as shown in Sect. 2.1. In the following, we describe our strategies for formation and representation of alert groups that enable group similarity computation.

Formation. Depending on the type of IDS, alerts may already contain some kind of classification provided by their detection rules. For example, the message "PAM: User login failed." contained in the alert shown in Fig. 2 could be used to classify and group every event caused by invalid logins. While existing approaches commonly perform clustering on such pre-classifications of IDSs,

```
{
        "timestamp": "2020-03-04T19:26:05.000000+0000",
        "rule": {
                "level": 5,
                "description": "PAM: User login failed.",
                "id": "5503",
                "firedtimes": 28,
                "groups": [
                        "pam",
                        "syslog",
                        "authentication_failed"
                ]
        },
        "full_log": "Mar  4 19:26:05 mail auth: pam_unix(dovecot:auth): authentication
                failure; logname= uid=0 euid=0 tty=dovecot ruser=daryl rhost=127.0.0.1
                user=daryl",
        "data": {
                "srcip": "127.0.0.1",
                "srcuser": "daryl",
                "dstuser": "daryl",
                "uid": "0",
                "euid": "0",
                "tty": "dovecot"
        },
        "location": "/var/log/forensic/auth.log"
}
```

Fig. 2. Simplified sample alert documenting a failed user login.

single alerts are usually not sufficient to differentiate between specific types of attacks or accurately filter out false positives (cf. Sect. 1). To alleviate this problem, we identify multiple alerts that are generated in close temporal proximity and whose combined occurrence is a better indicator for a specific attack execution. For example, a large number of alerts classified as failed user login attempts that occur in a short period of time and in combination with a suspicious user agent could be an indicator for a brute-force password guessing attack executed through a particular tool. Such a reasoning would not be possible when all alerts are analyzed individually, because single failed logins may be false positives and the specific user agent could also be part of other attack scenarios.

The problem of insufficient classification is even more drastic when alerts are received from anomaly-based IDS, because they mainly disclose unknown attacks. Accordingly, an approach that relies on clustering by alert classification attributes would require human analysts who interpret the root causes and assign a classifier to each alert. Temporal grouping on the other hand is always possible for sequentially incoming alerts and does not rely on the presence of alert attributes.

Our strategy for alert group formation is based on the interval times between alerts. In particular, two alerts $a, b \in \mathcal{A}$ that occur at times $a.t, b.t$ have an interval time $|a.t - b.t|$ and are allocated to the same group if $|a.t - b.t| \leq \delta$, where $\delta \in \mathbb{R}^+$. This is achieved through single-linkage clustering [3]. In particular, all alerts are initially contained in their own sets, i.e., $s_{\delta,i} = \{a_i\}, \forall a_i \in \mathcal{A}$. Then, clusters are iteratively formed by repeatedly merging the two sets with the shortest interval time $d = \min\left(|a_i.t - a_j.t|\right), \forall a_i \in s_{\delta,i}, \forall a_j \in s_{\delta,j}$. This agglomerative clustering procedure is stopped when $d > \delta$, which results in a number of sets $s_{\delta,i}$. Each set is transformed into a group $g_{\delta,i}$ that holds all alerts of set $s_{\delta,i}$ as a sequence sorted by their occurrence time stamps as in Eq. 6.

$$g_{\delta,i} = \{(a_1, a_2, \ldots, a_n), \forall a_i \in s_{\delta,i} : a_1.t \leq a_2.t \leq \cdots \leq a_n.t\} \tag{6}$$

Equation 7 defines the set of all groups for a specific δ as their union.

$$\mathcal{G}_\delta = \bigcup_{i \in \mathbb{N}} g_{\delta,i} \tag{7}$$

This group formation strategy is exemplarily visualized in Fig. 3. The figure shows alert occurrences of types $\{\square, \triangle, \circ, -\}$ in specific patterns duplicated over four timelines with different δ. The sequence $(\square, \triangle, \circ)$ at the beginning of the timelines occurs with short alert interval times and that a similar sequence $(\square, \triangledown, \circ)$ occurs at the end, but involves $\triangledown$ instead of its variant $\triangle$ and has an increased interval time between $\triangledown$ and $\circ$. Nevertheless, due to the similar compositions of these two alert sequences, it is reasonable to assume that they are two manifestations of the same root cause.

In this example, each tick in the figure marks a time span of 1 unit. In timeline (d), all alerts end up in separate groups, because no two alerts yield a sufficiently small interval time lower than $\delta = 0.5$, i.e., $\mathcal{G}_{0.5} = \{(\square), (\triangle), (\circ), (-), (\square), (\triangledown), (\circ)\}$. In timeline (c) where alerts are grouped using $\delta = 1.5$, two groups that contain more than a single alert are formed, because the grouped alerts occur within sufficiently close temporal proximity, i.e., $\mathcal{G}_{1.5} = \{(\square, \triangle, \circ), (-), (\square, \triangledown), (\circ)\}$. Considering the results for $\mathcal{G}_{2.5} = \{(\square, \triangle, \circ), (-), (\square, \triangledown, \circ)\}$ in timeline (b) shows that the aforementioned repeating pattern $(\square, \triangle, \circ)$ and its variant end up in two distinct groups. This is the optimal case, since subsequent steps for group analysis could determine that both groups are similar and thus merge them into a meta-alert as shown in Sect. 2.1. A larger value for delta, e.g., $\delta = 3.5$ that yields $\mathcal{G}_{3.5} = \{(\square, \triangle, \circ), (-, \square, \triangledown, \circ)\}$ in timeline (a), adds alert of type $-$ to form group $(-, \square, \triangledown, \circ)$, which is not desirable since this decreases its similarity to group $(\square, \triangle, \circ)$. This example thus shows the importance for an appropriate selection of the interval threshold for subsequent analyses.

Note that this strategy for temporal grouping has several advantages over sliding time windows. First, instead of time window size and step width, only a single parameter that specifies the maximum delta time between alerts is required, which reduces complexity of parameter selection. Second, it ensures that alerts with close temporal proximity remain in the same group given any delta larger than their interval times, while intervals of sliding time windows possibly break up groups by chance. Third, related sequences with variable delays result in complete groups as long as there is no gap between any two alerts that exceeds δ, e.g., two groups with similar alerts but varying delays are found for $\delta = 2.5$ in Fig. 3. However, time window sizes must exceed the duration of the longest sequence to yield complete groups, which is more difficult to specify in general.

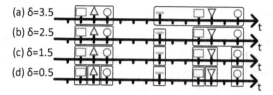

Fig. 3. Alert occurrences duplicated over four parallel timelines show the formation of alert groups based on alert interval times. Larger intervals (top) allow more elapsed time between alerts and thus lead to fewer and larger groups compared to smaller intervals (bottom).

Despite these benefits, pure time-based grouping suffers from some drawbacks compared to knowledge-based clustering methods, e.g., grouping by classification messages. As seen in the example from Fig. 3, the quality of the resulting grouping is highly dependent on a selection of the parameter δ that fits the typical time interval of the events to be grouped. Another issue is that randomly occurring alerts, e.g., false positives, are incorrectly allocated to groups if they occur in close proximity to one of the grouped alerts. Even worse, these alerts could connect two or more groups into a single large group if they happen to occur in between and in sufficiently high amount or close proximity to both groups. As we will outline in the following sections, our approach mitigates these problems by finding groups using several values for δ in parallel.

Similarity Computation. Other than clustering based on predefined alert types, time-based grouping only acts as a preparatory step for subsequent analyses. In particular, a similarity measure for alert groups is required that allows to determine which groups of alerts are likely generated from the same root cause. Only then it is possible to cluster groups by their similarities and in turn generate meta-alerts by merging alert groups that end up in the same clusters. We therefore define function $group\_sim$ in Eq. 8 that computes the similarity of any two groups $g, h \in \mathcal{G}_\delta$.

$$group\_sim : g, h \in \mathcal{G}_\delta \rightarrow [0, 1] \tag{8}$$

Analogous to alert similarity computation (cf. Sect. 2.2), the similarity between any non-empty group $g \in \mathcal{G}_\delta$ and itself is 1 and the similarity to an empty object is 0. However, we do not impose symmetry on the function, since it can be of interest to measure whether one group is contained in another possibly more abstract group, such as a meta-alert. Details on such a similarity function are discussed in [8]. In the following section, we first explain the representation of meta-alerts and then introduce matching strategies for similarity computations between groups.

2.4   Meta-alerts

We generate meta-alerts by merging groups, which relies on merging alerts within these groups. In the following, we first introduce features that support the representation of merged alerts and then outline group merging strategies for similarity computations and meta-alert generation.

Alert Merges. As outlined in Sect. 2.2, alerts are semi-structured objects, i.e., data structures that contain key-value pairs, and are suitable for similarity computation. However, aggregating similar alerts into a merged object that is representative for all allocated alerts is non-trivial, because single alert objects may have different keys or values that need to be taken into account.

For example, the failed login alert in Fig. 2 contains the attribute "srcuser" with value "daryl" in the "data" object. Since a large number of users may trigger such alerts, this event type occurs with many different values for attribute "srcuser" over time. An aggregated alert optimally abstracts over such attributes to represent a general failed login alert that does not contain any information specific to a particular event. The computed similarity between such an aggregated alert and any specific alert instance is independent of attributes that are known to vary, i.e., only the presence of the attribute "srcuser" contributes to similarity computations, but not its value. Note that this assumes that keys across alerts have the same semantic meaning or that keys with different names are correctly mapped if alert formats are inconsistent, e.g., keys "src_user" and "srcuser".

We incorporate merging of alerts by introducing two new types of values. First, a *wildcard* value type that indicates that the specific value of the corresponding key is not expressive for that type of alert, i.e., any value of that field will yield a perfect match just like two coinciding values. Typical candidates for values replaced by wildcards are user names, domain names, IP addresses, counts, and timestamps. Second, a *mergelist* value type that comprises a finite set of values observed in several alerts that are all regarded as valid values, i.e., a single matching value from the mergelist is sufficient to yield a perfect match for this attribute present in two compared alerts. The mergelist type is useful for discrete values that occur in variations, e.g., commands or parameters derived from events. Deciding whether an attribute should be represented as a wildcard or mergelist is therefore based on the total number of unique values observed for that attribute.

We define that each attribute key $k \in \kappa_a$ of an aggregated alert a that is the result of a merge of alerts $A \subseteq \mathcal{A}$ is represented as either a wildcard or mergelist as in Eq. 9.

$$a.k = \begin{cases} wildcard\,() \\ mergelist\,\left(\bigcup_{b \in A} b.k\right) \end{cases} \tag{9}$$

Note that Eq. 9 also applies for nested keys, i.e., values within nested objects stored in the alerts. Since our approach is independent of any domain-specific reasoning, a manual selection of attributes for the replacement with wildcards and mergelists is infeasible. The function *alert_merge* thus automatically counts the number of unique values for each attribute from alerts $A \subseteq \mathcal{A}$ passed as a parameter, selects and replaces them with the appropriate representations, and returns a new alert object a that represents a merged alert that is added to all alerts $\mathcal{A}$ as shown in Eq. 10–11.

$$a = alert\_merge(A), \quad A \subseteq \mathcal{A} \tag{10}$$
$$\mathcal{A} \Leftarrow a \tag{11}$$

Note that we use the operation $\Leftarrow$ to indicate set extensions, i.e., $\mathcal{A} \Leftarrow a \iff \mathcal{A}' = \mathcal{A} \cup \{a\}$. We drop the prime of sets like $\mathcal{A}'$ in the following for simplicity and assume that after extension only the new sets will be used. The extension of $\mathcal{A}$ implies that merged alerts are also suitable for similarity computation and merging with other alerts or merged alerts. We will elaborate on the details of the alert merging procedure in [8]. The next section will outline the role of alert merging when groups are merged for meta-alert generation.

Group Merges. Similar to merging of alerts that was discussed in the previous section, a merged group should represent a condensed abstraction of all groups used for its generation. Since each group should ideally comprise a similar sequence of alerts, it may be tempting to merge groups by forming a sequence of merged alerts, where the first alert is merged from the first alerts in all groups, the second alert is merged from the second alerts in all groups, and so on. Unfortunately, this is infeasible in practice, because alert sequences are not necessarily ordered, involve optional alerts, or are affected by false positives causing that alert positions in sequences are shifted. To alleviate this issue, it is necessary to find matches between the alerts of all groups to be merged. In the following, we describe three matching strategies used in our approach that are suitable for group similarity computation as well as meta-alert generation.

Exact Matching. This strategy finds for each alert in one group the most similar alert in another group and uses these pairs to determine which alerts to merge. The idea of finding these matches is depicted in the left side of Fig. 4, where lines across groups g_1, g_2, g_3 indicate which alerts were identified as the most similar. As expected, alerts of the same type are matched, because they share several common attributes and values that are specific to their respective types. The figure also shows that correct alerts are matched even though the second and third alert in g_2 are in a different order than in g_1 and g_3. In addition, note that the alert of type $\triangledown$ in g_1 is correctly matched to the related alert type $\triangle$ in g_2 and that the merged group thus contains the merged alert type $\boxtimes$ at that position. In addition, there is a missing alert of type $\circ$ in g_3 that leads to an incomplete match. Nevertheless, the alert of type $\circ$ ends up in the merged group, because it occurs in the majority of all merged groups and is therefore considered to be representative for this root cause manifestation.

When only two groups are considered, this matching method is also suitable for measuring their similarity. In particular, this is achieved by computing the average similarity of all matched alerts, where non-matching alerts count as total

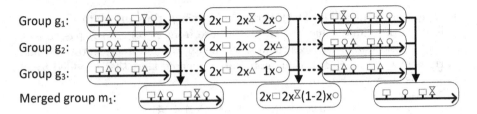

Fig. 4. Merging strategies for alert groups. Left: Finding exact matches between alert pairs. Center: Matching representatives using a bag-of-alerts model. Right: Matching using alert sequence alignment.

mismatches. The similarity score is further enhanced by incorporating an edit distance [10] that measures the amount of inserts, removes, and substitutions of alerts, i.e., misalignments such as the occurrence of $(\circ, \triangle)$ instead of $(\triangle, \circ)$ in g_2.

While the exact matching strategy yields accurate group similarities, it is rather inefficient for large groups. The reason for this is that computing the pairwise similarities of all alerts requires quadratic runtime with respect to group sizes. We therefore only use this strategy when the number of required comparisons for groups g, h does not exceed a limit $l_{bag} \in \mathbb{N}$, i.e., $|g| \cdot |h| \leq l_{bag}$, where $|g|$ denotes the size of group g. In the following, we outline an alternative strategy for larger groups.

Bag-of-Alerts Matching. For this strategy, we transform the alert sequences of all groups into a bag-of-alerts model following the well-known bag-of-words model [9]. This is accomplished by incrementally clustering [15] the alerts within each group using a certain similarity threshold $\theta_{alert} \in [0, 1]$. Thereby, each alert a that is sufficiently similar to one of the initially empty sets of cluster representatives R, i.e., $alert\_sim(r, a) \geq \theta_{alert}, \forall r \in R$, is added to the list C_r that stores all alerts of that cluster, i.e., $C_r \Leftarrow a$, or forms a new cluster with itself as a representative otherwise, i.e., $R \Leftarrow a$. Once all alerts of a group are processed, the bag-of-alerts model for that group is generated by merging all alerts in each cluster, i.e., $alert\_merge(C_r), \forall r \in R$.

The matching procedure then finds the pairs of these merged alerts that yield the highest similarities across groups and aggregates them by identifying lower and upper limits of their corresponding cluster sizes $|C_r|$ in each group. The advantage in comparison to the exact matching strategy is that the number of necessary similarity computations is reduced to the product of the number of clusters per group, which is controllable through θ_{alert}. Note that the speedup stems from the fact that the computation of the bag-of-alerts model only has to be carried out once for each group, but then enables fast matching with all other groups.

The center part of Fig. 4 shows bag-of-alert models for sample groups, where alerts of types $\triangle$ and $\triangledown$ in g_1 are merged to $\mathbb{X}$, which is then matched to $\triangle$ in g_2 and g_3 before they are once again merged for the generation of the meta-alert.

Since alert type $\circ$ occurs twice in g_1 and g_2, but only once in g_3, the meta-alert uses a range with minimum limit $l_{min} = 1$ and maximum limit $l_{max} = 2$ to describe the occurrence frequency of this alert type.

This strategy also supports measuring the similarity of two groups g, h by averaging the relative differences of occurrence counts, which yields the highest possible similarity of 1 if the respective counts coincide or their intervals overlap, and $min(l_{max,g}, l_{max,h})/max(l_{min,g}, l_{min,h})$ otherwise. Alerts without a match are considered as total mismatches and contribute the lowest possible similarity score of 0 to the average. We favored this similarity metric over existing measures such as cosine similarity [9], because it allows a more intuitive representation of lower and upper occurrence limits which supports human interpretation of meta-alerts.

The downside of the bag-of-alerts strategy is that information on the order of the alerts is lost. However, it is possible to resolve this issue by combining the original alert sequence with the bag-of-alerts model. In the following, we outline this addition to the bag-of-alerts matching.

Alignment-Based Matching. To incorporate alignment information for large clusters that are not suited for the exact matching strategy, it is necessary to store the original sequence position of all clustered alerts during generation of the bag-of-alerts model of each group. This information enables to generate a sequence of cluster representatives. For example, the right side of Fig. 4 shows that group g_1 has sequence $(\square, \lambdabar, \circ, \square, \lambdabar, \circ)$, because the occurrences of $\triangle$ and $\triangledown$ have been replaced by their cluster representative $\lambdabar$ that was generated in the bag-of-alerts model. Note that this strategy is much faster for large groups than the exact matching strategy, because it enables to reuse the matching information of representative alerts from the bag-of-alerts model instead of finding matches between all alerts. Since the corresponding sequence elements across groups are known, it is simple to use sequence alignment algorithms for merging and similarity computation.

We decided to merge the sequences using longest common sequence (LCS) [10], because it enables to retrieve the common alert pattern present in all groups and thereby omit randomly occurring false positive alerts [6]. The example in Fig. 4 shows that this results in a sequence of representatives $(\square, \circ, \square, \lambdabar)$ that occurs in the same order in all groups. Using the LCS also enables to compute the sequence similarity of two groups g, h by $|LCS(g, h)| / min(|g|, |h|)$, which we use to improve the bag-of-alerts similarity by incorporating it as a weighted term after averaging.

Equation 12 defines a function that takes a set of groups $G \subseteq \mathcal{G}_\delta$ and automatically performs all aforementioned merging strategies to generate a new group g.

$$g = group\_merge(G), \quad G \subseteq \mathcal{G}_\delta \tag{12}$$

$$\mathcal{G}_\delta \Leftarrow g \tag{13}$$

Analogous to merges of single alerts, Eq. 13 indicates that merges of alert groups have the same properties as normal groups and therefore support similarity computation and merging. In the previous sections, we defined several functions required for meta-alert generation. The following section will embed all aforementioned concepts in an overall procedure.

3   Application Example

The remaining section provides an application example for the proposed alert aggregation approach and introduces a Kibana[5] based Cyber Threat Intelligence (CTI) dashboard that visualizes alerts, alert groups, and meta-alerts, as well as their interdependencies in form of actionable CTI. The section first provides an overview of the example's process flow, then describes the test data, and finally depicts the results of the example and the CTI dashboard. A detailed evaluation of the alert aggregation approach is available in [8].

3.1   CTI Process Flow

Figure 5 depicts the process flow for the demonstrated application example. All tools and algorithms we use in course of the example are either open source or freely available for non-commercial use. The first step considers anomaly detection to generate alerts. In this example, we process log data that contains a baseline of normal system behavior, as well as traces of attacks. The next sections provide detailed information about the considered log data. Therefore, we apply the log-based anomaly detection system AMiner[6] [14,16] that generates alerts in JSON format (see Fig. 9). The AMiner forwards the alerts via a Kafka[7] message queue to a central elastic[8] search database that stores the alerts. The alert aggregation[9] continuously polls the alerts from the database and builds alert groups and generates meta-alerts. It forwards both alert groups and meta-alerts to the elastic search database. Finally, we developed a Kibana CTI dashboard[10] that visualizes the alerts, the alert groups, the meta-alerts, as well as their interdependencies. Section 3.3 describes the dashboard in detail.

3.2   Data Generation

For the demonstration of the alert aggregation and the CTI dashboard a representative use-case was prepared and implemented. This was accomplished in three steps applying the Kyoushi[11] testbed approach [7]: First, a testbed for log data generation was deployed and simulations of normal behavior were started. After several days of running the simulation, a sequence of attack steps was launched on the testbed. This was repeated four times to generate repeated

---

[5] https://www.elastic.co/kibana/.

[6] https://github.com/ait-aecid/logdata-anomaly-miner.

[7] https://kafka.apache.org/.

[8] https://www.elastic.co/.

[9] https://github.com/ait-aecid/alert-aggregation-generator.

[10] https://github.com/ait-aecid/alert-aggregation-dashboard.

[11] https://github.com/ait-aecid/kyoushi-environment.

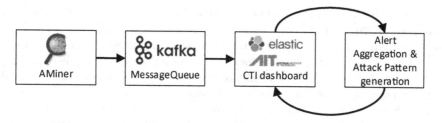

Fig. 5. The process flow used in the application example includes the log-based anomaly detection system AMiner, the message queue Kafka, a Kibana-based CTI dashboard developed by the authors, and the implementation of the alert aggregation.

manifestations of the same attack types that should then be aggregated to meta-alerts using the proposed alert aggregation approach. Thereby, we paid attention to vary the attack parameters so that the attack manifestations are not identical, but represent slight variations of the attacks that should then be reflected in the meta-alerts. Second, the log dataset was collected from the attacked webserver and labelled using a predefined dictionary of attack traces[12]. Third, the AMiner was used to analyze the dataset and generate alerts to be aggregated. In the following, we describe each of these steps in more detail.

The data generation approach is described in detail in [7]. In a nutshell, for the example at hand the virtual testbed environment consists of an Apache web server that runs an Exim mail server and Horde Webmail, as well as 16 virtual users that perform common tasks on the infrastructure, including sending emails, changing calender entries, and taking notes. The most relevant part for alert aggregation concerns the injection of attacks, since variations of attack parameters reflect in the meta-alerts. For our use-case, we prepared a multi-step intrusion that involves several tools commonly used by adversaries and exploits of two well-known vulnerabilities to gain root access on the mail server. The first two steps involve scans for open ports using the Nmap[13] scanner and Nikto[14] vulnerability scanner. Then, the attacker uses the smtp-user-enum tool[15] for discovering Horde Webmail accounts using a list of common names and the hydra[16] tool to brute-force log in to one of the accounts using a list of common passwords. The attack proceeds with an exploit in Horde[17] Webmail 5.2.22 that allows to upload a webshell (CVE-2019-9858[18]) and enables remote command execution. We simulate the attacker examining the web server for further vulnerabilities by executing several commands, such as printing out system info. In our scenario,

---

[12] The labeled testdata is available on https://zenodo.org/record/4264796#.YbG-2Loo9hE.

[13] https://nmap.org/.

[14] https://cirt.net/Nikto2.

[15] https://www.kali.org/tools/smtp-user-enum/.

[16] https://github.com/vanhauser-thc/thc-hydra.

[17] https://www.horde.org/apps/webmail.

[18] https://nvd.nist.gov/vuln/detail/CVE-2019-9858.

the intruder discovers a vulnerable version of the Exim package and uploads an exploit (CVE-2019-10149[19]) to obtain root privileges through another reverse connection. To realize the attacks, we use a sequence of predefined commands in a script, but do not specify values that are only known after instantiating the testbed, such as the IP addresses of the web server and user hosts, as well as parameters that are varied in each simulation, such as port numbers, evasion strategies, or commands executed after gaining remote access. This attack was purposefully designed as a multi-step attack with variable parameters to evaluate the ability of IDSs to disclose and extract individual attack steps and their connections, and recognize the learned patterns in different environments despite variations.

Once the testbed setup is completed, we run the simulation for five days to capture a baseline of normal system behavior. Afterwards, we run the attacks and collect one more day of log data to ensure that all attack consequences are completed (e.g., events corresponding to timeouts that are related to the attack could possibly only be generated some time after the attack is finished) and to allow the network and system behavior to stabilize itself back to the normal activities. At this point, we collect all the logs and label all events. This relates to the second step of the overall scenario and data generation procedure and is described in detail in [7]. Labeling data is essential for appropriately evaluating and comparing the detection capabilities of IDSs and alert aggregation approaches. However, generating labels is difficult for several reasons: (i) log data is generated in large volumes and manual labeling all lines is usually infeasible, (ii) single actions may manifest themselves in multiple log sources in different ways, (iii) processes are frequently interleaving and thus log lines corresponding to malicious actions are interrupted by normal log messages, (iv) execution of malicious commands may cause manifestations in logs at a much later time due to delays or dependencies on other events, and (v) it is non-trivial to assign labels to missing events, i.e., log messages suppressed by the attack.

We attempt to alleviate most of these problems by automatically labeling logs on two levels. First, we assign time-based labels to all collected logs. For this, we make use of an attack execution log that is generated as part of executing the attack scripts. We implemented a script that processes all logs, parses their time stamps, and labels them if their occurrence time lies within the time period of an attack stage. Assuming that attack consequences and manifestations are not delayed, it is then simple to check whether anomalies reported by IDSs lie within the expected attack time phases. Since exact times of malicious command executions are known, it is even possible to count correctly reported missing events as true positives.

---

[19] https://nvd.nist.gov/vuln/detail/cve-2019-10149.

While time-based labeling is simple and effective, it cannot differentiate between interleaved malicious and normal processes and does not correctly label delayed log manifestations that occur after the attack time frame. Therefore, our second labeling mechanism is based on lines that are known to occur when executing malicious commands. For this, we carry out the attack steps in an idle system, i.e., without simulating normal user behavior, and gather all generated logs. We observed that most attack steps either generate short event sequences of particular orders (e.g., webshell upload) or large amounts of repeating events (e.g., scans). We assign the logs to their corresponding attack steps and use the resulting dictionary for labeling new data. For the short-ordered sequences, we pursue exact matching, i.e., we compute a similarity metric based on a combination of string similarity and timing difference between the expected and observed logs and label the event sequence that achieves the highest similarity. For logs that occur in large unordered sequences, we first reduce the logs in the dictionary to a set of only few representative events, e.g., through similarity-based clustering. Our algorithm then labels each newly observed log line that occurs within the expected time frame and achieves a sufficiently high similarity with one of the representative lines. These strategies enable correct labeling of logs that occur with a temporal offset or are interrupted by other events, but obviously suffer from misclassifications when malicious and normal lines are similar enough to be grouped together during clustering.

In the final step of the overall scenario and data generation procedure, we use the anomaly-based detection engine AMiner. The AMiner learns a baseline of normal behavior and raises alerts for all deviations of this normal behavior in the testing phase. We add several detectors to the AMiner analysis pipeline: a detector for unparsed events that do not correspond to the parser model, a detector for new events that fit the parser but never occurred before (i.e., detection of new paths), detectors for new values that do not occur in the training phase in events of several log files (e.g., IP addresses in Exim log files or user agent strings in Apache log files), and detectors for new value combinations that do not occur in the training phase (e.g., file info in suricata event logs or user authentication info in Exim logs) [14,16].

3.3   CTI Dashboard

The remaining section describes the CTI dashboard in detail. The section presents the visualizations the dashboard provides as well as how it depicts data entities provided by the alert aggregation, such as alert groups and meta-alerts. Finally, it discusses how meta-alerts can be used to recognize reoccurring attack patterns. The CTI dashboard is implemented as Kibana dashboard[20] and uses an elastic search database. In the backend runs the proposed alert aggregation approach[21].

---

[20] https://github.com/ait-aecid/alert-aggregation-dashboard.
[21] https://github.com/ait-aecid/alert-aggregation-generator.

Visualization. Figure 6 shows the overview of the CTI dashboard. The general CTI dashboard shows three tables. The first one shows all currently existing meta-alerts, provides the time stamp when the meta-alert was observed for the last time, the meta-alert id, and the number of alerts the meta-alert consists of. The second table 'groups' shows the alert groups, the timestamp when a group was generated, which meta-alerts a group is assigned to[22], and the number of alerts a group consists of. The third table shows the alerts, the timestamp an alert was generated, the 'Componentname', i.e., the name of the detector that triggered the alert, the message of the alert, which groups it is assigned to[23], and the related meta-alerts[24].

The dashboard overview allows to filter for specific meta-alerts, alert groups, and alerts. For example, in Fig. 6, the user filters the meta-alert with the id 0 by clicking the box next to it. Hence, the second table shows all the groups that match meta-alert 0, and the third table provides all the alerts that relate to meta-alert 0.

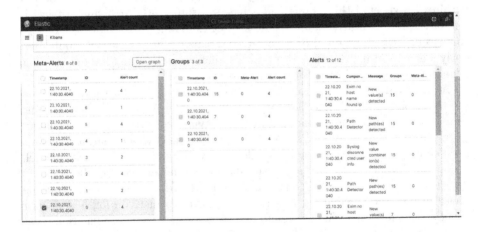

Fig. 6. Dashboard overview.

Additionally, the overview provides a button 'Open graph'. Once a user has filtered specific entities, it is possible to visualize their relations by clicking the 'Open graph' button. Figure 7 shows the visualization when filtering for meta-alert 0. The figure shows that groups 0 (G0), 7 (G7), and 15 (G15) match meta-alert 0 (MA 0). In this scenario groups G0 and G7 have triggered the generation of M0 and G15 matches the meta-alert. Moreover, the visualization shows that four alerts relate to each alert group. Detailed information on the single meta-alerts, alert groups, and alerts are provided by the 'Discovery' dashboard.

---

[22] Note, groups can match more than one meta-alert.
[23] Note, alerts can be assigned more than one alert group.
[24] Note, an alert can relate to more than one alert group.

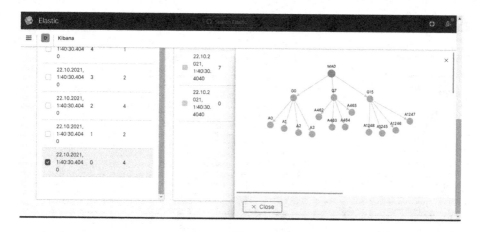

Fig. 7. Visualization of relations between meta-alerts, alert groups, and alerts.

Alerts and Alert Groups. The dashboard also provides a detailed view on alerts, alert groups, and meta-alerts that complements the graphical overview as a tree. In the following, we review the alert groups and the alerts they contain for the attack step visualized in the previous section. Figures 8, 9, and 10 depict the information of two alert groups provided by the CTI dashboard.

Figure 8 shows alert groups with ID 0 (left) and 7 (right) that both correspond to executions of the Nmap scan and are therefore similar. Note that these groups correspond to nodes G0 and G7 visible in the visualization of the alerts, alert groups, and meta-alert relationships in the previous section (see Fig. 7). As visible in Fig. 8, both alert groups are part of the same meta-alert MA0 with ID 0. Note that the timestamp visible in the figure describes the point in time where the groups were generated, and not the point in time where the alerts occurred, which is instead visible for each alert separately as we will show in the following screenshots. The delta time, i.e., the interval time that was used to build the groups by adding alerts to the same group if their interarrival time is lower than the threshold, is also visible in the JSON data. In particular, we used a delta time of 5 seconds to generate the alert groups. The field 'alerts' then depicts all alerts that are part of the alert group. Figure 8 provides a more detailed view on one of these alerts.

Figure 9 shows alerts A1 and A463. A1 represents the second alert of group G0 (left) and alert A463 the second alert of G7 (right). We picked these alerts as a representative example for all other alerts that are merged as part of the meta-alert generation procedure. Comparing these alerts shows that they have many similarities: First of all, they share the same fields. This makes sense, since the alerts are reported by the same detector from the same IDS, in particular, the NewMatchPathValueDetector from the AMiner. This detector detects new values in specific positions of events that did not occur as part of the training phase. Second, the alerts share common values for most of the attributes. This includes, for example, the type of the detector ('AnalysisComponentType'), the

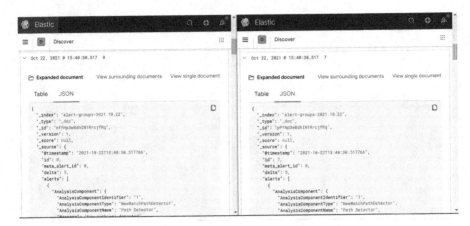

Fig. 8. Two similar alert groups.

name of the detector ('AnalysisComponentName'), as well as parts of the parsed
log line such as the message 'no host name found for IP address' in the parser
path '/parser/model/fm/no_host_found/no_host_found_str'. However, there are
also some differences between the two alerts that are especially interesting for
the purpose of alert aggregation. Most importantly, the value that triggered
the detection, which is stated in the field 'AffectedLogAtomValues' is different:
3232238098 in A1 and 3232238161 in A463. Note that these are IP addresses in
decimal format and correspond to 192.168.10.18 and 192.168.10.81 respectively.
The IP addresses can also be seen in the raw log data that is depicted in the
parser path '/parser/model'. These IP addresses are the addresses of the attacker
host in two executions of the attacks during the scenario where the alerts have
been collected from. Accordingly their detection as new values is correct. Besides
the IP addresses, also the timestamp of the raw log atom is different, because
the two attack executions have been launched at two different points in time.
The timestamps depicted in unix time are visible in path '/parser/model/time'
and in raw format in path '/parser/model'. We expect that these values are
independent of the attack itself, because in every system environment and for
every attack execution in real-world scenarios the IP address of the attacker
host and time of execution can be different. Consequently, in the meta-alert
these values are either represented as a list of possible options, or wildcards.

We do not show the remaining alerts of the groups, since they are interpreted
similarly. For completeness, we only state their types and important properties:
Two of the alerts are almost identical, because the anomalous value occurs in two
identical events. The third alert affects the following event that occurs during normal operation: Feb 29 06:40:49 mail-2 dovecot: imap-login: Disconnected
(auth failed, 2 attempts in 12 secs): user=<violet>, method=PLAIN, rip
=127.0.0.1, lip=127.0.0.1, secured, session=<3XdWO7GfOoN/AAAB>. However, during the attack execution the event appears as follows: Mar 4 13:51:
48 mail dovecot: imap-login: Disconnected   (disconnected before auth

was ready, waited 0 secs):   user=<>, rip=192.168.10.18, lip=192.168.
10.21, session=<+KO9uAeg4sPAqAoS>. Note that in this case, the message in
brackets states 'disconnected before auth was ready' instead of 'auth failed', which
never occurred before and is thus detected as a new path by the NewMatchPathDe-
tector. The same event also triggers the final alert in the alert group, which is raised
by the NewMatchPathValueComboDetector that monitors combinatinos of values. In particular, this detector monitors the user name as well as the 'secured'
and 'method' parameter in the event, which are all missing in the anomalous event.
Since this combination of missing values did not occur in the training phase, the
event is raised as an anomaly. We did not pick these alerts as examples, because
they are less expressive - the only difference is the timestamp and there is no IP
address that is different across the different attack executions. Other than that,
they are treated and interpreted in the same way.

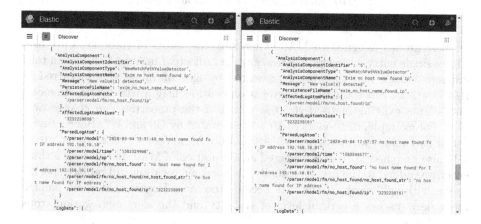

Fig. 9. Alerts of two similar alert groups

Figure 10 shows the meta-information of the alert group. In particular, it
shows the attribute alert_count, which states that four alerts occur in each of
the two groups. Moreover, the IDs of the alerts are explicitly mentioned. For the
first group, these IDs are 0, 1, 2, 3 corresponding to alerts A0, A1, A2, A3. In
the second group, the IDs correspond to A462, A463, A464, A465.

Meta-alerts. The following section describes how the 'Discovery dashboard'
depicts meta-alerts, using meta-alert 0 as example. Figure 11 shows a part of the
JSON that describes MA0, specifically the section that describes the second alert
of the attack pattern defined by meta-alert MA0. The second alert of MA0 relates
to the alerts A1 and A463, the second alerts of groups G0 and G7 visible in Fig. 9.
Figure 11 shows that some properties of the meta-alert have the same values in
all groups that are related to MA0. For example, the 'AnalysisComponentName',
the 'AnalysisComponentName', and the 'AffectedLogAtomPaths' are equal for

Fig. 10. Alert identifiers stated in alert groups.

all alert groups assigned to MA0. Therefore, the values of these keys are lists with a single entry. Other properties, such as 'AffectedLogAtomValues' can take different values, and thus are represented by lists of values that occurred in this locations. Since the alert aggregation continuously learns new meta-alerts and adapts existing meta-alerts, the values of the properties can change over time. For example, meta-alert MA0 was generated by G0 and G7. Hence, first a list of two values was assigned to 'AffectedLogAtomValues'. Afterwards, group G15 also matched MA0 and triggered an adaptation of MA0. In this case a third entry was added to the list. Eventually, the alert aggregation will replace specific values with wild cards, if the lists become too long. However, at some point a meta-alert reaches a certain level of stability and the alert aggregation stops modifying it.

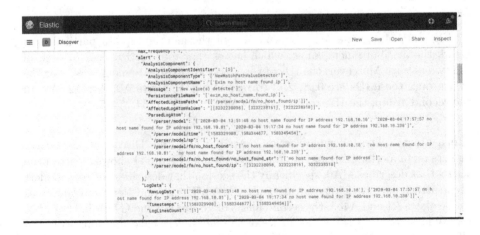

Fig. 11. Meta-alert example.

Figure 12 shows that each meta-alert also stores the relations between alert groups and alerts that are assigned to the meta-alert. This information is used to generate the visualization shown in Fig. 7.

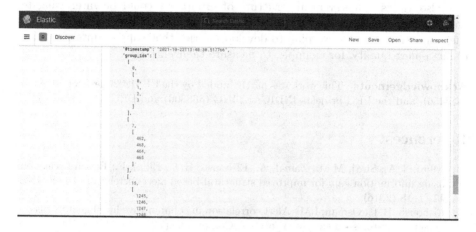

Fig. 12. Meta-alert structure.

4   Conclusion

In this chapter we introduced a novel approach for meta-alert generation based on automatic alert aggregation. Our method is designed for arbitrary formatted alerts and does not require manually crafted attack scenarios. This enables to process alerts from anomaly-based and host-based IDSs that involve heterogeneous alert formats and lack IP information, which is hardly possible using state-of-the-art methods. We presented a similarity metric for semi-structured alerts and three different strategies for similarity computation of alert groups: exact matching, bag-of-alerts matching, and alignment-based matching. Moreover, we proposed techniques for merging multiple alerts into a single representative alert and multiple alert groups into a meta-alert. We outlined an incremental procedure for continuous generation of meta-alerts using aforementioned metrics and techniques that also enables the classification of incoming alerts in online settings.

We presented an application example that demonstrates the alert aggregation approach. Additionally, we introduced a CTI dashboard that enables visualization of alert aggregation results, including alerts, alert groups, and meta-alerts. Finally, the dashboard allows to filter different entities and visualize their interdependencies.

We foresee a number of extensions for future work. We plan to develop a metric that measures how well a group is represented by a meta-alert could reduce the problem of noise alerts within groups and could even be used to separate alerts of overlapping attack executions into distinct groups. On the other hand, determining how well meta-alerts are represented by groups could allow to automatically recognize and improve incorrectly formed meta-alerts. Furthermore, we explained that group formation with different δ values enables generation of diverse meta-alerts. However, we do not make use of the fact that this also yields a hierarchical structure of groups. It could be interesting to transfer these relationships between groups to meta-alerts in order to improve their precision. Finally, we plan to develop metrics that support interpretation of meta-alert quality, for example, to measure their entropy.

Acknowledgements. This work was partly funded by the EU H2020 project GUARD (833456), and the FFG projects INDICAETING (868306) and DECEPT (873980).

References

1. Alhaj, T.A., Siraj, M.M., Zainal, A., Elshoush, H.T., Elhaj, F.: Feature selection using information gain for improved structural-based alert correlation. PLoS ONE **11**, 1–18 (2016)
2. Elshoush, H.T., Osman, I.M.: Alert correlation in collaborative intelligent intrusion detection systems - a survey. Appl. Soft Comput. **11**(7), 4349–4365 (2011)
3. Everitt, B.S., Landau, S., Leese, M., Stahl, D.: Cluster Analysis, 5th edn (2011)
4. Haas, S., Wilkens, F., Fischer, M.: Efficient attack correlation and identification of attack scenarios based on network-motifs. In: Proceedings of the 38th International Performance Computing and Communications Conference, pp. 1–11. IEEE (2019)
5. Julisch, K.: Clustering intrusion detection alarms to support root cause analysis. ACM Trans. Inf. Syst. Secur. **6**(4), 443–471 (2003)
6. Landauer, M., Skopik, F., Wurzenberger, M., Hotwagner, W., Rauber, A.: A framework for cyber threat intelligence extraction from raw log data. In: Proceedings of the International Conference on Big Data, pp. 3200–3209. IEEE (2019)
7. Landauer, M., Skopik, F., Wurzenberger, M., Hotwagner, W., Rauber, A.: Have it your way: generating customized log datasets with a model-driven simulation testbed. IEEE Trans. Reliab. **70**(1), 402–415 (2020)
8. Landauer, M., Skopik, F., Wurzenberger, M., Rauber, A.: Dealing with security alert flooding: using machine learning for domain-independent alert aggregation. ACM Trans. Priv. Secur. (2022, forthcoming). https://doi.org/10.1145/3510581. https://dx.doi.org/10.1145/3510581
9. Manning, C., Schütze, H., Raghavan, P.: Introduction to Information Retrieval. Cambridge University Press, Cambridge (2008)
10. Navarro, G.: A guided tour to approximate string matching. ACM Comput. Surv. **33**(1), 31–88 (2001)
11. Navarro, J., Deruyver, A., Parrend, P.: A systematic survey on multi-step attack detection. Comput. Secur. **76**, 214–249 (2018)
12. Ren, H., Stakhanova, N., Ghorbani, A.A.: An online adaptive approach to alert correlation. In: Kreibich, C., Jahnke, M. (eds.) DIMVA 2010. LNCS, vol. 6201, pp. 153–172. Springer, Heidelberg (2010). https://doi.org/10.1007/978-3-642-14215-4_9
13. Salah, S., Maciá-Fernández, G., Díaz-Verdejo, J.: A model-based survey of alert correlation techniques. Comput. Netw. **57**(5), 1289–1317 (2013)
14. Skopik, F., Wurzenberger, M., Landauer, M.: Smart log data analytics: techniques for advanced security analysis (2021)

15. Wurzenberger, M., Skopik, F., Landauer, M., Greitbauer, P., Fiedler, R., Kastner, W.: Incremental clustering for semi-supervised anomaly detection applied on log data. In: Proceedings of the 12th International Conference on Availability, Reliability and Security, pp. 1–6 (2017)
16. Wurzenberger, M., Skopik, F., Settanni, G., Fiedler, R.: AECID: a self-learning anomaly detection approach based on light-weight log parser models. In: ICISSP, pp. 386–397 (2018)

Blockchain-Based Task and Information Management in Computational Cloud Systems

Andrzej Wilczyński[1][(✉)] and Joanna Kołodziej[1,2]

[1] Department of Computer Science, Cracow University of Technology,
Warszawska 24, 31-155 Cracow, Poland
{andrzej.wilczynski,joanna.kolodziej}@pk.edu.pl
[2] Naukowa i Akademicka Sieć Komputerowa - Państwowy Instytut Badawczy
(NASK-PIB), ul. Kolska 12, 01-045 Warszawa, Poland
joanna.kolodziej@nask.pl

Abstract. Blockchain can be successfully utilised in diverse areas, including the financial sector and the Information and Communication Technology environments, such as computational clouds (CC). While cloud computing optimises the use of resources, it does not (yet) provide an effective solution for the secure hosting scheduling and execution of large computing and data applications and prevention of external attacks.

This chapter briefly reviews the recent blockchain-inspired task scheduling and information processing methods in computational clouds. We pay special attention to security, intrusion detection, and unauthorised manipulation of tasks and information in such systems. As an example, we present the implementation of a new blockchain-based scheduler in the computational cloud. We defined a new Proof of Schedule consensus algorithm, which works with the Stackelberg game, regulates checking and adding new blocks to the blockchain, and determines how to validate schedules stored in transactions. The proposed model assumes competition between different schedule providers. The winner of such a competition takes account of the client's requirements faster and prepares an optimal schedule to meet them. The presented scheduler extends the possibilities of using different scheduling modules by the end-users. By delegating the preparation of the schedules, providers can get benefits only for that, without executing customer tasks.

Keywords: Blockchain · Cloud computing · Security · Scheduling

1 Introduction

The recent digital revolution has contributed to increasing the volume, velocity and variety of data available on the Internet. In the era of Information and Communication Technology (ICT), one struggles with such problems as collecting and optimally managing such large amounts of data. The most important

J. Kołodziej et al. (Eds.): Cybersecurity of Digital Service Chains, LNCS 13300, pp. 162–201, 2022.
https://doi.org/10.1007/978-3-031-04036-8_8

research and challenging engineering tasks related to the ICT systems include ensuring secure network communication of users, data processing and data storage without the nefarious involvement of third parties. The financial aspects are also crucial. One of the possible solutions to such problems may be the application of the Blockchain (BC) technology and networks for the development of the new models of the networks and ICT systems, especially in the cases where security aspects are essential [29].

A rapid progress in developing the new distributed cyber-physical infrastructures of various scales leads to increased demand for computational resources such as computational and data servers, warehouses, databases, networks or services dedicated to data analysis and exploration. The Cloud Computing paradigm has been addressed as a methodology, computing services and architecture to manage these challenges. CC has been defined by Buyya et al. [10] as a simple extension of the grid infrastructure consisting of data centres, where the capabilities of business applications are provided as services that are available in the network. Cloud service providers receive profits for enabling their customers to access such services. On the other hand, consumers are motivated by reducing the related costs. Cloud Computing is not an entirely new model or paradigm but rather an evolution of the following models and technologies:

- **Computational Grid** [19] – a system composed of many connected computers in the distributed clusters [10] that cooperate in a large-scale network.
- **Virtualization of the available resources** – an architectural model, in which many virtual computing devices are visible as one large computing unit. There is no need in the Grid to overhaul the hardware infrastructure to obtain more computing power, and both the infrastructure and computing power are optimally used. Many software tools allow virtualizing machines, for instance: VMware, KVM, Xen [16], or OpenStack Platform [18] which is a more recent and innovative solution. Computational Grid may refer to the hardware resources and the data layer that provides a simpler interface and methods for accessing data. There can be many sources of data, but the user who relies on this data will see one abstract layer [48].
- **Utility Computing Networks** [11] - a model for providing specific resources on-demand and estimating fees based on their consumption;
- **Service-Oriented Architecture** (SOA) [37] - network architectural model focused on the defined services that meet the end users' requirements.

The most popular model of the cloud environment defines Cloud Computing as a multilayer system [39], where the following layer-stack can be specified:

- Infrastructure as a Service (IaaS) - the bottom layer of the system, it provides the client with IT infrastructure such as software, hardware or servicing,
- Platform as a Service (PaaS) - the middle layer, it provides ready-to-use and customized applications without the need to purchase hardware or software licenses,
- Software as a Service (SaaS) - the upper layer, it provides users with specific software features, such as e-mail access or calendar.

The world-leading cloud providers such as Google, Microsoft and Amazon initially used clouds in running their internal business operations. However, after the building of large data centres and data servers farms in many countries [7,8], they noticed a broader potential of the solution. They started offering the external enterprises the previously unused resources or services such as data storage or data processing. There are various methods of classification of cloud environments.

While designing and offering their products to customers, service providers have to take into account the end-to-end personalization of these services and their potential impact on end users' activities, including their business decisions. This is why it is essential to ensure the appropriate service level, which is usually done by concluding a specific contract between providers and consumers, i.e. Service Level Agreement (SLA). As many clients may want to use the same services at the same time, the providers must schedule tasks to achieve the desired quality and pace of service, under the provisions of the SLA. On the other hand, from the providers' perspective, it is essential to minimize the maintenance costs by shutting down resources where unused services are running. To do it quickly, proper scheduling of tasks is necessary.

In practice, the wide-area cloud infrastructure is usually defined as a collection of many cloud clusters working under the same or various cloud standards and administrators. Such distributed cloud clusters are connected by using the standard peer-to-peer (P2P) network. similar model works for the blockchain network, which was the first reason for trying to integrate both environments in order to improve the security policies in global clouds. There are two main methods of integration of the cloud with blockchain platforms:

- Using the cloud for the development of blockchain applications and supporting the integration with enterprise networks (private clouds) to facilitate storage, replication and access to transactional data;
- Using blockchain methods to improve the security of task, user and data management in the clouds.[1]

This chapter briefly reviews the recent blockchain–inspired task scheduling and information processing methods in computational clouds, which are mainly based on the second above mentioned integration method. We pay special attention to security, intrusion detection, and unauthorised manipulation of tasks and information in such systems. As an example, we present the implementation of a novel blockchain–based scheduler in the computational cloud. We defined a new Proof of Schedule consensus algorithm, which works with the Stackelberg game, regulates checking and adding new blocks to the blockchain, and determines how to validate schedules stored in transactions. Such an approach must result in competition between different schedule providers, won by the one who takes account of the client's requirements faster and prepares an optimal schedule to meet them. The presented scheduler extends the possibilities of using

---

[1] The model of the developed blockchain–based scheduler along with the comprehensive experimental analysis were published in A. Wilczyński's PhD dissertation [49] available at https://doktoraty.iet.agh.edu.pl/_media/2020:awilcz:phd_thesis_aw.pdf.

different scheduling modules by the end-users. By delegating the preparation of the schedules, providers can get benefits only for that, without having to execute customer tasks

The rest of the chapter is organized as follows. In Sect. 2 we present the basic definitions and the concept of the blockchain network. Section 3 presents the recent developments in security-aware scheduling in cloud computing. The new blockchain–based secure cloud scheduler is defined in Sect. 4 along with the examples of the a simple experimental evaluation (see Sect. 4.8). The chapter ends with the conclusions in Sect. 5.

2 Blockchain Backgrounds

There are many definitions of blockchain. Most of them refer to the origins of the blockchain technology that evolved from Bitcoin [36]. Blockchain is usually considered a distributed ledger of records containing cryptographically signed transactions grouped into blocks. The main properties of blockchain technology can be defined as follows [44, 55]:

- **decentralization** – in all standard transaction systems, there is typically a central unit called the supervisor, confirming the compliance of the transaction and recording it in the system. Since such a core unit must handle all the requests and approve them, it is often a bottleneck that determines the entire system's efficiency. BC lacks that problematic central supervisor because the decentralized nature of the BC system based on consensus algorithm jointly confirms each transaction, maintaining data consistency,
- **persistence** – since the transactions are validated, any attempt to approve transactions being incompatible with the established policies are immediately detected by confirming/mining nodes; blocks containing incorrect data are immediately detected, too,
- **anonymity** – each user in the network is assigned a generated address (hash) utilizing which they can perform operations. This address does not allow unambiguous identification of a real user,
- **auditability** – each transaction must refer to some previous transactions; hence there is a possibility to trace and verify what has happened with the processed data. For instance, in the bitcoin network, one can check how the balance of a given user has changed since the beginning of its existence in the system,
- **transparency** – transactions of any public address are available for inspection by every user having access to BC; each user of the public network has the same rights,
- **security** – chain of blocks are shared, tamper-proof, and cannot be spoofed due to one-way cryptographic hash functions. The use of cryptographic methods ensures the security of transactions. Roughly speaking, users can send data only if they have a private key. The private key is applied to generate a signature, which in, turn, serves to confirm that transaction was requested by a specific user and to prevent it from being changed,

- **immutability** – data stored in BC are immutable; each entry in the ledger must be confirmed by the network, so it cannot be a secret operation. Each block contains the previous block's hash, which is generated based on the data in the block. Therefore, even a minor change in the data results in the change of the hash and consequent interception and rejection of the modification by the other nodes.

2.1 Blockchain Network

Blockchain architectural model is defined as the distributed network composed of the nodes and users in the following way:

- nodes - individual systems that store the blockchain and ensure transactions are valid;
- users - persons or entities that can read the ledger;
- Peer–to–peer (P2P) – generic architectural model [13], in which each node can communicate with each other without the need of using a central information exchange point.

The abstract model of the BC network is presented in Fig. 1.

There is no general standard in creating a blockchain network that would allow communication between all blockchain networks. For now, each blockchain is made separately, and communications between different blockchain networks require special workarounds. Each BC network works on predefined rules that all nodes in the network agree on. These rules include conditions for adding and validating transactions and the mechanism of interaction between participating nodes. All standard communication rules used by the BC network are called the blockchain protocol.

2.2 Blockchain Components, Protocols and Algorithms

The ledger in the blockchain network is defined as a chain of blocks. Each block contains a hash digest of the previous block. A simple model of the block is presented by Yaga et al. in [54], and it consists of the following components:

1. Block Header:
   - block number;
   - hash of a current block – hash generated from the data contained in the block and previous blocks, usually determined using the Merkle tree (see Fig. 2), any modification of the data in the block will change the hash;
   - hash of a previous block;
   - timestamp;
   - nonce value – the value generated based on *Proof of Work* through solving the hash function, which allows adding the block to the chain.

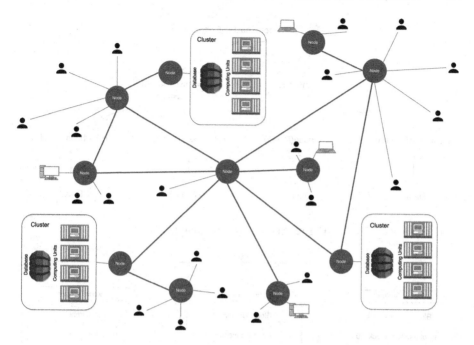

Fig. 1. Decentralized blockchain network Source: [49]

2. Block Data:
   (a) a list of transactions - a single transaction usually consists of:
       – inputs - the input data are usually digital assets to be sent; the source of the asset (its origin) is located here,
       – outputs - in the outputs usually the recipient of digital assets is defined, along with how many digital assets are receiving and conditions that must be met to spend this value,
   (b) other data.

Each ledger starts with a Genesis Block and each following block must be added to the chain after it. The Genesis block defines the initial state of the system. An example of chain of blocks is shown in Fig. 3.

The blockchain operation comprises a few simple steps:

1. The sending node prepares new data as a transaction and broadcasts it over the network.
2. The receiving node verifies the transaction and the data included in it. Each transaction must be signed and authorized using asymmetric cryptography [38]. The private key is used to sign transactions, while the public key is used to identify the user (user address) and verify the signature generated with the private key. This mechanism makes it possible to check whether the user who sent the message is its author. The procedure of signing and verification of the signature is shown in Fig. 4. Whenever the transaction and data pass

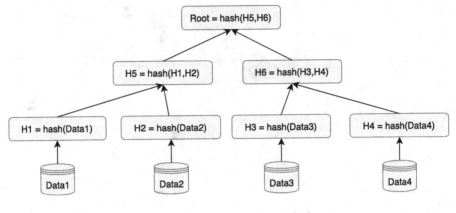

Fig. 2. Merkle tree Source: [49]

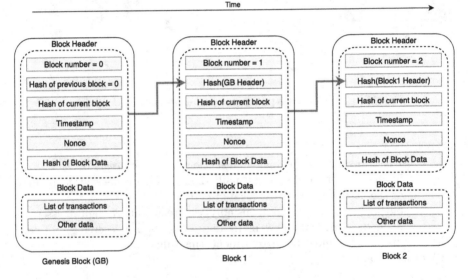

Fig. 3. Generic chain of blocks Source: [49]

the validation process, the node responds to the sending node and saves the transaction in the block.

3. After saving the appropriate number of validated transactions in a local block, nodes start the block confirmation procedure by the consensus adopted in the network.

4. The block is saved in the chain after the execution of the consensus algorithm (block confirmation by the appropriate number of nodes).

5. Every node in the BC network must locally save the approved block and include it in its chain.

It can be noted that many blocks may be published at the same time. Consequently, the existence of different versions of the blockchain in various places

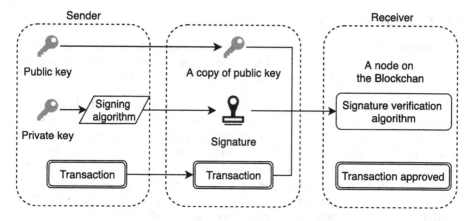

Fig. 4. The procedure of signing and verification of the signature Source: [49]

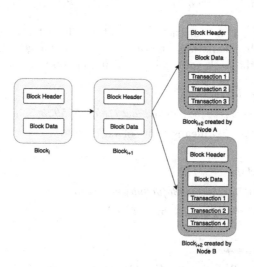

Fig. 5. Blockchain in conflict Source: [49]

is possible. It may happen for various reasons, such as network latency between nodes. This type of problem is shown in Fig. 5. As shown in the figure, a conflict occurs after adding the block $i + 2$. The block added by node A contains transactions 1, 2 and 3 while the block added by node B contains transaction 1, 2 and 4. Therefore, it is not the same block. Such differences do not result from the poor completion of the blocks. They arise from the almost simultaneous confirmation of different transactions by the nodes. Most BC networks deal with this problem while waiting for the addition of the next block by one of the nodes. It is assumed that the 'longer blockchain' wins. In other words, the winner is the node that is quicker to add the next block after the block, including the above conflict.

2.3 Consensus Models

A key aspect of blockchain technology is determining which node can publish the next block. It requires the implementation of a consensus model. The main techniques for obtaining consensus in blockchain networks include:

- Proof of Work (PoW) - this model is the most popular method of obtaining a consensus inBC network. The node can add a block after solving a computationally intensive puzzle or cryptographic function, which can only be done by brute force [9]. In PoW, the probability of mining a new block by a node depends on the ratio of its computing power intended to solve the puzzle to the total computing power of all miners connected to the network. An example of a puzzle is presented below. The node using the hash function SHA-256 [40] must find a hash value meeting the following criteria:

SHA256("schedule" + "nonce") = hash value starting with "09"

The nonce value is a numeric value that is added to the string *'schedule'*. After each hash calculation, the nonce value is changed. This operation is repeated until the hash value has the string beginning with "09".

SHA256("schedule" + "113") =
f8ac5c8094a5ebe334ebe4ba1cde6e29acc718743575933
d6c622406177a6aa4 - means "not solved"

SHA256("schedule" + "114") =
a8007fd4ef5eded7a095d958b3af9e89b48b1bc3a313555
d140f8aa400eb7a6a - means "not solved"

SHA256(schedule + "115") =
09ce2827da9ebc62bc2491ce96bdf366044247f17860826
2154d6eefb8f40721 - means "solved"

The above puzzle is not complex, but its complexity increases with each addition of a subsequent character to string 09. This model is adopted in such networks where suspicion prevails over the trust. Although it works well, its obvious disadvantage is consuming substantial energy to solve the puzzles. This type of consensus has been used in such networks as Bitcoin or Litecoin (cryptocurrencies).
- Proof of Stake (PoS) - this model combines generating blocks with the possession of a certain amount of digital assets in BC. The selection of a node to perform a function of a validator checking if the next block can be added to the chain is based on the number of assets it includes: the more assets a

node has, the more likely it is to be selected. Therefore, the strategy assumes that nodes with more assets can provide more reliable information than those with fewer assets. Usually, tokens are used to determine the number of assets. Assuming that a node in the network has a maximum of 100 tokens and the node has 20 tokens, it has a 20% chance to become a validator and mine a block. Such an approach may lead to a problem related to the monopolisation of the network, where the node with large assets accumulates the assets faster than others. Therefore, in some solutions, limitations associated with adding blocks are applied. After mining the block, the node must wait before confirming the next one. Other solutions introduce limitations of the lifetime of tokens: they are only valid for a specified time. Unlike PoW, PoS does not need to consume much energy to solve puzzles and work more economically. However, nodes have to merge into groups to choose a validator, which causes centralisation. This approach is used, for instance, in Decred [17] or Peercoin [14]. The algorithm proposed by Wilczyński et al. in [49] called *Proof of Schedule* is derived from this consensus model.

- Proof of Authority - in this model, nodes are not asked to solve puzzles or mathematical problems. Instead, the network includes hard-configured units called *'authorities'*, which are authorised to add new blocks and secure the blockchain network. This strategy tends to work well in private or consortium blockchains. Authorities receive a set of private keys with special permissions in the network. The networks based on proof of authority may have some issues concerning the distribution of mining load between signers and the control of the frequency of mining.

2.4 Blockchain Taxonomies

Although blockchain is a relatively new technology, few different blockchain taxonomies are defined in the literature. Lin and Liao [32] divided blockchain technologies into three types, depending on the character of data availability:

- public blockchain - everyone has access to the transaction and can participate in the process of obtaining a consensus; the examples of such a network are bitcoin or Ethereum [46], see Fig. 6,
- private blockchain - not every node can participate in the blockchain network and read the ledger; instead, access is limited and strict access rights management is implemented. A private BC is shown in Fig. 7,
- consortium blockchain - some pre-selected nodes have direct access to BC, and only the nodes from the consortium are allowed to add data; the data to be viewed can be open or private. A consortium BC is shown in Fig. 8.

Another taxonomy is defined for the blockchain network. Cohn et al. in [35] defined the following two classes according to the authorization criterion:

- permissioned blockchains - proprietary networks used by specific persons or entities, for instance, a group of cooperating banks that process financial transactions,

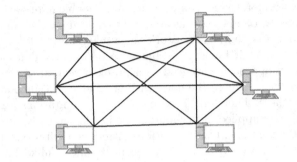

Fig. 6. Public blockchain Source: [49]

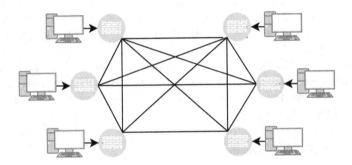

Fig. 7. Private blockchain Source: [49]

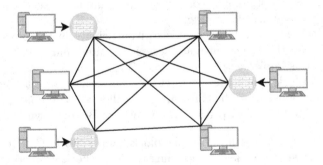

Fig. 8. Consortium blockchain Source: [49]

- permissionless blockchains - open networks to which anyone can access and use data located there.

Considering basic functionality and smart contracts [47] as the main classification criteria, Hileman and Rauches [21] considered two types of blockchain networks:

- stateless blockchain - *'transaction-optimes'*, networks limited to the functionality of the chain in terms of the computational complexity that they can perform (e.g. bitcoin),
- stateful blockchain - *'logic-optimised'*, networks that have expandable functionality in terms of expressing computation (e.g. dApps in ethereum [5]).

Blockchain technology is beneficial, and the particular type of blockchain network should be chosen depending on the service offered, and the market needs.

2.5 Security in BC Networks

Security in BC networks is provided through advanced cryptographic techniques, various methods for determining consensus and, above all, the core aspect of this technology, i.e. immutability of data. Joshi et al. in [24] defined the following important security principles in the blockchain network:

- defence in penetration - the use of multiple layers of security is more effective than the application of a single layer,
- minimum privilege - access to data should be limited to the lowest possible level,
- manage vulnerabilities - security vulnerabilities ought to be constantly checked and corrected,
- manage risks - the risk should be regularly assessed and managed at an environmental level,
- manage patches - faulty system components should be corrected, tested and developed as patches for the successive versions of the application.

Asymmetric-key cryptography is used in blockchain for the authorization of processed transactions. The private key is used here to sign transactions, the public key to identify addresses assigned to the user, and to verify the signatures generated using private keys. Due to asymmetric cryptography, it is possible to determine whether a user who gives a message to another user has a private key with which he has been signed and thus whether he has the right to send it. The transaction is signed with a private key, then together with the signature and public key is forwarded to the recipient. A node in the network based on this information using the verification algorithm can authorize the received transaction.

In practice, consensus models are responsible for providing the appropriate level of BC network safety. For example, in PoW to make the network fake, the node would have to possess at least 51% of the computing resources of the entire network to be able to falsify the information contained in the blocks, which is hardly possible in practice [52].

2.6   Blockchain Usecases

Blockchain technologies have found their way into many practical projects. Some of the most notable projects include:

- **Guardian**[2] – this project defines a token for a new global emergency response network that provides a framework for distributed emergency response systems, especially in locations far from wireless network transmitters and in hard-to-reach areas were calling for help using an emergency number (e.g. 112 or 911) is virtually impossible.
- **Blockchain Charity Foundation**[3] – it is a non-profit foundation whose mission is to create a decentralized network of charitable foundation centres, promote sustainable development, and ensure that they are as widely accessible as possible to those most in need.
- **Power Ledger**[4] - a system that allows customers to choose a source of electricity, enabling electricity trading with their neighbours and ensuring a fair return on investment, where energy is stable and affordable for everyone.
- **EthicHub**[5] - a system whose aim is to make available to all clients also individual investors the same access to traditional financial services by democratizing finances and making available investment opportunities around the world.
- **Grassroots Economics & Bancor**[6] – the decentralized blockchain-based community currencies in Kenya, aimed to combat poverty by encouraging local and regional trade.
- **VeChain**[7] – decentralized platform in which companies can quickly establish contacts and make transactions without intermediation.

The above examples show that the use of this technology ensures high security and quick execution of transactions and enables solving problems that have not been solved in any other way.

3   Security Criterion in Scheduling and Resource Allocation Problems in Computational Clouds

Task scheduling aims to build a schedule that determines when to execute each task and which resources should be selected to do it. For instance, tasks must be scheduled when there is a need to perform several calculations provided by the users and deliver the results within a specific time. To ensure a guaranteed Quality of Service (QoS) [27] to the clients, it is necessary to make as efficient

---

[2] https://guardtoken.net.

[3] https://www.binance.charity/.

[4] https://www.powerledger.io.

[5] www.ethichub.com.

[6] www.businesswire.com/news/home/20180621005727/en/Bancor-Launch-Blockchain-Based-Community-Currencies-Kenya.

[7] www.investinblockchain.com.

mapping of tasks to the given resources as possible; otherwise, the clients will not pay for them. Therefore, task scheduling is considered one of the burning issues to tackle in cloud computing systems.

A generic task scheduling model is shown in Fig. 9. In the figure, clients directing requests to the cloud can be seen. The cloud broker (task scheduler) collects the requests, responsible for decomposing requests for smaller tasks and running them to virtual machines. After the tasks are executed, the results are returned to the broker, passing them to the cloud client.

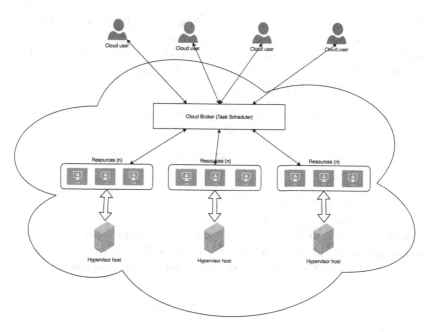

Fig. 9. Basic task scheduling process in cloud computing Source: [34]

Task scheduling in computational clouds can be considered, in fact, as a set of problems. Specification of the problem instances may be formulated based on various cloud scheduling attributes, namely:

- the environment (static or dynamic),
- cloud architecture (centralized, decentralized or hierarchical),
- task processing policy (immediate or batch),
- tasks' interrelations (independency or dependency).

Karatza et al. [20] defined the following instances of the cloud scheduling problems:

- bag-of-tasks scheduling - jobs consisting of independent tasks that can be processed in parallel,

- gang scheduling - jobs consisting of tasks that often communicate with one another, which can be processed in parallel,
- Directed Acyclic Graph (DAG) scheduling [45] - jobs consisting of tasks with a significant order of execution (workflow); tasks can be planned on different system nodes,
- real-time scheduling - composed of jobs in which the deadlines for executing tasks are defined,
- fault-tolerant scheduling - jobs in which there is a high probability of software failures that may prevent the execution of the schedule.

Most of the problem instances defined above are multi-objective global optimization problems. Such objectives, defined as the optimization criteria, are usually minimized to execute the generated schedules faster and cheaper for the clients or to do the individual tasks at a predetermined time. The most popular optimization criteria are the following:

1. Makespan – the time of finishing the last task from the batch; the smaller the makespan is, the faster the tasks are completed:

$$makespan = max\{ET_i, ET_{i+1}, ..., ET_n\} \qquad (1)$$

   where
   ET_i the ending time of the task i
   n number of tasks in the batch

2. Flowtime - the sum of the ending times of all tasks from the batch; this metric describes the response time to the client for the submitted task, and its minimization means a reduction in the average response time of the entire schedule:

$$flowtime = \sum_{i=1}^{n} ET_i \qquad (2)$$

   where
   ET_i the ending time of the task i
   n number of tasks in the batch

3. Economic cost - the total sum the client has to pay to the provider for the resource utilization

$$Economic\ Cost = \sum_{i=1}^{m} (C_i * T_i) \qquad (3)$$

   where
   C_i the cost of 1 second of utilization the resource i
   T_i time in which the resource i is utilized
   m number of resources

4. Resource utilization - maximizing the utilization of the resources, this metric is very important for the provider whose profit raises with the reduction of time gaps when the machine is not utilized:

$$Resource\ Utilization = \frac{\sum_{i=1}^{m} TR_i}{makespan * m} \tag{4}$$

where
TR_i the time of completion of all the tasks by the resource i
m number of resources

5. Deadline constraint - defines the time limit within which the task or batch must be executed.

More cloud scheduling criteria, such as tardiness, waiting time, turnaround time, fairness, throughput, priority constraint, dependency constraint, budget constraints, are defined in [25].

3.1 Security-Aware Cloud Schedulers – A Short Survey of Recent Schedulers

While the maximization of the resource utilization and profits of the resource owners are the key objectives of cloud scheduling, they may conflict with cloud users' security requirements and system reliability. Network security threats cause a significant hurdle to ineffective job and service outsourcing in the cloud. The cloud cluster or the cloud resource may not be accessible to the scheduler when infected with intrusions or malicious attacks. In such cases, the failures of the cloud resources and services during the tasks' executions can be observed.

The security-related scheduling criteria cannot be defined as the optimization ones. They are usually connected with monitoring all cloud users' system performance, decision strategies (including end-users), secure data, and information storage and processing.

In this section, we briefly survey the most influential models of secure cloud schedulers and demonstrate the usefulness of the blockchain methods.

In the first analyzed model, Kołodziej and Xhafa [30] proposed a scheduling model simultaneously allowing aggregation of task abortion and ensuring security requirements, which are the criteria for the cumulative objective function along with makespan and flowtime. They defined a meta-broker as being responsible for checking the security conditions and availability of resources. The level of security in their approach is determined based on trust level (tl) parameters defined for the resources and security demand (sd) defined for the tasks. These parameters depend mainly on the user's specific requirements, security policy, history of attacks, or the ability to self-defence. They are described in more detail in [28]:

- security demand - related to tasks, specified for each task in the job, refers to data integration, task sensitivity, peer authentication, access control and task execution environment, is defined as a vector:

$$SD = [sd_j, sd_{j+1}, \ldots, sd_n] \tag{5}$$

where
sd_j one of security demand parameters, assumes a value within the range [0,1],
where 0 represents the lowest and 1 the highest security requirements for
execution task j
n number of tasks in the job

- trust level - related to resources, specified for all resources in the system, this
metric determines the level of client trust to the resource manager, refers to
prior task execution success rate, cumulative grid cluster utilization, firewall
capabilities, intrusion detection capabilities, intrusion response capabilities,
is defined as a vector:

$$TL = [tl_i, tl_{i+1}, \ldots, tl_m] \tag{6}$$

where
tl_i one of trust level parameters assumes a value within the range [0,1], where
0 represents the riskiest and 1 fully trusted machine i
m number of resources

Having SD and TL vectors, it is possible to assess whether the condition of
ensuring security is met and, consequently, whether the task can be successfully
executed on a given machine. It means that $sd_j \leq tl_i$ for a given (j, i) task-
machine pair. In the experimental section, the authors compared the results of
scheduling carried out in 2 different modes: a secure mode where all the security conditions and resource uncertainty are verified for the task-machine pairs
and a risky mode where all risky and failing conditions are ignored. The measurement of the makespan showed that, in comparison to the classic approach,
some scheduling algorithms performed better in risky mode when put in Grid
environments having medium or large size. On the other hand, the secure mode
brought the best results in all grid instances. The referred article addresses security issues but its scope is fairly narrow and theoretical. It does not discuss such
issues as checking the inviolability of tasks and results, unauthorized modification or correctness of the prepared schedule.

Another model was developed by Li et al. in [31]. They defined a model
of the security and cost-aware scheduler (SCAS) for different types of tasks in
computational clouds, intended to minimize the total cost of workflow execution while meeting the assumed deadline and risk rate limits. Their approach
was based on the application of Particle Swarm Optimization algorithm (PSO)
to create a workflow schedule with tasks mapped to the resources and to the
type and number of virtual machines that should be used. To protect the tasks
against snooping, alteration and spoofing attacks, the authors used three security services: authentication, integrity, and confidentiality. Each task can require
all three security measures, with the security levels depending on the user's
specification. In the experimental section, four algorithms were tested against
three workflows. Then, the impact of security services and risk coefficient were
examined. The results confirmed the effectiveness and practicality of the used
algorithm.

Jakóbik et al. in [23] present an innovative architectural model based on a multi–agent scheme and security-aware meta scheduler controlled by genetic heuristics. The authors focused on the safety of task scheduling in cloud computing and described its behaviour in the event of a task injection attack. Namely, they considered a situation in which an attacker, logged in as an authorized consumer, tries to send an unauthorized task (see Fig. 10). It triggers a response from the system in the form of an alert sent to the correct place: its verification takes place before task scheduling. In addition, the authors proposed two models supporting users security requirements, a scoring model that allows task scheduling only on virtual machines that have an appropriate level of security and a model that considers the time needed for cryptographic operations associated with each specific task. These models are similar to those described by Kołodziej, and Xhafa [30]. In the experimental part, the influence of non-deterministic time intervals for the scheduling process on the environment performance was examined, and the makespan for different security levels was calculated. The results showed the effectiveness of the proposed models and their increasingly positive impact on the system's safety.

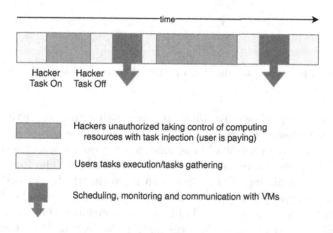

Fig. 10. Task injection attack proposed by Jakóbik Source: [23]

On the other hand, one should mention a relatively recent study by Lokhandwala [33] which is mainly related to the topic of this paper because its author resorted to blockchain technology to solve the problem of task scheduling. In Lokhandwala's approach, a decentralized blockchain network was used to allocate resources more efficiently, resulting in reduced energy consumption and, consequently, costs. A load of data centres stored in blocks is checked using smart contracts [47]. Then, the tasks to be executed are assigned to the data centres with the most negligible load. The algorithm on which the smart contract was based is shown in Fig. 11. In the experimental part, the correctness of the blockchain network was first checked and, subsequently, the model was evaluated. To conduct experiments *Shortest Job First* (SJF) algorithm was applied

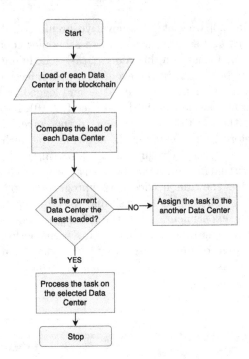

Fig. 11. Smart contract algorithm proposed by Lokhandwala Source: [33]

whose primary purpose was to minimize the waiting time of virtual machine (VM) response. However, the author did not measure the actual impact of the method on the waiting time of VM response, which would require its comparison with one of the classical methods not based on blockchain. The focus was more on testing the functioning of the blockchain network, which included assigning the tasks to the appropriate data centres and the security issues, i.e. blockchain resistance to manipulate the data. Lokhandwala concluded that blockchain was more suitable for data storage than calculating the load of Data Centres. The block mining process turned out to be very energy-consuming due to the chosen consensus algorithm (which probably should have been different for the case).

Hong et al. [22] discussed the problem of communication and task scheduling among users in device-to-device network (D2D) [26] to reduce the average time of task execution effectively. Their idea consisted of the wasted computing power of mobile devices, which are typically in an idle state with nothing but notification listeners and other low energy consumption applications activated. The possibility of using these static resources together with the storage can lead to highly profitable and profitable cooperation in executing tasks in D2D networks. There are, however, some doubts if task scheduling in such systems is fair to everyone. It may look unfair if the users contributing a lot of their computational resources to others receive little being in dire need. Hence, Hong et al. proposed an innovative blockchain-based credit system that can be used for task

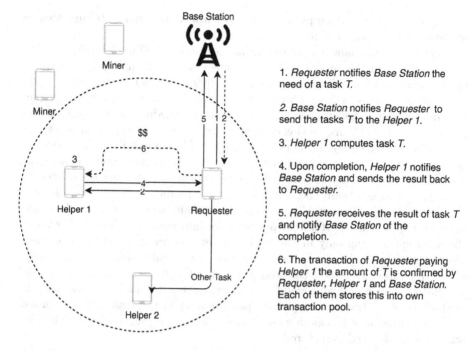

Fig. 12. Task scheduling in D2D network proposed by Hong Source: [22]

scheduling to enforce justice among D2D network users. Their solution consists of cooperative task scheduling to reduce the average task execution time among the users and a blockchain-based credit system to ensure fairness in the network. The system model and the principle of its operation are presented in Fig. 12. The authors checked the impact of various initial credits provided to each user, different maximum waiting times, task sizes, and time elapsed on the performance. According to the results, the proposed model significantly shortens the average task execution time for the requesters in D2D networks.

4   Blockchain-Based Secure Cloud Scheduler

Task scheduling systems available on the market (e.g., Amazon ECS[8]) use many variations of scheduling algorithms (FCFS [53], SJF [12] etc.) that are, nevertheless, not publicly available. Cloud service providers such as Amazon Web Services (AWS)[9], or Azure[10] use their algorithms to prepare schedules. The clients wishing to use their services send the task to them and can only trust that it will be done according to their expectations at the lowest possible cost. The internal

---

[8] https://docs.aws.amazon.com/AmazonECS/latest/developerguide/Welcome.html.
[9] https://aws.amazon.com/.
[10] https://azure.microsoft.com/pl-pl/.

algorithms used by service providers are not always optimal in taking account of the specific customer requirements.

In this section, a new *Secure Blockchain Scheduler* (BS) model defined in [50] was described. In this model, the specific customer needs and security requirements are considered. We implemented the public blockchain to make the model available to every scheduler provider who would like to participate in preparing the schedule. The provider who prepares the schedule meeting the client's requirements faster wins. In this case, the inter-clouds [41] approach is referred to, in which the cooperation between cloud providers is possible whenever they need additional services or computing resources. The defined model is based on a similar idea according to which the providers can use the services offered by other providers to obtain the best schedule. Communication between different cloud providers is determined by a public blockchain, which is decentralized and does not require the use of unique protocols for information exchange. Therefore, the units specializing only in one field and not necessarily providing other services can freely participate in the generation of schedules. The general concept of the developed model is presented in Fig. 13. The main actors in that model are clients (end users) and cloud service providers. Its main elements are the pool of requests, transactions, nodes participating in the transaction approval process and chain of blocks in which transactions with prepared and confirmed schedules are located and stored.

4.1   Clients and Cloud Service Providers

Clients formulate their requirements and direct them to the cloud in our scheduling model. These can be jobs related to running the executable file or executing a source code fragment that solves some mathematical problem. Together with a specification of their needs, they can also provide some specific conditions, for instance:

- executing tasks on a machine with special security parameters (firewall, antivirus, etc.) due to data sensitivity and confidentiality,
- data processing only on servers located in a defined geographical location due to legal reasons,
- quick execution of tasks regardless of costs or the exact opposite.

Cloud service providers collect requests from clients, which are then forwarded to *Task Managers* (TMs). Based on the received data describing the tasks and the specific requirements of the client, TM who knows the available resources/virtual machines (VMs) in his cloud, chooses the ones that will be the most suitable for their execution. The choice is made considering requirements in terms of security, the physical location of machines, the short waiting time for results, or the client's small budget. After that, the task manager performs a description of the selected VMs and tasks to be executed.

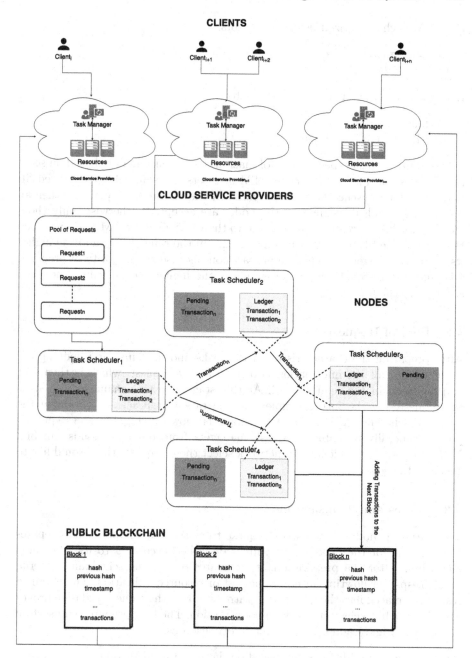

Fig. 13. Secure blockchain scheduler model Source: [49]

Each VM is characterized using two factors:

- computing capacity cc,
- trust level tl (Eq. 6).

Each task is characterized using two factors:

- workload wl,
- security demand sd (Eq. 5).

In addition to the specification of machines and tasks, mainly based on security aspects specified by the client, TM also sets the value of the expected SL parameter for the schedule to be prepared. If the SL value is equal to 0 then all proposed schedules designed by the nodes are accepted; otherwise, only those whose SL value is greater than or equal to the value given by TM are considered as correct. The SL parameter assumes values in the range [0, 3], and the higher its value, the longer the schedule preparation because the majority of prepared schedules are rejected. On the other hand, the higher the SL value, the more secure the schedule is.

4.2   Pool of Requests

After preparing the characteristics of the tasks and machines and defining the expected SL, all the information is defined as the request, which is then sent and collected in the request pool. At this stage, the task manager also signs the request, i.e. the future recipient of the target transaction containing the prepared schedule. A body of such request is shown in Fig. 14. The requested pool is generally available, and task managers from different clouds can bid. Nodes located in the blockchain network select those requests they would like to generate the schedule.

4.3   Nodes and Transactions

The initiating node retrieves the request from the request pool and prepares the schedule for the tasks and machines described according to its scheduling algorithm. After the preparation, it calculates one of the scheduling criteria, i.e. makespan or flowtime or economic cost or resource utilization. The obtained results are placed into the transaction with data from the request and then broadcast over the blockchain network for confirmation. The fully prepared transaction is shown in Fig. 15 and contains such information as:

- id - transaction id generated based on data contained therein,
- sender (PKN) - the public key of the node preparing the transaction,
- recipient (PKTM) - the public key of the task manager creating the request,
- signature (DS) - digital signature made by the node,
- request id - id of the request sent by the task manager,
- information about the prepared schedule:

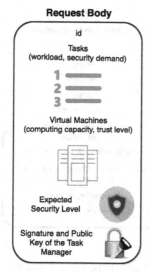

Request Body

Fig. 14. Body of request from the pool of requests Source: [49]

- tasks - id, workload and security demand of the tasks;
- machines - id, computing capacity, trust level and ids of tasks to execute; each machine includes the assigned ids of tasks that should be executed on it;
- scheduling criterion (SC) - makespan, flowtime, economic cost or resource utilization.

In the defined transaction, SC is the factor that determines whether the schedule is optimal. This factor will be replaced by makespan, flowtime, economic cost or resource utilization. In the experimental part, the model will be evaluated for each criterion. After obtaining the appropriate number of transaction confirmations, the node places it in the block. Before adding the transaction to the block, the SL value of the prepared schedule is calculated. If the value of SL is, at least, at the security level specified by TM, the transaction is added to the block. Otherwise, it is omitted because further processing and saving in the chain of blocks would be pointless.

4.4 Chain of Blocks

The block is created and validated after collecting a sufficient number of transactions, and the number of required transaction confirmations is defined as a global parameter for the entire BC network. Each block consists of:

- the block hash value (Bhv) - calculated on the basis of previous block hash value, a timestamp and the Merkle tree root hash value,
- the previous block hash value (PBhv),

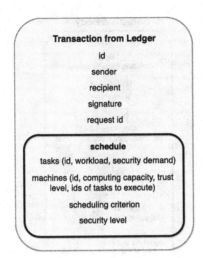

Fig. 15. Body of the transaction Source: [49]

- a timestamp (Tim),
- the Merkle tree root hash value (MTRhv) (see Fig. 2), generated using the SHA-256 hash function [40],
- a list of transactions - transactions with prepared schedules, containing the information presented in the Fig. 15.

Once all the block building requirements are met, it is mined by mining node and distributed across the BC network. During block propagation, some conflicts may occur because several nodes may try to add many blocks simultaneously. As a result, different versions of the chain of blocks may be provided (see Fig. 5). Such situations are resolved by adopting a rule to wait for the next added block and invariably recognize a more extended sequence of blocks as official; in other words, the first node successful in adding the following block prevails. After confirming the chain throughout the BC network and recognizing it as official (a fragment of such a chain is shown in Fig. 16) task managers can load the schedule prepared for them. They obtain it using their public key; each transaction with a prepared schedule is addressed to the TM whose PKTM was given in the pool of requests. Having the schedule, TM can allocate tasks to the resources and monitor them. At this moment, the whole process ends.

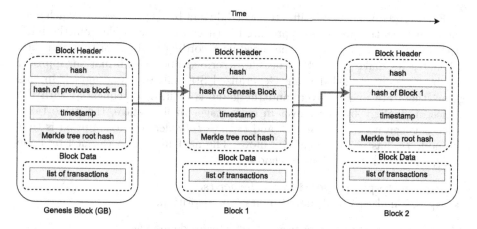

Fig. 16. The first few blocks from the chain of blocks of the model Source: [49]

4.5   Proof of Schedule – Generalized Stackelberg Game

We introduce in our model a new consensus algorithm – *Proof of Schedule* (PoSch) [50], based on the Stackelberg game. Our consensus algorithm is dedicated to regulating schedule checking and adding new blocks to the chain.

Let us denote by i to l the nodes (task schedulers), which participate in the approval of the schedule (transaction). Node ts_i, based on the pool of tasks and their workloads and the collection of virtual machines and their computing capacities, prepares the most optimal schedule according to its algorithm and gives its adopted scheduling criterion; let's assume that in this case, it is makespan. After the preparation, the schedule is placed in the transaction and disseminated across the network. The nodes that receive the transaction for confirmation also prepare the schedule according to their algorithms and calculate its makespan. The following notation will be used to present the described procedure:

- $TS = \{ts_i, ts_{i+1}, \ldots, ts_l\}$ - the set of nodes involved in confirming transaction,
- wl_j - characterization of the task j,
- $wl(schedule)$ - the sum of vector elements $[wl_1, \ldots, wl_n]$, defined for all tasks from schedule,
- ts_i - node initiating the transaction,
- ts_{i+1} - first node confirming the transaction,
- M_{ts_i} - makespan of the schedule determined by node ts_i,
- $M_{ts_{i+1}}$ - makespan of the schedule determined by node ts_{i+1},
- SF_{ts_i} - scheduling factor of the ts_i node, the sum of $wl(schedule)$ for all schedules in the blockchain added by node ts_i,
- $SF_{ts_{i+1}}$ - scheduling factor of the ts_{i+1} node, the sum of wl_{sch} for all schedules in the blockchain added by node ts_{i+1},
- BW_t - the sum of $wl(schedule)$ for all schedules added to the blockchain within a given period of time t.

Each subsequent node verifies the schedule sent by its predecessor, which does not mean that the predecessor prepared it (it can be a schedule from the initiating node). First, it prepares the schedule according to its algorithm and then calculates its makespan. The schedule described above confirmation/approval can be formally modelled using Generalized Stackelberg Game model. In this game, there are many players and the game is defined as sequential with the choice of strategy by one player in each stage. In first stage, the game takes place between nodes $ts_i - leader$ and $ts_{i+1} - follower$; the assumption is that the node ts_i has already made its move. The next move is performed by node ts_{i+1}, which has two options to choose:

- M_{ts_i} - makespan proposed by the *leader* ts_i;
- $M_{ts_{i+1}}$ - makespan calculated by its own algorithm.

The *follower* chooses one of two pure strategies defined as:

- s_1 - choosing makespan M_{ts_i};
- s_2 - choosing makespan $M_{ts_{i+1}}$;

where $s_1, s_2 \in \{0, 1\}$.

To determine the utility function for the follower, the scheduling factors, which are treat as confidence coefficients must be scaled, which is carried out as follows:

$$\overline{SF_{ts_i}} = \begin{cases} 1 & \text{if max } \{SF_{ts_{i+1}}, SF_{ts_i}\} = SF_{ts_i} \\ \frac{SF_{ts_i}}{SF_{ts_{i+1}}} & \text{if max } \{SF_{ts_{i+1}}, SF_{ts_i}\} \neq SF_{ts_i} \end{cases}$$

$$\overline{SF_{ts_{i+1}}} = \begin{cases} 1 & \text{if max } \{SF_{ts_i}, SF_{ts_{i+1}}\} = SF_{ts_{i+1}} \\ \frac{SF_{ts_{i+1}}}{SF_{ts_i}} & \text{if max } \{SF_{ts_i}, SF_{ts_{i+1}}\} \neq SF_{ts_{i+1}} \end{cases}$$

(7)

The utility function for the *follower* depends on both strategies s_1 and s_2 and scaled confidence coefficients of players:

$$u(s_1, s_2, M_{ts_i}, M_{ts_{i+1}}) = M_{ts_i}\overline{SF_{ts_i}}s_1 + M_{ts_{i+1}}\overline{SF_{ts_{i+1}}}s_2 \qquad (8)$$

Looking for a strategy is tantamount to solving the following problem:

$$\begin{cases} \underset{s_1,s_2}{\text{argmax }} u(s_1, s_2, M_{ts_i}, M_{ts_{i+1}}) \\ s_1 + s_2 = 1 \\ s_1, s_2 \in \{0, 1\} \end{cases} \qquad (9)$$

The problem 9 is a maximization problem with constraints, which was solved using the simplex method [42]. Once the solution, i. e. strategies s_1 and s_2, are found, node ts_{i+1} chooses:

- the option M_{ts_i}, if $s_1 = 1$ and $s_2 = 0$,
- the option $M_{ts_{i+1}}$, if $s_2 = 1$ and $s_1 = 0$.

If node ts_{i+1} loses the game (it chose the option M_{ts_i}), it sends transaction from node ts_i to the next node ts_{i+2} and notifies the node ts_i about the correctness of its schedule, so the next stage of the sequential game is taking place, where node ts_i remains the leader and the follower is the next node ts_{i+2}. Otherwise, node ts_{i+1} initiates a new transaction according to its own schedule, becoming a *leader* and sends it for verification to the node ts_{i+2}, which is the first *follower*. The game is carried out until the node receives confirmation from the appropriate number of TS sequence items. The fewer confirmations the system requires, the more transactions it can produce in a given period. On the other hand, the more confirmations, the more secure and reliable the system is in comparison to the other systems [6]. This value should be selected individually, depending on the system implementation. In the proposed approach, the minimum number of transaction confirmations (MTC) is defined as a global parameter during blockchain initialization. SF_{ts_i}, $SF_{ts_{i+1}}$ coefficients must be non-zero, so if nodes participating in the game do not yet have such data, they must be randomly selected. Similarly, the initiating node ts_i, having no predecessor, will choose its time of schedule.

4.6   Blocks Mining

The block can contain many transactions. It is ready to be confirmed if the sum of $wl(schedule)$ for all schedules within all block transactions exceeds the set value:

$$\text{block is ready to mine if} \quad \sum_{i=1}^{p} wl(schedule_i) \geq B_{wl} \tag{10}$$

where

- $wl(schedule)$
- B_{wl} minimum block workload defined as a global parameter set during blockchain initialization
- p number of transactions in the block

When the appropriate B_{wl} indicator is obtained, the mining node can add a block to the blockchain. Each transaction in the block must be validated. Validation is intended to check whether the providers of the transaction inputs have cryptographically signed the transaction. The signature verifies if they have the right to transfer funds for participation in preparing the schedule. Confirmation nodes check the published block, demonstrating that each transaction it contains has been validated, after which the block can be added to the blockchain. The subsequent blocks are added by nodes called *validators*. *Validators* are nodes that have so far participated in the transaction creation process and have also expressed a desire to mine a block. One leader is selected from the pool of validators. The election is based on adding a node's transaction history covering a specified period. The selection criterion is defined as:

$$\begin{cases} L_t = max(TF_{(v_i,t)}, TF_{(v_{i+1},t)}, ..., TF_{(v_{i+n},t)}) \\ TF_{(v_i,t)}, TF_{(v_{i+1},t)}, ..., TF_{(v_{i+n},t)} \leq \frac{1}{2}BW_t \end{cases} \tag{11}$$

where

- L_t - a leader for adding the given block in the given time t
- $TF_{(v_i,t)}$ - trust factor - the sum of all I added to the blockchain by validator v_i during time t
- BW_t - the sum of all I added to the blockchain during time t

The above approach originates from the idea of *Proof of Stake*, namely from its specific case referring to the hybrid of coin ageing systems and delegate systems [54]. A node can become a leader only if its current trust factor does not exceed the value of $\frac{1}{2}BW_t$, which protects BC network against the 51% attack (or majority attack) to which such systems are vulnerable [1].

4.7   Profits for Task Schedulers

Nodes involved in creating or confirming transactions and block mining can be rewarded in various ways. They usually charge a fee for performing specific actions. One of the possibilities is presented below. According to it, nodes (task schedulers) can receive profits for participating in operations on which the functioning of BC network is based. The task scheduler profit for creating or confirming one transaction (schedule) $P(schedule)$ within an entire block can be defined as follows:

$$P(schedule) = \frac{wl(schedule)}{CN * 0.8} \tag{12}$$

where

- $wl(schedule)$
- CN the number of all nodes confirming the schedule (including the creating node)

However, profit for mining the block $P(block)$ can be defined as follows:

$$P(block) = wl(block) * 0.2 \tag{13}$$

where

- $wl(block)$ the sum of $wl(schedule)$ for all transactions in the block

The proposed reward approach mainly depends on whether the blockchain is public or private. In the case of this approach, blockchain is public, but it can be freely changed to private. Therefore, the profits model may also vary depending on the given implementation, improved version of profits model was proposed in [50].

4.8   Evaluation Examples

In this section, we present the exemplary results of a simple experimental study, where 4 different cloud schedulers were implemented along with the blockchain algorithms[11]

We consider the following simple scenario:

1. The task scheduling process is run on 4 different scheduling modules; each module uses one of the RR, FCFS, HSGA or SJF algorithms (detailed description of the algorithms can be found in [29]).
2. BS is launched and 16 nodes are defined in the BC network. Each of them uses one of the four algorithms used by the scheduling modules described in point 1 to prepare the schedule. As a result, BS saves the best schedule selected by the network in the blockchain.
3. Schedules from points 1 and 2 are carried out for different datasets (different number of tasks and different number of virtual machines).
4. Each of the prepared schedules is evaluated according to different metrics. Points 1 and 2 are repeated to evaluate the schedule in terms of the values of makespan, flowtime, economic cost and resource utilization; the security level of the schedule is not taken into consideration (expected SL = 0). The value of each criterion is calculated on the basis of the results of schedule execution using the CloudSim simulator[12].
5. Points 1 and 2 are repeated for different expected SL, taking into account the makespan as a schedule evaluation criterion.

The following test datasets were prepared with the task and virtual machines characteristics (workloads and computing capacities) together with the security demand and trust level parameters. Tasks characteristics ($[wl_1, \ldots, wl_n]$, $[sd_1, \ldots, sd_n]$) and virtual machines characteristics ($[cc_1, \ldots, cc_m]$, $[tl_1, \ldots, tl_m]$) were generated according to the Gaussian distribution:

$$\mathcal{N}(\mu, \sigma^2) \tag{14}$$

where:

− μ mean
− σ^2 variance of random variable

In the literature, there are many cases where test data is generated for several different scenarios (different number of machines and tasks). The number of virtual machines usually ranges between 32 and 256, while the number of tasks from 512 to 4096. Kołodziej [28] provided four different scenarios where different numbers of tasks and machines were defined and data was generated according to the normal distribution for machines $\mathcal{N}(5000, 875)$ and for tasks

---

[11] A comprehensive experimental analysis with a lot of scenarios and full statistical analysis is presented in https://doktoraty.iet.agh.edu.pl/_media/2020:awilcz: phd_thesis_aw.pdf.

[12] http://www.cloudbus.org/cloudsim/.

Table 1. Characteristics of virtual machines

	Dataset 1	Dataset 2
Number of VM	32	128
Distribution of computing capacity (cc) values	$\mathcal{N}(7,4)$	
Measure of cc	MFLOPS	
Minimum value of cc	1	
Maximum value of cc	12	
Distribution of trust level (tl)	$\mathcal{N}(0.5, 0.04)$	
Minimum value of tl	0.2	
Maximum value of tl	1	

Table 2. Characteristics of tasks

	Dataset 1	Dataset 2
Number of tasks	1024	4096
Distribution of workloads (wl) values	$\mathcal{N}(600, 90000)$	
Measure of wl	MFLO	
Minimum value of wl	100	
Maximum value of wl	1000	
Distribution of security demand (sd)	$\mathcal{N}(0.8, 0.0225)$	
Minimum value of sd	0.6	
Maximum value of sd	0.9	

$\mathcal{N}(250000000, 43750000)$, respectively. The real characteristics of the computational units can be found on the webpages [2–4] where different processors are compared. Taking account of the experiments conducted by Kołodziej, it was decided to generate 2 different datasets of characteristics of virtual machines and 2 different datasets of characteristics of tasks, whose key parameters are presented in Tables 1 and 2. Datasets were generated applying the Commons Math library [15] using the *NormalDistribution* class. Due to the fact that 2 datasets of characteristics of tasks and 2 datasets of characteristics of virtual machines were generated, each task scheduling process took place on 4 different datasets:

- 32 VM and 1024 tasks;
- 32 VM and 4096 tasks;
- 128 VM and 1024 tasks;
- 128 VM and 4096 tasks.

The main configuration parameters of the extended CloudSim presented in Tables 3 and 4.

Table 3. BCSchedCloudSim configuration

Number of records in the pool of requests	96
MTC	8
B_{wl}	1000000 MFLO
Time for which TF of validators is determined	30 days
Initial value of SF of each node in the BC network	583329 MFLO
Failure coefficient α (see Eq. 15)	2.5

Table 4. CloudSim configuration

1 data center	
Size of VM image	10000 MB
Memory of VM	4096 MB
Number of CPUs in VM	4

Each schedule execution was repeated 48 times. Then, the obtained results were compared with those returned by BS, where 96 requests with the same data were placed.

Evaluation of the Secure Blockchain Scheduler Based on Makespan [50]

According to the previously presented scenario, an experiment was carried out where makespan was adopted as a criterion for schedule evaluation. Size of the BC network was set to 16 nodes. In this part of experiments, the security level criterion was omitted and will be considered in the next section. The algorithm for calculating the value of makespan was presented in Eq. 1. The results of this experiment are shown in Fig. 17. The shorter the time necessary to execute the entire schedule, the better the schedule was. As demonstrated in the obtained results, in most cases the best result was achieved by BS. In three cases, the best makespan was returned. In one case, the returned makespan was not the best but it is not the worst either. Discrepancy between the minimum and maximum values returned by the scheduler is the smallest in the case of BS, which confirms the stability of its operation.

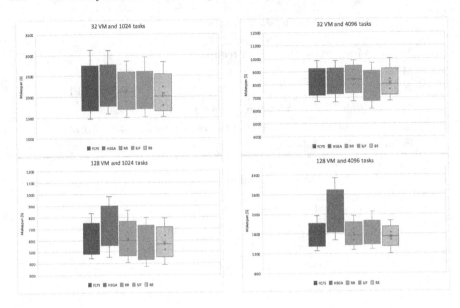

Fig. 17. Evaluation of the model performance using makespan Source: [49]

Evaluation of the Secure Blockchain Scheduler Based on the Security Level of the Schedule [51]

In the previous section, the security level criterion was omitted. In this section, the results of experiment assessing primarily this aspect are presented. Table 5 present the parameters of the considered scheduling scenarios.

Table 5. Experiments outline - expected security level equal to 1.5

SC	Expected SL	Size of the BC network
makespan	1.5	16 nodes

The SL was calculated based on the values of $P^{failure}$, P^{fake} and $P^{hacking}$ parameters [51].

$P^{failure}$ determines the probability of machine failure during task execution due to the high security requirements specified for this task. This factor is estimated the same for each scheduler used in the experiments. $P_{i,j}^{failure}$ for specific machine i and task j was defined by Kołodziej [28] as follows:

$$P_{i,j}^{failure} = \begin{cases} 0 & sd_j \le tl_i \\ 1 - e^{-\alpha(sd_j - tl_i)} & sd_j > tl_i \end{cases} \tag{15}$$

where

- α failure coefficient defined as a global parameter
- sd_j described in Eq. 5
- tl_i described in Eq. 6

P^{fake} defines the probability that the schedulers send a false or incorrectly prepared schedule. The following schedulers – (FCFS, HSGA, RR and SJF) – were not intgrated with the blockchain algorithms, and in such cases we set the parameter P^{fake} to 0.5. In the case of blockchain-based scheduler BS, where the schedule is checked by other nodes from the network, the value of P^{fake} is calculated by using the following formula:

$$P^{fake} = 1 - \frac{N_c}{N_v} \tag{16}$$

where

- N_c number of all confirmations that the schedule is correct obtained by the node from the verification nodes
- N_v number of all verification of the schedule regardless of whether the answer was positive or negative

Assuming that there are 16 nodes in the network and MTC is equal to 8, it can be seen that in the case of BS this factor assumes a value within the range $[0, 0.5]$, depending on how many requests the node must send to the network to receive 8 confirmations.

The value of the last factor $P^{hacking}$ indicates the probability of manipulation or modification of the prepared schedule by unauthorized entities. In the case of a single schedule module (FCFS, HSGA, RR and SJF), it can be assumed that $P^{hacking}$ is equal to 0.5. For BS, this value depends on TF_t of the attacking node. The higher the TF_t the block adding node has, the greater the probability that it may launch a majority attack [43] to modify parts of the blockchain. The $P^{hacking}$ value in that case is calculated according to the following formula:

$$P_t^{hacking} = \begin{cases} 0.5 & TF_t \geq \frac{1}{2}BW_t \\ \frac{TF_t}{BW_t} & TF_t < \frac{1}{2}BW_t \end{cases} \tag{17}$$

where

- TF_t the sum of $wl(schedule)$ for all schedules added to the blockchain by attacking node within a given period of time t (in this simulation t is equal to 30 days)
- BW_t

The Eq. 17 shows that $P^{hacking}$ in the case of BS assumes a value within the range $[0, 0.5]$, depending on how high the attacker's trust factor is in the moment of adding the block to the blockchain.

Provided experiments show how much advantage BS module has over the other scheduling modules when it comes to the security level criterion. The results of these experiments are presented in Figs. 18 and 19. As can be seen, the difference in the number of virtual machines and tasks is not significant because the results are very similar. However, it is worth noticing that BS has a significant advantage over the other modules. In the case of BS these are values around 2 while in the case of other schedulers the values are close to 1.5. In the simulation, the expected SL was set to 1.5 and all schedulers managed to achieve such a result.

It could be also observed, that the security level of the schedule prepared by BS is about 0.5 larger than in other cases. The effect of changing the number of nodes and MTC in the BC configuration on the P^{fake} value was checked. The results demonstrate that the P^{fake} value raises with the number of nodes in the network, which means that for larger networks there is a higher transaction rejection rate before it receives the appropriate number of confirmations. The impact of the chain of blocks size, specifically the BW_t value, on the $P^{hacking}$ factor. It turns out that the more transactions and blocks are in the chain, the lower the $P^{hacking}$ value is, which means that the security level of schedules grows with the length of blockchain and number of transactions placed in it. The highest SL achieved value was 2.266, a very good result compared to the 1.518 obtained by the other modules.

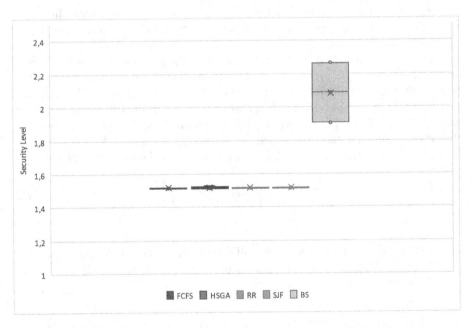

Fig. 18. Evaluation of the model performance using security level - 32 VM and 1024 tasks Source: [49]

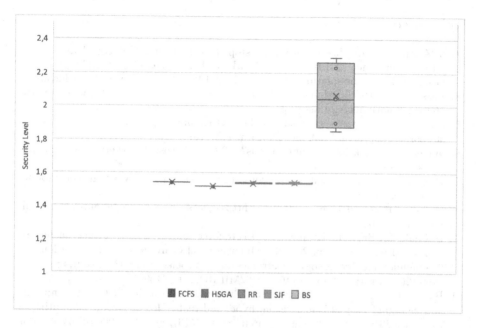

Fig. 19. Evaluation of the model performance using security level - 128 VM and 4096 tasks Source: [49]

5   Conclusions

Blockchain is a popular financial technology that uses ICT environments for virtual financial transactions using cryptocurrencies (e.g. Bitcoin). Blockchain customers store their transaction records in the blockchain P2P network, which effectively utilises the computing resources of its peers. A proof of work and a proof of stake are blockchain consensus algorithms used to improve the security of blockchain transactions.

This chapter briefly discussed the benefits of integrating the blockchain network with the elastic, scalable cloud environment to enhance the trustfulness of data servers and the security of data and user management. We also identified the challenges posed by this integration process. We presented a new concept of integrating the clouds infrastructure and schedulers with the blockchain algorithms to monitor the execution of the security-aware task scheduling in the cloud, one of the most important research topics in today's cloud and fog computing. We believe that the new blockchain-based scheduling model will allow us to overcome the problem of implementing the existing models in real-life scenarios.

Acknowledgements. Joanna Kolodziej's work was supported in part by the GUARD European Commission project under Grant Agreement no. 833456.

References

1. 51% attack (2019). https://www.investopedia.com/terms/1/51-attack.asp
2. CPU performance (2019). https://setiathome.berkeley.edu/cpu_list.php
3. Geekbench 5 - cross-platform benchmark (2019). https://www.geekbench.com/
4. Passmark - CPU benchmarks - list of benchmarked CPUs (2019). https://www.cpubenchmark.net/cpu_list.php
5. State of the dapps - ranking the best ethereum dapps (2019). https://www.stateofthedapps.com/rankings/platform/ethereum
6. What are blockchain confirmations? (2019). https://www.ethos.io/what-are-blockchain-confirmations
7. Discover our data center locations (2020). https://www.google.com/about/datacenters/locations/
8. Global infrastructure (2020). https://aws.amazon.com/about-aws/global-infrastructure/
9. Bošnjak, L., Sreš, J., Brumen, B.: Brute-force and dictionary attack on hashed real-world passwords. In: 2018 41st International Convention on Information and Communication Technology, Electronics and Microelectronics (MIPRO), pp. 1161–1166 (2018). https://doi.org/10.23919/MIPRO.2018.8400211
10. Buyya, R., Yeo, C.S., Venugopal, S., Broberg, J., Brandic, I.: Cloud computing and emerging IT platforms: vision, hype, and reality for delivering computing as the 5th utility. Future Gener. Comput. Syst. **25**(6), 599–616 (2009). https://doi.org/10.1016/j.future.2008.12.001
11. Chana, I., Kaur, T.: Delivering IT as A utility- A systematic review. CoRR abs/1306.1639 (2013). http://arxiv.org/abs/1306.1639
12. Chowdhury, S.: Survey on various scheduling algorithms. Imp. J. Interdiscip. Res. (IJIR) **3**, 4 (2018)
13. Ding, C.H., Nutanong, S., Buyya, R.: P2P networks for content sharing. CoRR cs.DC/0402018 (2004). http://arxiv.org/abs/cs/0402018
14. Dorovskaya, D.: Review of peercoin cryptocurrency: history of creation and predictions (2018). https://peercoin.net/
15. The Apache Software Foundation: Commons math: The apache commons mathematics library (2016). https://commons.apache.org/proper/commons-math/
16. Gagniuc, M.G.: Virtual machines technologies. In: Proceedings of 9th International Conference on Development and Application Systems, Suceava, Romania, pp. 200–205 (2008)
17. Garner, B.: What is decred (DCR)? — a guide on decentralized blockchain governance (2019). https://coincentral.com/decred-lowdown-decentralized-blockchain-governance/
18. Grzonka, D., Szczygiel, M., Bernasiewicz, A., Wilczynski, A., Liszka, M.: Short analysis of implementation and resource utilization for the openstack cloud computing platform. In: Mladenov, V.M., Georgieva, P., Spasov, G., Petrova, G. (eds.) ECMS 2015 Proceedings of European Council for Modeling and Simulation, Albena (Varna), Bulgaria (2015). https://doi.org/10.7148/2015
19. Guharoy, R., et al.: A theoretical and detail approach on grid computing a review on grid computing applications. In: 2017 8th Annual Industrial Automation and Electromechanical Engineering Conference (IEMECON), pp. 142–146 (2017). https://doi.org/10.1109/IEMECON.2017.8079578
20. Karatza, H.D.: Performance evaluation and analysis of large scale distributed systems: issues, trends, problems and solutions (2016). http://chipset-cost.eu/wp-content/uploads/2016/05/EK-SummerSchool-Bucharest-Sep2016.pdf

21. Hileman, G., Rauchs, M.: Global Cryptocurrency Benchmarking Study. Cambridge Centre for Alternative Finance, Cambridge Judge Business School, University of Cambridge (2017). https://EconPapers.repec.org/RePEc:jbs:altfin:201704-gcbs

22. Hong, Z., Wang, Z., Cai, W., Leung, V.C.M.: Blockchain-empowered fair computational resource sharing system in the D2D network. Future Internet **9**, 85 (2017)

23. Jakóbik, A., Grzonka, D., Palmieri, F.: Non-deterministic security driven meta scheduler for distributed cloud organizations. Simul. Model. Pract. Theory **76**, 67–81 (2017). https://doi.org/10.1016/j.simpat.2016.10.011. http://www.science direct.com/science/article/pii/S1569190X16302532. High-Performance Modelling and Simulation for Big Data Applications

24. Joshi, A.P., Han, M., Wang, Y.: A survey on security and privacy issues of blockchain technology. Math. Found. Comput. **1**, 121 (2018). https://doi.org/10.3934/mfc.2018007. http://aimsciences.org//article/id/d27803a2-7ce7-46e8-900d-30001fd4785a

25. Kalra, M., Singh, S.: A review of metaheuristic scheduling techniques in cloud computing. Egypt. Inform. J. **16**(3), 275–295 (2015). https://doi.org/10.1016/j.eij.2015.07.001. http://www.sciencedirect.com/science/article/pii/S1110866515000353

26. Kar, U.N., Sanyal, D.K.: An overview of device-to-device communication in cellular networks. ICT Express **4**(4), 203–208 (2018). https://doi.org/10.1016/j.icte.2017.08.002. http://www.sciencedirect.com/science/article/pii/S2405959517301467

27. Khatibi Bardsiri, A., Hashemi, S.M.: QoS metrics for cloud computing services evaluation. Int. J. Intell. Syst. Technol. Appl. **6**, 27–33 (2014). https://doi.org/10.5815/ijisa.2014.12.04

28. Kołodziej, J.: Evolutionary Hierarchical Multi-Criteria Metaheuristics for Scheduling in Large-Scale Grid Systems (2012)

29. Kołodziej, J., Wilczyński, A.: Blockchain secure cloud: a new generation integrated cloud and blockchain platforms - general concepts and challenges. Eur. Cybersecur. J. **4**(2), 28–35 (2018)

30. Kołodziej, J., Xhafa, F.: Integration of task abortion and security requirements in GA-based meta-heuristics for independent batch grid scheduling. Comput. Math. Appl. **63**(2), 350–364 (2012). https://doi.org/10.1016/j.camwa.2011.07.038. http://www.sciencedirect.com/science/article/pii/S089812211100592X. Advances in context, cognitive, and secure computing

31. Li, Z., et al.: A security and cost aware scheduling algorithm for heterogeneous tasks of scientific workflow in clouds. Future Gener. Comput. Syst. **65**, 140–152 (2016). https://doi.org/10.1016/j.future.2015.12.014. http://www.sciencedirect.com/science/article/pii/S0167739X15003982. Special Issue on Big Data in the Cloud

32. Lin, I.C., Liao, T.C.: A survey of blockchain security issues and challenges. Int. J. Netw. Secur. **19**, 653–659 (2017)

33. Lokhandwala, F.A.: A Heuristic Approach to Improve Task Scheduling in Cloud Computing using Blockchain technology. Master's thesis, Dublin, National College of Ireland. http://trap.ncirl.ie/3299/

34. Madni, H., Shafie, A.L., Abdullahi, M., Abdulhamid, S., Usman, M.: Performance comparison of heuristic algorithms for task scheduling in IAAS cloud computing environment. PLoS ONE **12**, e0176321 (2017). https://doi.org/10.1371/journal.pone.0176321

35. Michael, J.W., Rennock, A.C., Butcher, J.: Blockchain technology and regulatory investigations. Practical Law (2018)

36. Nakamoto, S.: Bitcoin: a peer-to-peer electronic cash system. Cryptography Mailing list (2009). https://metzdowd.com

37. Perrey, R., Lycett, M.: Service-oriented architecture. In: Proceedings of 2003 Symposium on Applications and the Internet Workshops, pp. 116–119 (2003). https://doi.org/10.1109/SAINTW.2003.1210138

38. Pointcheval, D.: Asymmetric cryptography and practical security (2002)

39. Prasanth, A.: Cloud computing services: a survey. Int. J. Comput. Appl. **46**, 975–8887 (2012)

40. Rachmawati, D., Tarigan, J., Ginting, A.B.C.: A comparative study of message digest 5(MD5) and SHA256 algorithm. J. Phys.: Conf. Ser. **978**, 012116 (2018). https://doi.org/10.1088/1742-6596/978/1/012116

41. Rani, B.K., Rani, B.P., Babu, A.V.: Cloud computing and inter-clouds - types, topologies and research issues. Procedia Comput. Sci. **50**, 24–29 (2015). https://doi.org/10.1016/j.procs.2015.04.006. http://www.sciencedirect.com/science/article/pii/S1877050915005074. Big Data, Cloud and Computing Challenges

42. Reeb, J.E., Leavengood, S.A.: Using the simplex method to solve linear programming maximization problems (1998)

43. Saad, M., et al.: Exploring the attack surface of blockchain: a systematic overview. arXiv abs/1904.03487 (2019)

44. Tasca, P., Tessone, C.: A taxonomy of blockchain technologies: principles of identification and classification. Ledger **4** (2019). https://doi.org/10.5195/ledger.2019.140. https://ledgerjournal.org/ojs/index.php/ledger/article/view/140

45. Taufer, M., Rosenberg, A.: Scheduling DAG-based workflows on single cloud instances: high-performance and cost effectiveness with a static scheduler. Int. J. High Perform. Comput. Appl. **31**, 19–31 (2015). https://doi.org/10.1177/1094342015594518

46. Vujičić, D., Jagodić, D., Randić, S.: Blockchain technology, bitcoin, and ethereum: a brief overview. In: 2018 17th International Symposium INFOTEH-JAHORINA (INFOTEH), pp. 1–6 (2018). https://doi.org/10.1109/INFOTEH.2018.8345547

47. Wang, S., Ouyang, L., Yuan, Y., Ni, X., Han, X., Wang, F.Y.: Blockchain-enabled smart contracts: architecture, applications, and future trends. IEEE Trans. Syst. Man Cybern.: Syst. **49**, 2266–2277 (2019). https://doi.org/10.1109/TSMC.2019.2895123

48. Wilczyński, A., Kołodziej, J.: Virtualization model for processing of the sensitive mobile data. In: Kołodziej, J., Pop, F., Dobre, C. (eds.) Modeling and Simulation in HPC and Cloud Systems. SBD, vol. 36, pp. 121–133. Springer, Cham (2018). https://doi.org/10.1007/978-3-319-73767-6_7

49. Wilczyński, A.: Blockchain-based task scheduling in computational clouds. Ph.D. thesis, AGH University of Science and Technology (2020). https://doktoraty.iet.agh.edu.pl/_media/2020:awilcz:phd_thesis_aw.pdf

50. Wilczyński, A., Kołodziej, J.: Modelling and simulation of security-aware task scheduling in cloud computing based on blockchain technology. Simul. Model. Pract. Theory 102038 (2019). https://doi.org/10.1016/j.simpat.2019.102038. http://www.sciencedirect.com/science/article/pii/S1569190X19301698

51. Wilczyński, A., Kołodziej, J., Grzonka, D.: Security aspects in blockchain-based scheduling in mobile multi-cloud computing. In: 2021 IEEE/ACM 21st International Symposium on Cluster, Cloud and Internet Computing (CCGrid), pp. 696–703 (2021). https://doi.org/10.1109/CCGrid51090.2021.00084

52. Wilczyński, A., Widlak, A.: Blockchain networks - security aspects and consensus models. J. Telecommun. Inf. Technol. **2**, 46–52 (2019). https://doi.org/10.26636/jtit.2019.132019
53. Xoxa, N., Zotaj, M., Tafa, I., Fejzaj, J.: Simulation of first come first served (FCFS) and shortest job first (SJF) algorithms (2014)
54. Yaga, D., Mell, P., Roby, N., Scarfone, K.: Blockchain technology overview. NIST Interagency/Internal Report (NISTIR) - 8202 (2018). https://doi.org/10.6028/NIST.IR.8202
55. Zheng, Z., Xie, S., Dai, H., Chen, X., Wang, H.: An overview of blockchain technology: architecture, consensus, and future trends. In: 2017 IEEE International Congress on Big Data (BigData Congress), pp. 557–564 (2017). https://doi.org/10.1109/BigDataCongress.2017.85

Ethics in Cybersecurity. What Are the Challenges We Need to Be Aware of and How to Handle Them?

Denitsa Kozhuharova, Atanas Kirov(✉), and Zhanin Al-Shargabi

Law and Internet Foundation, Sofia, Bulgaria
{denitsa.kozhuharova,atanas.kirov}@netlaw.bg

Abstract. In the field of research, the role of ethics grows more and more every year. One might be surprised but even in the field of technology there is a necessity for experts to understand and to implement ethical principles. Ethics itself could be understood as a code or a moral way by which a person lives and works. But within the field of information technology and cybersecurity research there is a chance that even the most technical appropriate solution does not go in line with the corresponding ethical principles. Experts need to implement fundamental ethical principles in their technical products in order not to cause harm or have any negative effect on their users. To the vast majority of challenges that will be reflected in this chapter are discussed within the EU-funded project GUARD, namely what are the proper actions which need to be taken to ensure ethical compliance. Challenges such as ensuring the privacy of the users, reporting and handling incidental findings, testing the technological product, mitigating biases etc. could have different negative effect on humans if not dealt with properly. The current chapter would explore the questions posed above alongside a description of a methodology resulting in the combined efforts of experts both in the field of cybersecurity and ethics.

Keywords: Cybersecurity · Ethics · Cyberethics · Data · Privacy · Hacking · Information · Incidental findings · Assessment · Risk · Measures · Guidance · Mitigation

1 Introduction

Ethics can be understood as the code by which one should live, work, and treat others. Humanity has always been in pursuit of guiding principles, which would lead its actions and shape its communities. There are numerous schools of thought that seek to understand what makes certain actions ethical and how people can make ethically sound choices. Consequentialists for example link the morality of actions to their effects, with utilitarianists justifying all actions if in the end they are in pursuit of the greater good. Deontologists seek fundamental rules and principles which should guide individuals throughout their life. The list of conflicting views on what is ethical is ever-growing. Different cultures and religions also differ in their understanding of ethics.

© The Author(s) 2022
J. Kołodziej et al. (Eds.): Cybersecurity of Digital Service Chains, LNCS 13300, pp. 202–221, 2022.
https://doi.org/10.1007/978-3-031-04036-8_9

Still, there are some views that seem to be universal. For example, every individual would condemn any harm done to innocent people or every individual puts high value on their right to privacy and freedom. There are certain ethical principles that are overarching and shape our understanding of the world around us. They guide us during our private life and often they can also shape the way we carry out our work and professional arrangements. In this trail of thought, there are many ethical principles that different professional field have accepted as values linked to loyalty and honesty. There are certain moral expectations we have when thinking of professionals. This is because we are dependent on them, their professionalism and moral integrity. We have become accustomed to erase the human element to all things linked to technology. But with the evolution of technology and our almost absolute dependency on it, cybersecurity professionals are facing increasingly more moral and ethical dilemmas.

When thinking of cybersecurity professionals, we seem to undermine the humanitarian aspect of their profession. However, on the other side of our screen there is a whole team of professionals that strives to protect our personal data, fight off malicious attacks, and manage a wide range of security risks. These individuals are left in a field with little or no legal guidelines to ensure a universal standard of protection. With the evolution of newer and newer technologies, like cloud computing, artificial intelligence (AI), Internet of Things (IoT), the risks continue to grow and to test our understanding of what is ethical and what is not. Can hacking be justified if it is in response to an established breach? Is the market for zero-day exploits something that should be supported? How do we ensure the privacy of users in the era of big data and cloud computing? These and more questions continue to challenge both professionals and scholars. This chapter seeks to examine some of the key ethical discussions in cybersecurity.

Firstly, under Sect. 2 it will focus on contemporary ethical issues in cyber security. This includes some of the well-known issues, such as data privacy and security breaches. A detailed analysis will cover questions relating to hacking, the reasons behind hacking and types of hackers. Furthermore, it is also important to examine risks in new and emerging technologies in relation to that under the next subsection this chapter will focus on topics concerning Internet of Things and Cloud computing. Here the ethical dilemmas are again connected to issues similar as the above-mentioned ones. The next subsection will examine the morality of testing new technologies which could have an effect on individuals and their well-being. Lastly, Sect. 3 will focus on some possible mitigation measures in order to ensure not only ethical compliance but also compliance with the relevant legal provisions.

2 Contemporary Ethical Issues in Cybersecurity

The ethical issues that arise in the field of cybersecurity vary in terms of the activities implemented by the stakeholders and the legal requirements in regard to the level of security. The intensity of the risks that may arise to the individuals should be also considered. With the increasing advent of new technologies, cybersecurity related ethical risks could occur in any area of everyday life – the economy, healthcare, public safety, transportation, etc. and to cause different level of harm to the individuals.

The risks themselves have different effects on them – some have a direct consequence on their rights such as violation of their privacy and dignity [20], others can have a detrimental effect on their economic activity such as hacking and other types of security breaches [7]. Before any mitigation measures are taken to address the specific risk, the concerned entities must become well acquainted with it so they are able to take the most appropriate measure to address it and to reduce any harmful effect that may be caused.

2.1 Data Privacy of Users

Processing of personal data presents some inherent risks to the rights of individuals [5]. The data may be lost, destroyed, subject of an unlawful change, disclosed to unauthorized parties or processed in an unlawful manner. The risks that could occur from the processing of personal data could vary depending on the nature and scale of processing. Large-scale processing including the processing of sensitive data, have a higher risk for individuals [16]. It is important to properly identify, address and mitigate any risks in advance, significantly limiting the negative impact on data subjects as a result of the processing.

Besides a fundamental human right, data privacy is of great importance since it tackles information inequality. Usually, individuals are in adverse position when negotiating contracts about the use of their data and do not have the means to check if their counterparties are living up to the terms of the agreement. Data protection regulations ensure fair conditions and adequate protection measures when transferring data [40]. Furthermore, data privacy protects individuals from discrimination [19]. It is well known that personal information when used in different context may lead to unfair treatment and disadvantages for the data subjects. This is especially the case with the uncontrolled use of new technologies with the motive of protecting public security. Privacy regulations are restricting the usage of sensitive information thus protecting individuals especially in marginalized communities from unfair treatment and harm [24]. Finally, privacy regulations will preserve human dignity and protect people from outside forces that could have negative effect on their decision-making process.

Special attention should be granted to some types of data that processing would require the implementation of additional protection measures. Such example is the data managed by healthcare systems and organisations or the so-called health data. This according to the General Data Protection Regulation (GDPR) is any data related to the physical or mental health of an individual including information that is related to the provision of health care services. Health data is considered as special category of personal data and could be processed only on several explicitly stated grounds in the GDPR. This chapter will not emphasize the grounds for processing this type of data, but it will present some challenges and mitigation measures that need to be considered. In any case, data controllers that are processing health data and medical institutions should do any activity related to this specific type of data in secure environments that are ensuring the security of the information.

Here we should conclude that the establishment of common ethical principles for lawful data processing is essential for risk governance and mitigation. The principles should take into consideration basic fundamental rights envisaged in international conventions and cover how to obtain, use, process, and store personal data. With their help data controllers must always demonstrate transparency and guarantee the data subjects rights under the GDPR.

2.2 Security Breaches and Risks. Contemplating the Idea of "Ethical Hacking"

When discussing cybersecurity issues, most people would equate this field to any and all efforts to combat hacking and cyber intrusions. All of us face concerns that malicious individuals will manage to gain access to our devices, our personal data, financial information, etc. and misuse it for personal gain. Still, this chapter seeks to question these ideas. Is hacking always unethical? What are the current ethical dilemmas linked to hacking and cyber intrusions?

Types of Hackers
Scholars in the field of cyberethics differentiate hackers based on their intention and practices [3, 36]. Some researchers have even set apart the hackers from the early days of the Internet [27]. These hackers were not at most driven by malicious intent but engaged in hacking activities for personal satisfaction or recognition [27]. This raises the question if these hacker's activities did not pursue material gain and cause material harm, are they still ethically reprimandable? Here, the answer should be in the affirmative. No matter the incentive, hackers still breach the privacy and security of private devices and data, this cannot be accepted, even if it was done with no serious intentions behind it.

These considerations are no longer as relevant. Hackers now by large are incentives by their personal and material gain. With the development of the Internet, the main intentions behind hacking have substantially changed [27]. As we become more and more dependent on technologies, all spheres of our life become linked to the Internet and to a wide range of devices. The cyber sphere today contains everything linked to a person: personal information, intellectual property, banking information, trade secrets, security passwords, etc. [27]. This should not only be said in the context of the individual, most services also are heavily dependent on the Internet, as more and more public and private services become digitalized. The banks, hospitals, schools, military, small business as well as transnational corporations are intangibly linked to the cyber sphere. This creates millions of opportunities for people skilled in programming and cyber intrusions to generate large profit in exchange for access to critical data [27]. A hacker can not only steal our banking information and go on a spending spree, but they can also carry out an attack against our online election systems under the guidance of a third party (which can be a foreign government or terrorist group for example) and get millions in payment. There is a multitude of lucrative opportunities that can incentivize modern hackers to carry out their cyberattacks. Thus, it seems that the early days where online savvy youngsters broke into systems for fun and recognition, but had no ill intent, have become out-of-date and a different classification, more aware of the intentions behind hacks, must be used.

Such a classification for hackers, which is based on the reasons behind their actions, is: white hat hackers, black hat hackers and grey hat hackers.

White Hat Hackers
White hat hackers are those that pursue legitimate goals and have gained authorization for their activities [36, 51]. Often these individuals are hired by different companies to test their security systems and find security vulnerabilities. For example, regarding a potential security issue, a group of white hat hackers would utilize similar methods used

by malicious hackers in order to find the potential exploits. But instead of causing harm or stealing data, this would be done in order to pinpoint vulnerabilities and create guidelines how to cure them [30]. An important contribution of white hackers in business, would be their impact of securing company networks and in this way protecting trade secrets and business practices. Furthermore, authors have recognized how white hat hackers help guarantee a seller's product security [30].

It is important to note that the white hat hackers can be employed solely by one company or work as a freelancer and help numerous companies. Interestingly, there are situations where white hat hackers offer their services for free for certain institutions or other bodies in need. For example, during the COVID-19 pandemic there was a rise of cyberattacks against hospitals, which led to a group of professionals to create the Cyber Alliance to Defend Our Healthcare, which aims to help hospitals strengthen they cybersecurity systems and avoid risks and counter attacks [54].

Black Hat Hackers
Black hat hackers on the other hand act in an illegal manner [3, 27, 36]. Often when we think of hackers, we think of this subgroup which in the pursuit of monetary gain, for example cause harm to us and our communities. Some of the methods used most often by these hackers include [26]:

– Phishing
– Ransomware
– Worms
– Viruses
– DoS/DDoS Attacks
– Cookie theft

Grey Hat Hackers
These hackers sit on the intersection between white and black hats, thus their activities raise the most ethical debates. They could be in pursuit of higher ideological goals, or they could be influenced again by purely personal incentives such as looking for entertainment [3, 27, 36]. They may break certain legal restraints, but ultimately, they would not seek out causing harm. Most grey hats abide by their personal understanding of ethical questions and their own established ethical principles.

Another concept that causes ethical questions is 'hacktivism' [52]. This phenomenon is linked to instances where hacking was carried out with a particular social or political goal which would seemingly justify the use of illegal methods of intrusion, or any harms caused by the actions. Such instances could include attacks carried out by abusive governments, leaking information of pedophiles, attacks against businesses that are known for environmental abuses. Evidently, there is much diversity in ethical reasoning and hacking methods that fall under the umbrella of 'hacktivism', thus this chapter will elaborate in detail whether there could be an ethical framework that would justify illegal hacking based on the goals it pursues.

Are White Hat Hackers Always Ethical?
At first glance it seems easy to address ethical questions connected to hacking. When

discussing black hat hackers, they would always be deemed unethical. In essence they harm innocent individuals for personal gain, they cause financial and emotional strain, and they may even threaten the fundamental structures of our societies. On the other hand, white hat hackers could always be justified, they are seeking to help the individuals whose securities they check and abide by all legal requirements.

This would be a very narrow-minded view on such questions. Jaquet-Chiffelle and Loi discuss an interesting hypothetical case where a white hat hacker, who was hired to check the security systems of a company, finds information connected to unethical practices of the company [27]. The question is whether this hacker should share these findings with the authorities or other relevant third parties. One argument against sharing is that this would ruin the trust between companies and hackers, which in the long run will make them less likely to commission security checks and would lower their level of overall protection [27]. Another argument is that in some jurisdiction sharing such findings may even be a breach of the legal regulations that protects company secrets [27]. Still, this does not answer the ethical dilemma of a hacker keeping information that exposes grave violations of the company.

Furthermore, another ethical issue is the mere existence of such a category of hackers. It is important to note that these classifications are neither static, nor are they linked to the individual, but to their actions [3, 27, 36]. That is to say that a hacker can carry out business as a white hat hacker, but also at some point carry out illegal intrusions for personal gain. The danger then lies in all the information and skills they have acquired working for corporations and learning their security methods and secrets. Another consideration is linked to white hat hackers that work for many companies based on freelancing. There may be a risk that one of these individuals who worked for one company also gets into contact with a competing company and shares critical information for monetary gain.

Such and similar concerns cause some scholars to question the mere practice of teaching technology students how to hack, since in essence this gives them the ability to later on cause a wide range of issues and harms [21]. In our view, the current developments in the field of cybersecurity have reached a point of no return. Amateur hackers are spending their time engrossed in a multitude of online resources that teach them newer and newer ways to find exploits and carry out intrusions. Botnet systems are automizing different processes of online abuse and leading to unimaginable levels of harm. For example, a ransomware attack against Colonial Pipeline led to widespread gasoline shortages in a number of states in the USA, and in the end the company was forced to pay $4.4 million dollars in bitcoin to the hacker group to stop further damages [48]. While the US government managed to return some of the money, this is one instance from a large pool of similar crimes that becoming widespread in today's digital age. Another similar example is the attack against Keseya, a company that manages IT infrastructure for several firms and enterprises. This attack influences a number of their clients, businesses such as the Swedish supermarket Coop had to temporarily close 800 of their shops due to the attack, which would have led to large financial loses [38]. Even governments are finding zero-day exploits and are not notifying system holders in order to be able to exploit them later on if needed as part of investigations [32].

In such circumstances, no matter the moral considerations, our only option is to invest even more in cultivating experts that can carry out intrusions against malicious systems and that can check our own systems for any weakness. We need to put our resources into educating professionals and promoting a strong moral code and work ethic in order to ensure they do not decide to engage in illegal and unethical activities. In the end, we must also accept that there will also be questionable instances when discussing hacking and cyber intrusions. Sometimes a hacker may stumble upon information they were not supposed to find or in order to ensure there are no weaknesses in a system they may have to resort to some technical methods that breach to some extent the privacy of certain users. Then we must accept that the course of action is left to that individual and their discretion. As the judge who may be put in a position to balance two conflicting interests or to find an answer to an ethical conflict, the white hat hacker must decide their course of action and carry the professional consequences if that decision proves to be unsound. Still, their actions should not be discussed through the lenses of right and wrong. The people that hired the hacker have already consented to the actions and decisions carried out by that individual.

Can Hacktivism Be Justified?

Another important ethical issue concerns the existence of so-called 'hacktivists'. These individuals carry out illegal cyber intrusions in the alleged pursuit of an ideological goal and/or the protection of ethical values such as free speech, equality, etc. A proposed definition of the types of attacks they carry out would regards instances where *'the hack is used in relation to some political or social agenda carried out by private individuals for their own political ends, often with this political element acting as a central justification for the hack'* [4]. This raises several ethical dilemmas.

Firstly, some argue that instances of hacktivist are of a non-violent nature. Delmas discusses them precisely as a means of civil disobedience [13]. Some prominent online hacktivists even link their actions to the core values of the Internet [28]. Such descriptions would place such activities within the grounds of civil protests and would make them justified [13].

However, it must be noted that often hacktivism can be linked to harms and damages [4]. These damages can be of a diverse character: financial, physical, reputational, etc. Bellaby raises the concern that hackers lack the moral authority to engage in political violence [4]. It has been argued that only the state has the authority to engage in political violence, based on political theories such as the 'Social Contract Theory' [4]. Individuals have renounced authority to the state to protect their rights and interests and have given up their rights to seek out justice on their own. Under this framework, the actions carried out by hacktivists are not ethically sound.

Still, it must be noted, that in certain cases where the state has not carried out its obligations accordingly, individuals can then resort to actions on their own. Bellaby however narrows them to cases of state negligence, which would concern potential harms to individuals due to the state's continuous inaction or misconduct [4]. For example, a singular misstep taken by the state, would not justify counteractions by vigilantes. However, cases of largescale state abuse can lead to a justified response by a hacktivist group.

For example, this precisely concerns operations of the hacktivist group Anonymous, such as Operation Tunisia and Operation Egypt, where hackers broke into the security systems of governmental organizations in order to help protesters and to aid dissidents from online censorship [46]. In this case not only the state did not protect its citizens, but it also actively infringed their rights and interests. Thus, seemingly the actions of the hacktivists while illegal, were morally justifiable.

During the coronavirus pandemic, Anonymous also shared information about COVID-19 cases in Nicaragua, which the government was hiding. This again would fall under measures taken due to the government's inaction or ill-intent [50]. Another similar example raised by Bellaby are the attacks carried out by Anonymous with the intent of protecting minority rights [4]. The organization executed a number of intrusions against the Ugandan government in order to stop a bill that would have harmed the rights of members of the LGBT+ community [49].

Such cases are on one hand controversial, since they in fact seek to impose a certain political view through coercive measures. In this instance, the actions of the group were in clash with the cultural understandings of the state in question, still they can be justified since they were in the pursuit of the basic human rights of the minority in question. We would argue that such examples of hacktivism always seek to strike a balance between conflicting principles and political ideologies. Some authors have recognized that sometimes these clashes can be so extreme, that a hacktivist's actions can also be justified as measures of self-defense [4]. It could be argued that Anonymous not only sought to achieve a political change in the societies they influenced, they sought to protect the basic integrity and life of the individuals that were threatened by the state.

These considerations are more difficult to justify in the case of attacks against businesses. It is generally recognized that the state is authorised to regulate and overlook business activities as well as sanction those that carry out illegal activities or otherwise harm consumers or their own employees. When the state does not in fact take action against a malicious company, some would claim that hacktivists are justified in intervening in order to protect human rights or other similar values. For example, there have been a number of attacks carried out by hackers with the aim of sabotaging corporations that harm the environment, like the taking down of the French company Areva's website, which is in the nuclear power business [4]. Attacks on businesses are more problematic. Often political activists will have their own personal or political biases [4]. While state actions will include thorough investigations and numerous levels of checks and balances before retributive actions are carried out against companies and enterprises, hackers can carry out attacks based on their own personal opinions about a certain company and its perceived misconduct. Furthermore, the attacks carried out by hackers may lead to much collateral damage, the financial and material damages to corporations will not only harm the corporate itself, but may also influence its employees, many of whom might not even be aware, let alone complicit, in the actions of the company that lead to the attacks.

Thus, when discussing political hacktivism, it should be noted that any conclusions on the moral character of such actions will be very case specific and will call for a very detailed analysis of the proportionality of such actions and their intent.

2.3 New Risks in Developing Fields – IoT and Cloud Computing

A key characteristic of cybersecurity is that it is ever-developing. With the emergence of new technologies, new ethical questions arise as well. This chapter will focus on two emerging technologies that may pose cybersecurity risks and some interesting ethical questions.

Internet of Things

Internet of Things (IoT) would refer to the rise of devices that are linked to the Internet and are able to communicate, send and receive data and help individuals in their everyday life [1]. The IoT is said to lead to a revolution in our physical relationship with our devices [1, 23]. But as revolutionary as these devices are, there are a wide range of ethical issues that these technologies create.

Privacy and Consent

The issue with IoT devices is that often users might not know what kind of information their devices collect. For example Allof discusses how a sex toy collected a wide range of information about its user: vibration settings, dates and times the device was used, email addresses of users [1, 42]. This anecdote while humorous, should cause great concern. Currently, we have become accustomed to the idea that the Internet has created an enormous market for our data and personal information. Still, it is frightening how this breach of our private life can reach such intimate spheres of our life as those discussed above.

The rise of IoT devices is driving these processes forward. As more and more everyday devices are being linked to the cybersphere and are starting to collect data, carry out different services, etc., we will have to be as aware as possible about what we give our consent to prior to using a device. From smart watches, smart kitchen appliance, even smart water bottles to digitalized personal assistants, the risks are never ending. For example, smart watches that track our fitness routines could give away precise information of our daily routine or whereabouts [1]. The use of smart kitchen appliance could give away information when we are in our home and when we are absent, which in turn may create a security risk [1]. In such circumstances it is extremely important for individuals to be able to decide what information to give to devices and what not to share.

This raises the question of informed consent. If an individual is given full information about what the device collects and how it will use the information, and if individual gives their informed consent, then many of the ethical issues can be dealt with. It is important to highlight that the informed consent should cover the requirements under Article 4 of the GDPR, namely that consent should be freely given, specific, informed and unambiguous. Moreover, the data controller must be able to demonstrate that consent is given at any time during the processing and to give the possibility for the data subject to withdraw it. Consent is an integral part of the data subjects' right to be informed and its violation leads to non-compliance with data protection law, but it is also an ethical issue. Apart from that there are also some other considerations that needs to be taken care of:

- Firstly, an ethical dilemma is whether we can expect users who lack technological knowledge to be able to make sound decisions when facing complex issues such as data processing, collection, storage and potential risks [1].
- Secondly, it has been pointed out by many experts that often the Terms and Conditions of companies and devices are very technical in character or prolonged in order to

disincentivize users who are traying to familiarize themselves with them [1]. This is an infringement of the right of the data subject to be informed under which any information provided to the data subject must be easily accessible, understandable and provided in clear and plain language [43]. In the end many users just look over these documents and give their consent just to access the service or use the device to its full capacity.

- Third, some device/service providers may even link the use to accepting all of the applicable Terms and Conditions [1]. Maybe some of us have faced this when trying to access a certain website. It could have even been a reason we decided to switch to another website where we could gain similar content but with less privacy breaches. Thus, we could be tempted to overlook all of these considerations. If someone does not want their smart bracelet to collect private information on their location, they can go running with a normal chronometer. But one must analyze these issues with a look towards the future.

In the near future, where IoT would have become an omnipresent part of our daily lives, we might not have the luxury to refuse their use. Furthermore, the use of such devices may no longer be just an individualistic decision, they may become integrated in the systems we use, in our healthcare, education, government [10]. Thus, now in the beginning of their implementation we must make sure that all privacy concerns are thoroughly dealt with. Such devices must not become a "Pandora's box", filled with sensitive information we do not even know we shared.

Security
Another issue is linked to the safety of users [1, 44, 53]. IoT is beginning to reach all spheres of our lives. At the same time, the risks of malfunction or malicious cyber intrusions are rising. The fact that smart devices are linked to networks and are programmable raises many concerns that they can easily be compromised.

There are already many well-known cases of security failures of smart devices. There have been numerous cases of baby monitors being hacked by criminals who use it to spy on infant children [41] or of IoT children's dolls also serving as surveillance devices [22], there is a plethora of other household devices that also were discovered to pose surveillance weaknesses [39]. All of these cases pose a large threat to individuals, they can cause emotional damage or even expose sensitive data to malicious individuals that can then use it for their own benefit. Imagine a criminal knowing when your child is left alone at home based on the surveillance data they have access to. Or imagine your family was one of the victims of the hacked Cayla doll[1]. Trough the doll, criminals would be able to communicate with your child, manipulate it into sharing data or even make it open a door or window they can later use to infiltrate your house when you least expect it.

---

[1] This toy was able to connect to Bluetooth networks, communicate with families, ask questions, collect data, share that data with a voice recognition company in the USA. More on this can be found in: Erickson A.: This pretty blond doll could be spying on your family, https://www.washingtonpost.com/news/worldviews/wp/2017/02/23/this-pretty-blond-doll-could-be-spying-on-your-family, Accessed 2022/02/03;

What is even more frightening is that some security threats pose direct and unmanageable threats. If a security breach in the form of data leakage can be managed by changing passwords or limiting the amount of data a device can collect and share, some threats cannot be mitigated and must completely be eliminated. For example, some IoT health devices such as implantable cardiac devices can be hacked and stopped or used to administrate irregular pacing or shocks [31].

Such cases are extremely troubling as they pose even life-threatening risks to consumer. They also would have detrimental effects on public trust and may have dire financial and reputational consequences for businesses and developers. A survey by Internet Society shows that 75% of consumers do not trust the way their data is shared and 28% of users that do not own a smart device would not buy one due to security risks [25].

It is an ethical question who should bear the responsibility of ensuring there are enough countermeasures to guarantee user security. The survey of Internet Society also discovered that 88% of consumers believe security standards should be assured by regulators, 81% trust manufacturers and 80% retailers [25]. These positions cause several points of conflict. On one hand, governments and state regulators often are left behind when it comes to emerging technologies and cannot keep up with the newest risks and tendencies in cybersecurity. On the other hand, retailers do not in fact have a direct say on the designs of devices and the safety precautions that can be installed in them. This would call for a level of self-regulation by manufacturers. Some may argue that expecting manufacturers to ensure security standards on their own discretion would not be effective as this would be in conflict with their business interests.

As discussed by many, businesses have as a main priority profit and growth. If a new product is set to launch and has already promised large gains for the company, there may be pressure to overlook any potential security threats that have emerged last minute. However, it must be noted that businesses recognize how important security is to users and cannot afford to compromise their reputation. Thus, we would argue that businesses themselves in fact have taken the burden of ensuring consumer safety, even if bases on profit incentives. Regulators must then work in cooperation with them to ensure threats are avoided or mitigated.

Cloud Computing

Cloud computing systems can be defined as "*software-related activities performed by users thanks to pools of computing resources, which are accessible through a network, where they are made available by some providers*" [47]. Many of us have used such services when working with products such as Google Drive, Microsoft Share Point, Dropbox, Gmail, Facebook. Broadly cloud computing can be classified under the following types [35]:

- Infrastructure as a service (IaaS) – cloud service providers supply consumers with basic computer resources such as storage, servers, etc.
- Platform as a service (PaaS) – cloud service providers supply consumers with platforms they can use to create and deliver their own applications.
- Software as a service (SaaS) – cloud service providers build, host and supply application to consumers.

This emerging technology also poses many ethical questions and considerations.

Ownership of Data

One of the important questions is whether when using a cloud service, the users can retain ownership of their data and products. Here there is a multitude of issues. Firstly, some cloud services not only store data, they are used by users to create the data itself. This raises questions whether this data can be claimed by the cloud service provider. Secondly, the data retained by a certain cloud service may be created or uploaded from one location, but fall within a different jurisdiction based on the location of the services [45]. This conflict of jurisdictions is even more confusing, due to the fact that there is no set standard that can be established [12]. Questions of ownership are often dealt with in the terms and conditions of the cloud service providers [12]. For example, major cloud service providers, such as Office 365, Amazon Web Service and Google have similar positions on ownership and reserve all rights over the data and content stored for the users [8].

These are important considerations since they would later influence the consequences of a data breach or how information can be stored and shared. In order to ensure that users have a wide range of rights in regard to their data, as well as the ability to make decisions how it is stored and shared, they must retain ownership over it. Scholars have discussed the phenomenon of younger generation becoming less concerned over the question of data ownership [11]. De Bruin and Floridi focus on the way public perception has shifted 'from the product to the services the product represents' [11]. For example, they describe how contemporary users will focus less on who owns a certain photograph when it is uploaded and more on where they can share the photograph, whether they can edit it and other similar service based assessments [11].

Here a counterbalance would be again ensuring users are well informed of the importance of data protection and privacy as well as what consequences the decisions they make could have. De Bruin and Floridi argue against a strong regulatory role of the state and propose an approach dubbed interlucency, where consumers can make decisions after being thoroughly informed by providers [11]. This information should be effectively communicated, aimed at the particular individual and the provider must ensure the user genuinely was able to grasp the information that was shared with him.

We would also consider such an approach extremely fruitful, but one should not completely disregard the importance of government regulation as well. Through the ethical lens, the state as established was given the authority to regulate such important questions in order to protect the safety of its citizens. In this regard, the EU has taken large steps in regulating cloud services in the extent needed to protect EU citizens and their rights.[2]

Security Risks

The potential intrusions from third parties constitute the larger risk when it comes to cloud computing. This risk has some unique dimensions when it comes to cloud computing. Imagine you and your colleagues store vital information in a cloud service. One of your

---

[2] The European institutions and bodies have published an extensive guide: European Data Protection Supervisor, Guidelines on the use of cloud computing services, https://edps.europa.eu/sites/edp/files/publication/18-03-16_cloud_computing_guidelines_en.pdf Accessed 2022/02/08;

colleagues compromises the security of that cloud environment. All of you now will face the potential consequences of such a development. Or maybe, the centralized server of that cloud provider was hacked, and this puts you in danger along with a multitude of other users.

Still, traditional mechanisms of protection could be implemented: security checks, encryption, etc. In this sense, there may be a heightened risk of intrusions, but these can be thoroughly mitigated. At the same time, many authors have pointed out the benefits cloud services provide. Users are able to save large financial investments that would have otherwise been used for machines, storage space, maintenance, etc. For this they gain a cheaper, easily accessible product maintained and protected by a third party with more expertise in cybersecurity in the face of a cloud service provider. Thus, when balancing the ethical considerations of user security and the practical implications of a convenient service such as cloud computing, it is understandable why users would accept any potential but small harms that this new technology may bring.

2.4   Risks While Testing New Technology

Another ethical concern is how to proceed with the testing of future products. Ethical testing is nothing new, our society has faced a multitude of ethical issues when testing for example pharmaceutical products or cosmetics. A central issue in all such ethical debates is the potential risks the test subjects are exposed to [29]. Here the main argument to justify this is the consent given by the participants as well as the overarching societal interest in such testing activities. Participants often have altruistic reasons for joining test studies, but they also gain financial stimulus to award their participation or even compensate any shortcomings.

These justifications can be carried on to the field of new technology testing. However, there are also some unique considerations. Firstly, when discussing new technologies there are unforeseen risks that might not be anticipated by the experts. Unforeseen risk may be applicable to all new products, even one should expect such, but specifically in the field of technology these risks could not only be unexpected, they may be of a character that has not yet been dealt with. For example, scientists still do not know for sure how certain Bluetooth earphones and their waves can influence the brain of their users [2]. On one hand, such concerns are for what it seems unfounded with no real evidence for harm. On the other hand, if they prove to be rightfully placed, they may cause harms that we are not yet sure how to proceed with.

Secondly, another issue that can be raised is that in some instances participant consent is not always clearly given. For example, Uber is testing its self-driving cars in real life environments within urban populated areas such as San Francisco, Phoenix, Pittsburgh [34]. While the direct participants in the testing have consented to take part, all pedestrians in the testing areas have not. This is worrying, especially when one considers that such testing has already led to a casualty [33]. Defenders argue that if implemented such technologies will substantially lower casualties caused by human error. Still, this does not justify the risks bystanders are exposed to when in proximity to a product that is yet to finish all safety tests.

3   Required Measures to Ensure Ethical Compliance

In view of the above-mentioned risks and liabilities to the overall compliance with ethical principles, certain actions need to be taken in order to ensure full compliance. The measures that could be taken vary from simple organisational activities to the introduction of special technologies that ensure the protection of specific rights and freedoms of the persons concerned. In order to establish which measures should be taken, particularly with regard to new technological systems that should be integrated, appropriate conformity and impact assessments should be carried out. The best that can be done is before any new technology is developed to create a list of requirements that could be taken with regards the actual development. Such approach was taken in framework of the GUARD project funded by the European Commission's Horizon 2020 programme, under which a set of requirements (functional, design, performance, ethical, data protection and etc.) were established to be followed during the development of the platform under the project.

3.1   Implementing Organisational Measures to Ensure Ethical Compliance

Envisaging and implementing organisational measures is the base minimum for ensuring compliance with the fundamental ethical principles. What measures should be included is decided on case-by-case basis and should be pointed out that more than one measure could require to be implemented in order to reach ethical compliance. Another important thing that should be considered is that in most cases the sole implementation of organisational measures is not sufficient, and additional technical measures must be included. This depends on the variety and severity of cybersecurity risks that could occur, while the definition of the exact measures should be taken after a proper assessment of the risks, that could affect the individuals is concluded.

The measures that could be implemented are the following: 1) internal trainings for staff members and technical developers on fundamental ethics, 2) preparation of ethical codes of conduct for staff members and technical developers, 3) conducting follow-up audits to assess the level of compliance with the core ethical principles, 4) adoption of incidental findings policy that will indicate how to handle any unforeseen information, 5) introduction of ethical personnel, which goal is to advice and oversee how ethical standards should be properly implemented.

One measure that could be implemented continuously and indefinitely is the establishment of procedures for periodic monitoring of the compliance with the fundamental ethical principles. It should be noted that monitoring procedures should not be applied to every system. Before such measure is adopted an assessment of the nature of the system, its purpose and what impact it has on individuals should be conducted. For example, a system that stores and processes data that is publicly available should not be subject to a detailed monitoring procedure, unlike a similar system that processes personal data. Once this has been determined, it should be decided over what period the monitoring activities will take place [9]. As has been mentioned many times, a judgement should also be made here with regard to the nature of the system to be monitored in order the monitoring period to be determined. After all, continuous monitoring is too time and resource consuming, leading to additional difficulties.

Each of the above measures is relevant to achieving ethical compliance. Whichever, of the above measures is adopted, they should be strictly adhered to in order to avoid any loss and to prevent any damage to those implementing them. The improper implementation of the measures would impede the fulfilment of their objectives and could lead to harm to the individuals.

3.2   Carrying Out an Impact Assessment

An assessment of the impact on the rights and freedoms of citizens and the persons concerned is an appropriate measure to take in order to minimize any risks and ensure ethical compliance. Such assessment is envisaged both by the Council of Europe and EU regulations. Specifically, EU law under Article 35 of the GDPR envisages that a data protection impact assessment should be carried out when the nature of the processing is likely to result in high risk to the rights and freedoms of natural persons. This requirement is envisaged to be carried out by the data controller[3] and could also cover an assessment on the impact of fundamental rights and freedoms explicitly stated in international legislative acts such as the European Convention of Human Rights (ECHR)[4]. The main implication of the results of the impact assessment is to ensure accountability and compliance with relevant legislation and ethical principles.

GDPR does not define how the likelihood of a risk is to be assessed but it indicates what those risks might be[5]. The impact assessment should identify appropriate measures to address these risks. Where an impact assessment is required, data controllers must assess the necessity and proportionality of the processing and the possible risks of the individuals.

The Article 29 Working Party have developed guidelines under which there is criteria to determine whether or not an impact assessment is required for the specific processing activities. The criteria includes: 1) evaluation or scoring; 2) automated decision-making with legal or similar significant effect; 3) systematic monitoring, 4) sensitive data; 5) data processing on a large scale; 6) datasets that have been matched or combined; 7) data concerning vulnerable data subjects; 8) innovative use or applying technological or organisational solutions; when the processing in itself "prevents data subjects from exercising a right or using a service or a contract [18]".

Under the GDPR, there is no specific guidance on how an impact assessment should be carried out, but there are various methodologies that provide guidance on how should be proceeded with such assessment. An example of such methodology is the Standard Data Protection Model (SDM)[6], which is explicitly recommended by the Article 29 Working Party Guidelines on Data Protection Impact Assessment, and embraces the legal requirements set by the GDPR. This methodology was used in the preparation of the Data Protection Impact Assessment under the GUARD project and with its help the legal

---

[3] Article 35, paragraph 1, General Data Protection Regulation;

[4] Singed 4 November 1950, Effective from 3 September 1953;

[5] Recital 75, General Data Protection Regulation;

[6] This can be found at: SDM Methodology, https://www.datenschutzzentrum.de/uploads/sdm/SDMMethodology_V1.0.pdf. Accessed 2022/02/02.

requirements envisaged under the EU Data Protection Regulation were transformed into proper technical and organisational measures which will minimize any possible risks.

The methodology introduces the concept of "Data Protection Goals". It defines this term to describe certain categories of requirements derived from data protection law. It is through them that the transformation from legislative requirements into technical and organisational measures takes place. The term is also referred in the case law of the German Constitutional Court (Judgement of 27 February 2008 – 1 BvR 370/07, 1 BvR 595/07, Official Record of Decisions [BVerfGE] 120, 274). In this decision, the court pointed out that the individuals should be protected when their personal data is processed by modern technological solutions from unlimited collection, storage, usage, transfer and misuse ensuring compliance with fundamental data protection goals such as data minimization, confidentiality, integrity etc.

3.3 Adopting Privacy Enhancing Technologies

Privacy Enhancing Technologies (PETs) are technological measures that aim at protecting personal identity. These measures usually are involving different levels of encryption such as blind signatures, digital signatures, pseudonyms etc. [6]. They are effective measures to ensure privacy by design and could minimize the amount of data processed to help protect any personal information. PETs have to be distinguished from the rest of the data-security technologies. The difference is that data security is about ensuring the security of the processing activities regardless their legitimacy. On the other hand – PETs are seeking to restrict the usage of personal data or to give control of the revelation of personal data to the concerned individuals [6]. PETs are strongly related to big data, which includes the usage of a huge volume, variety and real-time data (from physical sensors, social media etc.). This leads to a very high plausibility that big data may contain personal identifiers and to an extensive variety of issues concerning data privacy such as lack of control and transparency, reusability of the data, re-identification and data inference, profiling and automated decision making [17]. Although the usage of big data is crucial for the economic and technical development, enterprises should be cautious since the risk of misuse is high making the achievement of privacy by design the best possible way to ensure compliance with the GDPR.

One of the ways in which privacy by design could be ensured is exactly with the help of PETs. Again, it should be evaluated which PETs should be implemented on a case-by-case analysis. The correct choice of technology will depend on different factors, including the type of data that it is used, volume of the data, the source, the purpose of the processing etc.

In summary there are many positive aspects to the use of PETs which could help protect data subjects from a wide range of ethical risks. The discussions related to the use of PETs will continue to evolve and be directly linked to the use of new technologies that could have negative effect to data subjects. In relation to that is important when using or designing privacy-preserving systems to follow the proper ethically informed methodologies when using or developing such systems in order to identify and mitigate any possible risks.

4 Conclusions

This article presents some of the ethical risks and issues that could occur in the field of cybersecurity, and it was based to some extend on the findings under the EU funded project GUARD. It also represents some of the measures dedicated to protecting the privacy of data subjects that were implemented during the project's lifetime regarding the technology developed within it. What can serve as a basic recommendation, especially when developing new technologies is to establish a list of requirements, including ethical ones that the system must cover before any action is taken. This will ensure compliance with the ethical principles at highest level and mitigate any negative effect on the individuals.

Regarding the ethical risks that may occur, one must be aware that they are of varying intensity and may affect different human rights and freedoms and different areas of our lives. The fields that pose many ethical issues and were thoroughly discussed include hacking and cyber intrusions, both authorized and unauthorized, risk in newer technologies such as IoT devices and cloud computing, among others. All these areas have some issues in common such privacy concerns, harms to businesses, etc., but each area proved to have its own specific issues. It is highly important to be aware of the risk that may occur in order to implement proper measures that will minimize any harmful effect to the individuals. This requires proper understanding of the issues and additional input from experts in the field.

In conclusion, we could summarize that the issues regarding ethical problems in the field of cybersecurity are complex and require a robust approach. Each emerging risk must be assessed in order to determine the negative effect it will have on the individual. Such an assessment would then make it possible to choose an appropriate response. Stakeholders taking the measures should be flexible and combine diverse measures in order to achieve better results and envisage the participation of ethical experts all together with technical developers and cybersecurity experts. Their combined work will be the best way to ensure ethical compliance and that no harm will be caused to individual.

References

1. Allhoff, F., Henschke, A.: The Internet of Things: foundational ethical issues. Internet of Things **1–2**, 55–66 (2018)
2. Are Bluetooth Headphones Dangerous? Here's What Experts Think, Healthline. https://www.healthline.com/health-news/are-wireless-headphones-dangerous. Accessed 16 Jan 2022
3. Barber, R.: Hackers pro-filed—who are they and what are their motivations? Comput. Fraud Secur. **2001**(2), 14–17 (2001)
4. Bellaby, R.W.: An ethical framework for hacking operations. Ethical Theory Moral Pract. **24**(1), 231–255 (2021). https://doi.org/10.1007/s10677-021-10166-8
5. Bishop, L.: Big data and data sharing: ethical issues. UK Data Service, UK Data Archive (2017)
6. Burker, H.: Privacy-enhancing technologies: typology, critique, vision. In: Agre, P.E., Rotenberg, M. (eds.) Technol. Privacy New Landscape, pp. 125–142. MIT Press, London (1997)
7. Cekerevac, Z., Zdenek, D., Prigoda, L., Cekerevac, P.: Hacking, protection and the consequences of hacking. Komunikacie **20**(2), 83–87 (2018)

8. Chima, R.: Cloud Security – Who Owns The Data? Blueberry Consultants. https://www.bbc onsult.co.uk/blog/cloud-security-who-owns-the-data. Accessed 3 Mar 2022

9. Cybersecurity ethical obligations. https://resources.infosecinstitute.com/topic/cybersecurity-ethical-obligation/. Accessed 4 Feb 2022

10. Dahlqvist, F., Patel, M., Rajko, A., Shulman, J.: Growing opportunities in the Internet of Things, growing opportunities in the Internet of Things. https://www.mckinsey.com/ind ustries/private-equity-and-principal-investors/our-insights/growing-opportunities-in-the-int ernet-of-things. Accessed 8 Feb 2022

11. De Bruin, B., Floridi, L.: The ethics of cloud computing. Sci. Eng. Ethics **23**(1), 21–39 (2016). https://doi.org/10.1007/s11948-016-9759-0

12. Delgado, R.: The ongoing question of data ownership in the cloud, socPub. https://socpub.com/articles/the-ongoing-question-of-data-ownership-in-the-cloud-13749. Accessed 3 Feb 2022

13. Delmas, C.: Is Hacktivism the new civil disobedience? Raisons Politiques **69**(1), 63–81 (2018)

14. Durant, A.: The Enemy Within. Business XL, pp. 48–51 (2007)

15. Erickson, A.: This pretty blond doll could be spying on your family. https://www.washin gtonpost.com/news/worldviews/wp/2017/02/23/this-pretty-blond-doll-could-be-spying-on-your-family/. Accessed 3 Feb 2022

16. Ertem, A.: Sensitive Data and Receiving Consent according to GDPR. https://blog.scrintal.com/sensitive-data-and-receiving-consent-according-to-gdpr-a31c9ee8ea28. Accessed 8 Feb 2022

17. European Union Agency for Cybersecurity: Privacy by design in big data. An overview of privacy enhancing technologies in the era of big data analytics (2015)

18. European Union Agency for Fundamental Rights and Council of Europe. In: Handbook on European Data Protection Law, 2018 edn. Publications Office of the European Union, Luxembourg (2018)

19. Favaretto, M., De Clercq, E., Elger, B.S.: Big data and discrimination: perils, promises and solutions a systematic review. J Big Data **6**, 12 (2019)

20. Floridi, L.: On human dignity as a foundation for the right to privacy. Philos. Technol. **29**(4), 307–312 (2016). https://doi.org/10.1007/s13347-016-0220-8

21. Hartley, R.D.: Ethical Hacking: Teaching Students to Hack, East-Carolina University. https://doi.org/10.13140/RG.2.1.3580.8085. Accessed 16 Jan 2022

22. Hautala, L.: Smart toy flaws make hacking kids' info child's play. https://www.cnet.com/home/smart-home/cloudpets-iot-smart-toy-flaws-hacking-kids-info-children-cybersecurity/. Accessed 3 Feb 2022

23. Henschke, A.: The Internet of Things and dual layers of ethical concern. In: Lin, P., Abney, K., Jenkins, R. (eds.) Robot Ethics 2.0, pp. 229–243. Oxford University Press, New York (2017)

24. How GDPR Stops Discrimination and Protects Equalities. https://www.openrightsgroup.org/how-gdpr-stops-discrimination-and-protects-equalities/. Accessed 8 Feb 2022

25. Internet Society: The Trust Opportunity: Exploring Consumer Attitudes to the Internet of Things. https://www.internetsociety.org/resources/doc/2019/trust-opportunity-exploring-con sumer-attitudes-to-iot/. Accessed 3 Feb 2022

26. Ivanov, I..: What is a Black Hat Hacker? Techjury. https://techjury.net/blog/what-is-a-black-hat-hacker. Accessed 11 Jan 20222

27. Jaquet-Chiffelle, D.-O., Loi, M.: Ethical and unethical hacking. In: Christen, M., Gordijn, B., Loi, M. (eds.) The Ethics of Cybersecurity. TILELT, vol. 21, pp. 179–204. Springer, Cham (2020). https://doi.org/10.1007/978-3-030-29053-5_9

28. Johnson, B., Stephens, D.: Is 'hacktivism' a force for good … or chaos?, Marketplace. https://www.marketplace.org/2017/04/28/hacktivism-force-good-or-chaos/. Accessed 2 Feb 2022

29. Kapp, M.: Ethical and legal issues in research involving human subjects: do you want a piece of me? J. Clin. Pathol. **59**(4), 335–339 (2006)
30. Kumar, S., Agarwal, D.: Hacking attacks, methods, techniques and their protection measures. Int. J. Adv. Res. Comput. Sci. Manag. **4**(4), 2353–2358 (2018)
31. Larson, S.: FDA confirms that St. Jude's cardiac devices can be hacked, CNN. https://money.cnn.com/2017/01/09/technology/fda-st-jude-cardiac-hack/. Accessed 3 Feb 2022
32. Legal Frameworks for Hacking by Law Enforcement: Identification, Evaluation and Comparison of Practices, Study for the LIBE Committee, 6 April 2017
33. Levin, S., Wong, J.: Self-driving Uber kills Arizona woman in first fatal crash involving pedestrian. https://www.theguardian.com/technology/2018/mar/19/uber-self-driving-car-kills-woman-arizona-tempe. Accessed 6 Jan 2022
34. Marshall, A.: The lose-lose ethics of testing self-driving cars in public, Wired. https://www.wired.com/story/lose-lose-ethics-self-driving-public/. Accessed 16 Jan 2022
35. Maurer, T., Hinck, G.: What Is the Cloud? In: Cloud Security: A Primer for Policymakers, Carnegie Endowment for International Peace (2020)
36. Milin-Ashmore, J.: What Is Ethical Hacking and Why Is It Important? https://ethical.net/ethical/what-is-ethical-hacking. Accessed 5 Jan 2022
37. O'Leary, A.: Horrified mum hears chilling man's voice on hacked baby monitor saying child is 'cute', Mirror. https://www.mirror.co.uk/news/world-news/horrified-mum-hears-chilling-mans-24959669. Accessed 3 Feb 2022
38. Osborne, C.: Updated Kaseya ransomware attack FAQ: What we know now, ZDNet. https://www.zdnet.com/article/updated-kaseya-ransomware-attack-faq-what-we-know-now/. Accessed 2 Feb 2022
39. Palmer, D.: 175,000 IoT cameras can be remotely hacked thanks to flaw, says security re- searcher, ZDNet. https://www.zdnet.com/article/175000-iot-cameras-can-be-remotely-hacked-thanks-to-flaw-says-security-researcher/. Accessed 3 Feb 2022
40. Privacy and Information Technology. Stanford Encyclopedia of Philosophy (2019). https://plato.stanford.edu/entries/it-privacy/. Accessed 4 Feb 2022
41. Pyman T.: 'Creepy hacker used baby monitor to SPY on my son': Parents fear restless 15 month-old boy was being woken by 'local man' accessing cot camera after hearing 'deep male voice' at 2.30 am, Mailonline. https://www.dailymail.co.uk/news/article-10287527/Parents-fear-creepy-hacker-used-baby-monitor-spy-son.html. Accessed 3 Feb 2022
42. Redden, M.: Tech company accused of collecting details of how customers use sex toys. The Guardian. https://www.theguardian.com/us-news/2016/sep/14/wevibe-sex-toy-data-collection-chicago-lawsuit. Accessed 16 Jan 2022
43. Right to be informed. https://www.dataprotection.ie/en/individuals/know-your-rights/right-be-informed-transparency-article-13-14-gdpr. Accessed 31 Jan 2022
44. Roberts, P.: Pretty much all consumer internet of things vulnerabilities are avoidable. The Security Ledger. https://securityledger.com/2016/09/pretty-much-all-consumer-internet-of-things-vulnerabilities-are-avoidable/. Accessed 16 Jan 2022
45. Rocchi, M., Murphy, B.: Ethics and cloud computing, data privacy and trust. In: Cloud Computing, pp. 105–128. Palgrave Macmillan, Cham (2020)
46. Ryan, Y.: Anonymousand the Arab uprisings, Al Jazeera. https://www.aljazeera.com/news/2011/5/19/anonymous-and-the-arab-uprisings. Accessed 02 Feb 2022
47. Turilli, M., Floridi, L.: Cloud computing and its ethical challenges. https://dx.doi.org/10.2139/ssrn.3850031. Accessed 24 Feb 2022
48. Turton, W., Mehrotra, K.: Hackers breached colonial pipeline using compromised password, Bloomberg. https://www.bloomberg.com/news/articles/2021-06-04/hackers-breached-colonial-pipeline-using-compromised-password. Accessed 2 Feb 2022

49. Uganda Government websites hacked by anonymous in defense of gay pride: LGBT Rights, Huffpost. https://www.huffpost.com/entry/uganda-government-websites-hacked-ano nymous-gay-rights_n_1789623. Accessed 2 Feb 2022

50. Vida, M.: Anonymous group hack reveals hidden government data about COVID-19 cases in Nicaragua. https://globalvoices.org/2020/08/31/anonymous-group-hack-reveals-hidden-gov ernment-data-about-covid-19-cases-in-nicaragua/. Accessed 22 Feb 2022

51. Western Governors University: Ethical hacking and how it fits with cybersecurity. https://www.wgu.edu/blog/ethical-hacking-how-fits-with-cybersecurity1908.html#close. Accessed 4 Feb 2022

52. White, T., Gutierrez, B.: Protest or Criminal Activities?. The Ethics of Hacktivism. https://taw hite88.wordpress.com/2014/03/24/protest-or-criminal-activities-the-ethics-of-hacktivism/. Accessed 24 Feb 2022

53. Yoo, C.: Centre for international governance, the emerging internet of things: opportunities and challenges for privacy and security. In: Governing Cyberspace During a Crisis in Trust: An Essay Series on the Economic Potential — and Vulnerability — of Transformative Technologies and Cyber Security, Center for International Governance (2019)

54. Zarley, B.: 'White hat hackers are defending hospitals from rising cyber attacks'. Freethink. https://www.freethink.com/technology/cyber-attacks. Accessed 22 Feb 2022

A Discussion on Ethical Cybersecurity Issues in Digital Service Chains

Frédéric Tronnier(✉) , Sebastian Pape , Sascha Löbner ,
and Kai Rannenberg

Goethe University, Frankfurt, Germany
{frederic.tronnier,sebastian.pape,sascha.loebner,
kai.rannenberg}@m-chair.de

Abstract. Enabling cybersecurity and protecting personal data are crucial challenges in the development and provision of digital service chains. Data and information are the key ingredients in the creation process of new digital services and products. While legal and technical problems are frequently discussed in academia, ethical issues of digital service chains and the commercialization of data are seldom investigated. Thus, based on outcomes of the Horizon2020 PANELFIT project, this work discusses current ethical issues related to cybersecurity. Utilizing expert workshops and encounters as well as a scientific literature review, ethical issues are mapped on individual steps of digital service chains. Not surprisingly, the results demonstrate that ethical challenges cannot be resolved in a general way, but need to be discussed individually and with respect to the ethical principles that are violated in the specific step of the service chain. Nevertheless, our results support practitioners by providing and discussing a list of ethical challenges to enable legally compliant as well as ethically acceptable solutions in the future.

Keywords: Data protection · GDPR · Cybersecurity · Ethical issues · Digital service chain

1 Introduction

Information and data, including personal data, are the main drivers of the constantly advancing digitalization and digital economy. In this economy, traditional product and service chains are supplemented and replaced by digital service chains that transform the way products and services are created, processed, distributed and experienced. Products, services and processes are increasingly being connected to create new insights and information from data. With these drivers, ethical and legal issues are arising on the appropriate protection of individuals and their data. While the legislative response in Europe through the General Data Protection Regulation (GDPR) is widely regarded as a major step towards the protection of data subjects and (their) personal data, ethical issues remain. The GDPR

Supported by H2020 Science with and for Society Programme [GRANT AGREEMENT NUMBER – 788039 – PANELFIT].

J. Kołodziej et al. (Eds.): Cybersecurity of Digital Service Chains, LNCS 13300, pp. 222–256, 2022.
https://doi.org/10.1007/978-3-031-04036-8_10

aims to give individuals the control over (their) personal data by laying down a set of rules clarifying how personal data may be used by individuals and organizations. Compliance with data protection regulation does however not automatically equal ethical organizational procedures. With respect to research projects, the European Commission defines this point accurately as: "the fact that your research is legally permissible does not necessarily mean that it will be deemed ethical" [23, p. 4]. We argue that the same holds for the development of products and services in digital service chains where ethical issues are rarely discussed.

Ethical issues concerning data and cybersecurity are often – and rightly so – discussed from the perspective of individuals as they are likely to be the stakeholders suffering from them. However, in this work, we aim to discuss ethical issues from the perspective of both, individuals and organisations, using the framework of digital service chains as a point of reference. As ethical issues arise due to the different needs and interests of various stakeholders, individuals, data subjects, small and multinational organizations as well as states and state agencies, ethical issues need to be discussed with all stakeholders in mind.

The objective of this work is therefore to cluster existing ethical issues with regards to cybersecurity and data commercialization in the different phases or steps of digital service chains. Our objective is not to define the "right decision" for stakeholders in an ethical issue, but rather collect a list of such issues arising in digital service chains. We imagine that service providers in the chain can go through that collection and identify ethical issues, which are relevant to their services, too. To a certain degree, we follow the call from Schoentgen and Wilkinson [77] to expand the ethics debate on recent technologies.

The structure of this work is as follows: In section two related work on digital service chains, cybersecurity, and data commercialization is provided. As there exist numerous ethical issues, we concentrate on the most pressing or timely ones, based on the methodology outlined in the third section. The fourth section discusses ethical issues following the framework of a digital service chain. The results are then discussed in a separate section. The last section concludes this work and identifies opportunities for future work.

2 Background and Related Work

The following subsections provide an introduction to the topics relevant for this work. In the first subsection, the topics of cybersecurity and data protection are established. As multiple ethical issues in digital service chains relate to the selling and purchasing of data, we define the term of data commercialization in the subsequent section before outlining digital service chains themselves. Fundamental ethical principles are then introduced before giving an overview on related work on ethics in cybersecurity in research.

2.1 Cybersecurity and Information Security

Cybersecurity, often also called IT security or ICT security before "cyberspace" became a popular term, refers to the safeguarding of individuals, organizations and society of cyber risks. As computer and information systems are increasingly relied on as the backbone of organizations and the daily working environment of large parts of the workforce, ensuring cybersecurity is a crucial factor for organisations and individuals alike. With the advancement of the internet, new wireless network standards and technologies such as "internet of things", "smart devices" or connected vehicles, the importance of ensuring cybersecurity is only increasing. The primary focus of cybersecurity is often described as the provision of confidentiality, integrity, and availability of data, also called the CIA-triad. In this context, confidentiality aims to prevent data and information from unauthorized access while integrity aims to maintain the accuracy and consistency of data and information in all stages of the processing of the data. Lastly, availability encompasses the consistent accessibility of data and information for all authorized entities. Integrity and availability are then also considered relevant for the systems handling the data. Cybersecurity can be seen as a significant aspect of the broader concept of information security. Information security, the protection of information and data, encompasses both non-technical and technical aspects, whereby cybersecurity solely focuses on the technical aspects of it. For instance, the creation of shredding or recycling procedures of printed information would fall under the domain of information security but does not fall under the domain of cybersecurity. In this work, we address information security in general, as the management of information security includes the management of cybersecurity and offers a more holistic approach to study ethical issues of cybersecurity in digital service chains.

To ensure information security, it is essential to understand the different types of vulnerabilities that can lead to information disclosure or the disruption of services in a system. The International Organization for Standardization (ISO) and the International Electrotechnical Commission (IEC) define a vulnerability in ISO/IEC 27005:2018 as *"weakness of an asset or control (3.1.12) that can be exploited so that an event with a negative consequence occurs"* [25].

Such vulnerabilities were classified in ISO/IEC 27005 into their related asset types: hardware, software, network, personnel, physical site and organizational site. Here, vulnerabilities may not only be caused by insecure or unprotected hardware or software but also by the susceptibility of external factors such as humidity for hardware, natural disasters for a physical site or a lack of security training for personnel. A wide range of causes for vulnerabilities exist that need to be individually evaluated [84]. As the definition of a vulnerability also relates the concept of threats, it is necessary to define a threat in the context of information security. According to the European Union Agency For Cybersecurity (ENISA), a threat may be defined as: *"Any circumstance or event with the potential to adversely impact an asset through unauthorized access, destruction, disclosure, modification of data, and/or denial of service"* [19]. A plethora of different threats exists for which various possible classification schemes exist[1].

---

[1] For an overview of threat types, see the threat classification model of the Horizon2022 CyberSANE project: https://www.cybersane-project.eu/taxonomy-of-threat-landscape/.

2.2   Data Commercialization

According to the European Commission, in 2019, *"the value of the European Data Market is expected to reach 77.8 billion Euro, with a growth rate of 97% in 2018, and at an average rate of 4.2% out to 2020"* [58, p. 67][2] In 2025, *"...the Data Market will amount to more than 82 billion Euro in the EU27, against 60.3 billion Euro in 2018 (a 6.5% CAGR 2020–2025)..."* [58, p. 41]. The same estimate predicts that, if policy and legal framework conditions for the data economy are put in place in time, its value will increase to EUR 680 billion by 2025 for the EU28 (550 billion for the EU27), representing 4.2% (4.0%) of the overall EU GDP for a baseline scenario. Still, the term 'data commercialisation' is one that causes diverging reactions among different stakeholders in the environment of data protection and ICT research. While some people regard it as a reality that is indeed lawful - whether commercially and/or socially desirable or not -, others assess it to be unlawful, unethical and unacceptable for personal data in general. This could be explained by the fact that there does not exist one generally approved definition of the term. As the lawfulness of commercialising and processing data highly depends on its specification, it is crucial to define the context first. Hereby, one should differentiate between:

- The type of data, that is either personal or non-personal data [14, p. 4–5];
- The amount of data, that is either multiple data records in a database or individual data records;
- The source of the data, that is either collected by the data controller, by a third party or publicly available data;
- The form of commercialisation, that is the licensing or granting access of data.

In order to discuss ethical considerations on this subject in the context of this work, the commercialization of data is defined as: the processing of personal data as regulated under the GDPR, in the form of licensing by granting third parties access to collected personal data for a monetary profit. While it is assumed that personal data possesses economic value that may be transferred between parties, the specifics of the commercialisation of data however may differ, depending on the licensor, licensee and the purpose of the data.

Ethical Considerations on Data Commercialization: The commercialisation of data does not only create issues and gaps through unclear or missing regulation but also needs to be reviewed from an ethical perspective. The European Commission states in a non-guiding document on Ethics and Data Protection (2018) for researchers that: *"...the fact that your research is legally permissible does not necessarily mean that it will be deemed ethical"*. So also ethical requirements need to be met for the commercialisation of data. The GDPR already encompasses some ethical aspects such as transparency and accountability in the relations between data subjects, data controllers, and data processors. The GDPR also aims to foster the societal interest to protect data and ensure privacy, for instance in Art.

---

[2] Disaggregated data can be found at The European Data Market Monitoring Tool: http://datalandscape.eu/european-data-market-monitoring-tool-2018.

57(1)(b), stating that public authorities must "promote public awareness" on the aspects of data processing. Moreover human dignity and personal autonomy are moral values, covered by constitutions and laws that need to be respected through the protection of data, also when data is being commercialised.

However, several ethical issues and questions arise when looking at the commercialisation of data, as defined in this document. Should it be possible to renounce fundamental rights to allow for data altruism? How can data indeed be ethically commercialised if the ownership of data is not defined? Unless an established pricing mechanism for personal data is developed, fair data markets that ensure an adequate remuneration of individuals relinquishing their personal data are unlikely to occur. As long as privacy is not transparently priced, individuals are not aware of the value of their personal data, do not know whether they are getting a fair deal if they accept to monetise their data, and remain unaware of their market power. This demonstrates that legal and ethical issues are closely connected and that the commercialisation of data needs to be reviewed with both, ethical and legal issues in mind.

2.3   Digital Service Chains

The book "Service Chain Management" by [86] provides a comprehensive introduction to the topic and defines the sub-category of digital service chains. The authors state that digital service chains "depend on the digital transportation and processing of information from "raw" inputs to "finished" outputs delivered over bandwidth-rich computer networks to a variety of computationally powerful consumer devices" [86]. Digital service chains are therefore comparable to traditional service chains and consist of the steps outlined in Table 1.

Table 1. Examplary digital service chains, adapted from [86]

Content creation	Aggregation	Distribution	Data transport	Digital experience
Software	Software suites	J2EE, .Net, Application servers	Cables, Wireless	Terminals and mobile devices
Advertising	Combining personal data	Ad-networks	Cables, Wireless	Terminals and mobile devices

The first step, Content Creation, is defined as a process through which software, music, art or other services are created. While [86] defines this step as an intense human process, we argue that this step could also take place automatically, given the emergence of new technologies and services that allow the creation of other goods and services without the need of a human. Examples of this are ML/AI algorithms that can create music, texts, or software on their own [31,61].

In the second step, Aggregation, data and information are aggregated from different sources, for instance from multiple data subjects or platforms. In the third step, Distribution, the data is placed on a suitable platform, using a distribution system, to be delivered to the respective users or customers. This could for instance be advertising servers at a social media organization or application servers for a software solution. In the fourth step, Data Transport, the data is transported to users or customers using fixed or wireless network solutions. Lastly and in the fifth step, Digital Experience, the service or product is experienced by customers or users, using mobile or stationary devices.

Digital service chains have been researched extensively from a technological perspective [20] and also with respect to cybersecurity. Repetto et al. [74] argue that traditional security models are not suitable anymore for increasingly agile service chains and develop a reference architecture to manage cybersecurity in digital service chains. Concrete use cases of such a framework are detailed in [75]. However, in both articles, there is no consideration of how to ensure that the deployed services consider potential ethical issues.

2.4   Ethics in Cybersecurity

When discussing ethical issues relating to cybersecurity and the commercialization of data, ethical issues need to be discussed first. Vallor et al. [85] argue that "ethical issues are at the core of cybersecurity practices" as they retain "the ability of human individuals and groups to live well". Research on ethics in cybersecurity has been an emerging topic [67] with a particular focus on ethics in cybersecurity in the context of AI [82]. Manjikian [55] provides an comprehensive introduction to the topic. A variety of ethical frameworks and approaches towards ethics in cybersecurity exists. Formosa et al. [28] distinguish the existing approaches into two categories:

- The first category applies moral theories such as utilitarianism, consequentialism, deontological, and virtue ethics. The authors state that this approach may lead to conflicting results, depending on the moral or ethical theory applied.
- The objective of the second category is "to develop a cluster of mid-level ethical principles for cybersecurity contexts" [28].

Based on the shortcomings of existing approaches, the authors develop a new framework, depicted in Fig. 1. The ethical principles depicted in Fig. 1 will be utilized when discussing the ethical issues relating to digital service chains identified in this work.

In the following sections the framework will be used as a point of reference on which ethical issues in digital service chains and with regard to the commercialization of data are to be clustered upon. The five basic principles of cybersecurity ethics, adapted from [28] are the following:

- **Non-maleficence:** The technologies, services, and products envisioned and implemented in the digital service chains do not to intentionally harm users or make their lives worse.
- **Beneficence:** The technologies, services and products envisioned and implemented in the digital service chains should be beneficial for humans, that is, improve users overall live.

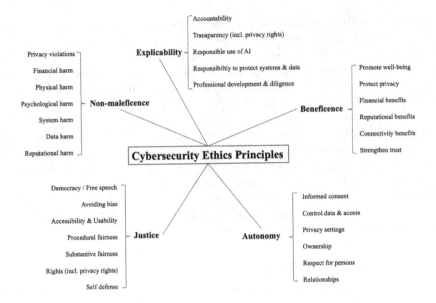

Fig. 1. Five cybersecurity ethics principles adopted from Formosa et al. [28]

- **Autonomy:** The technologies, services and products envisioned and implemented in the digital service chains should retain users' autonomy. That is, users are able to make informed decisions on how these services and products impact their lives and how they may use them.
- **Justice:** The technologies, services, and products envisioned and implemented in the digital service chains should not discriminate or undermine solidarity between users. Instead, fairness and equality are to be promoted.
- **Explicability:** The technologies, services, and products envisioned and implemented in the digital service chains are to be transparent. Users are to be able to understand them and know which entities are responsible and accountable for them.

2.5 Related Work

While a plethora of research on technology-related ethical issues exists, research on ethics in cybersecurity and digital service chains is less omnipresent.

Ethical issues in cybersecurity are often studied in the domain of academic research, in which ethical standards are to be met by researchers when working with data. Macnish and van der Ham [51] investigate different ethical issues and discuss the difference between ethical issues in research and practice using two case studies. The authors find that researchers are able to draw on feedback from research ethics committees, an option that is not available to practitioners. The authors advocate for a stronger focus and discussions on ethical topics in computer science courses. The book of Manjikian [55] provides an extensive introduction into the topic of cybersecurity ethics. The author introduces several concepts and ethical frameworks and applies them to multiple issues in cybersecurity, such as data piracy and military cybersecurity. Finally, the author discusses codes of ethics for cybersecurity. While the author follows a comparable approach to this work, the ethical issues discussed in this work were identified through a different structure, expert workshops and encounters, and take place in a particular setting, the focus on digital service chains and the commercialization of data.

Similarly, the interdisciplinary book of Christen et al. [13] discusses various topics of ethics in cybersecurity. Here, van de Poel [72] analyses values and value conflicts in cybersecurity ethics, clustering them into security, privacy, fairness and accountability. The author identifies and discusses several value conflicts, not only between security and privacy, but also between privacy and fairness or accountability. The chapter of Loi and Christen [50] discusses several ethical frameworks for cybersecurity and creates a first methodology for the assessment of ethical issues. The methodology follows the privacy framework of Nissenbaum [68] that views privacy as contextual integrity and extends it with "social norms and expectations affecting all human interactions that are constitutive of an established social practice" [50]. When discussing ethical issues in the context of business, the book focuses more on specific domains, such as healthcare, or on ensuring cybersecurity for businesses (see [59,80]).

Mason [56] discusses policy for personal data as an overarching framework in a socio-technical system. He focuses on respect for persons and the maintenance of individual dignity. In the same manner, Nabbosa and Kaar [63] investigate ethical issues of digitalization with a strong focus on the economics of personal data. They conclude that user's awareness to data privacy needs to be strengthened and the control over the data needs to be shifted back to the users, but this cannot be done by regulation alone and all shareholders should take responsibility. Schoentgen and Wilkinson [77] present several ethical frameworks and investigate the implementation of ethics by governments and companies. Royakkers et al. [76] focus on ethical issues emerging from the Internet of Things, robotics, biometrics, persuasive technology, platforms, and augmented and virtual reality. They connect the presented ethical issues with values set out in international treaties and fundamental rights.

Hagendorff [33] analyzes 22 guidelines for ethical artificial intelligence and also investigates to what extent these were implemented in practice. His conclusion is that artificial intelligence ethics are failing in many cases. Mostly, because there are neither consequences for a company not following the guidelines nor for the individual developer not implementing them when developing a new service.

However, none of this work has a specific focus on the digital service chains and maps the ethical challenges to its corresponding phases.

3   Methodology

The methodology of this work is based on a two-step approach. Starting point for the identification and analysis of ethical, and also legal, issues was a workshop with four legal and four industry experts from Spain, Finland, England, the Netherlands, Germany, and France, which took place on 3 June 2019 in Bilbao, Spain. The workshop, corresponding to work-package 3 of the Horizon2020 PANELFIT project[3], was structured into four sessions:

- Ownership of Data
- Usage of External Databases
- Monetising Internal Databases
- Good Commercialisation Governance

Each of the experts was asked to give a short presentation on one of the topics, followed by a discussion with all attendees (experts and present projects partners). Based on the results of the workshop, several attendants have also produced academic papers on the commercialisation of data, leading to a special issue in the European Review of Private Law.[4] While the workshop focused primarily on legal issues and gaps in the GDPR relating to the commercialization of data, the workshop also raised first ethical issues that have been subsequently expanded on in a second workshop on 28th of June 2021 in an online event. Similarly, the workshop was structured into four sessions:

1. Data Altruism
2. The value of data
3. A pricing mechanism for data
4. Data as payment for a service

Again, experts on ethics and information privacy were asked to give short presentations on the topics, whereby the topics were first chosen by a larger set of experts on ethics, chosen by the PANELFIT project consortium, via mail correspondence, based on their topicality and priority. Based on the conducted workshops, the previously mentioned topics that relate to ethical consideration on the commercialization of data are discussed in this work. Two additional workshops, following the same structure as outlined above, were held regarding ethical and legal issues of cybersecurity specifically, corresponding to work-package 4 of the PANELFIT project.

In a second step, a literature review was conducted on ethics in cybersecurity and digital service chains in particular to elaborate further on the issues identified through the workshops and encounters. The objective was twofold. Firstly, to identify possible ethical issues that were not voiced, or not of concern, in the workshops and encounters. Secondly, to analyze the previously identified issues in detail and in particular in the context of digital service chains.

---

[3] The PANELFIT project (Participatory Approaches to a New Ethical and Legal Framework for ICT) aims to reduce ethical and legal issues with regards to the European data protection regulation. To this end, the project develops openly accessible guidelines that help stakeholders overcome such issues in various areas, including the processing of data in ICT and the provision of cybersecurity. PANELFIT is a related project of GUARD.

[4] Volume 29, Issue 5 (p. 699–830), 2021 of the European Review of Private Law. kluwerlawonline.com/journalIssue/European+Review+of+Private+Law/29.5/19933.

4   Ethical Issues

The following section provides a discussion on the ethical issues that have been identified through the methodology defined in the prior section. All ethical issues are structured into the five steps of a digital value chain. Ethical issues are furthermore structured to firstly provide the context of the issue. Next, the ethical issues itself is defined and, where applicable, examples are provided. Lastly, a risk assessment and the possible impact are discussed in detail.

4.1   Content Creation

Overall, this section is structured using the CRISP-DM framework [90]. Regarding the business understanding we start by discussing the ethical issue of different definitions of fairness that were provided by a variety of machine learning researches. Then we discuss the issue of data altruism for data acquisition. Regarding data understanding we investigate examples for common biases that can occur and should be solved in the phase of data preparation.

Selecting the "Right" Definition for Fairness

Context: It is obvious that a user will expect a fair design of an AI model. But how to achieve such a fair model is not an easy task for the developers as fairness is not clearly defined and may differ between users, developers and the context of a service. In this paragraph we will have a closer look on different fairness definitions and the problem of selecting the "right" definition for fairness.

Ethical Issues: Although the GDPR states in Article 5 and 14 that personal data should be processed lawfully, transparent and fairly, a clear definition of fairness is not trivial. Malgieri [53] argue that fairness is a substantial balancing of the interested parties that are predominantly data controllers and data subjects. They further declare that fairness is separated from lawfulness and transparency by not being a legal construct. In their opinion, fairness aims to mitigate situations of unfair imbalances, the data subject feels vulnerable.

Kusner et al. [45] declare that the classic fairness criteria such as demographic fairness or statistical parity are limited because they ignore the discrimination of subgroups or the individual level. Therefore, Kusner et al. [45] introduce the principle of counterfactual fairness that is achieved when individuals and their structural counterfactual part are equally treated.

Zafar et al. [91] introduce another definition of fairness that is based on the principles of disparate treatment[5] and disparate impact[6]. They line out that maximizing fairness under accuracy constraints is a major issue when designing AI applications. Especially if the sensitive attribute in the training set is very high this can lead to unacceptable performance with regard to the business objectives.

---

[5] Disparate treatment: A decision making process, e.g. a classification suffers if it is built on a subject's sensitive attributes [4].

[6] Disparate impact: A decision making process suffers if subgroups with certain sensitive attributes are hurt [4].

Example: A well known example for the problem of choosing the right definition of fairness is the discussion about the risk assessment tool Correctional Offender Management Profiling for Alternative Sanctions (COMPAS) that predicts the risk of a defendant committing a misdemeanor or felony within 2 years, from 2016. In a detailed analysis the investigative news organization ProPublica claimed the model to be unfair as under their definition of fairness the model was found to be biased against black citizens [2]. On the opposite side, the developing company Northpoint argued that their definition of fairness holds including more standard definitions of fairness [17, 21].

Risk Assessment and Discussion: While we have included only a limited selection of fairness definitions, this already demonstrates that there is not one ethically correct definition of fairness. In general, two different types of fairness can be identified, that are the fairness of a group and the fairness of individuals and subgroups. While Zafar et al. [91] show one way to weight these definitions, Selbst et al. [79] argue that a social concept such as fairness cannot be resolved by mathematical definitions because fairness is procedural, contextual and contestable. Moreover, also Mehrabi et al. [57] provide a taxonomy for fairness to avoid bias in AI systems. Finally, this argumentation shows that whether an algorithm is fair or not can barely be assessed by a programmer alone and will always require a diverse team as controlling instance, defining a definition that fits the specific requirements of the service and its users.

Data Altruism

Context: During multiple encounters and workshops, the notion of data altruism was raised as a pressing issue that needs consideration when discussing the commercialization of data. Data altruism refers to the instances in which data is voluntarily made available for organizations or individuals to (re)use without compensation. Such instances may be for the common good, for scientific research or the improvement of public services, as stated in the proposal for the European Data Governance Act (DGA) [1]. Data altruism is related to the concept of data solidarity and particularly crucial for clinical, health and biomedical research as such research is in need of large amounts of data. Citizens are increasingly generating data that might prove valuable for researchers and public institutions.

Ethical Issues: It is presently unclear how to ensure ethical conduct when defining data altruism in the context of the commercialization of data. This issue is particularly intervened with the legal challenge of ensuring consistency between legislation of the GDPR and the DGA.

Example: Data altruism may occur in the content creation phase of digital service chains and is particularly connected to health and biomedical data. Private individuals consent to the processing of their health data for research or medical purposes. An ethical issue arises know if the controller of the data decides to re-purpose the data for new processing activities by giving other, commercial entities access to the data. These new controllers use the data to create services that are sold to other organizations or individuals for a monetary profit. While the re-purposing of the data does compulsorily needs a legal basis, such as consent from the data subject, the question remains whether commercial entities should profit of data altruism in the first place.

Risk Assessment and Discussion: In the DGA, data altruism is referred to as the reuse of data without compensation for "purposes of general interest, such as scientific research purposes or improving public services" [1]. The DGA does not only regulate data altruism and the free reuse of data but also the sharing of data among businesses, "...against remuneration in any form" [1], emphasizing its relationship with the commercialization of data.

Several initiatives and proposals are aiming at fostering data altruism by providing a legal framework on the matter. Individual countries like Denmark are currently studying the introducing of safe spaces to store citizen generated data that can later be used for research [16, p. 86]. In Germany, the draft legislation for the Patient Data Protection Act encompasses the notion of a "data donation" through which patients may consent to the free use of their data. Data is then to be stored in an electronic patient record that is available for research [9]. On a European level, THEDAS, the Joint Action Towards the European Health Data Space aims at promoting the concept of secondary use of health data to benefit public health and research in Europe.[7]

In a joint opinion on the proposal for the DGA, the EDPB and the EDPS emphasize the importance of consistency between the GDPR and other regulation such as the DGA and address the main criticalities of the proposal [24]. It can be seen that especially some elements of the DGA require further clarification in order to foster data altruism while ensuring consistency with the GDPR and ethical conduct. The first element refers to the European data altruism consent form as introduced in Art. 22 DGA. It is advised that the European Commission adopts a modular consent form through which data subjects are able to give and withdraw consent for the processing of personal data for data altruism purposes. Here, the EDPB and EDPS argue that:

"In particular, it is unclear whether the consent envisaged in the Proposal corresponds to the notion of "consent" under the GDPR, including the conditions for the lawfulness of such consent. In addition, it is unclear the added value of 'data altruism', taking into account the already existing legal framework for consent under the GDPR, which provides for specific conditions for the validity of consent" [24].

Furthermore, the GDPR does not allow a data subject to renounce one's rights, even if the data subject might be willing to do so, for instance for research in the public interest. Informed consent, public and legitimate interest remain the legal bases of choice for such instances, creating a collision between the concept of data altruism in the DGA and the GDPR. Individuals might be willing to "offer"

---

[7] See Joint Action Towards the European Health Data Space – TEHDAS Available under: https://tehdas.eu.

personal data for research even if they do not know exactly how, and how much of, the data will be used, for what specific purposes and by which entity. The GDPR does not allow for such a general consent, for this level of data altruism. Thus, it is not clear whether the concept of consent in the DGA acts as a lawful basis for the processing of personal data or as an extra safeguard that is to be combined with the existing legal basis for the processing for public interest. Similarly, the notions of processing of data for the general interest, as introduced in the DGA, and public interest, in the GDPR, need to be harmonized. Lastly, the DGA introduces "Data Altruism Organizations registered in the Union". Such legal entities should be enabled to gain access to personal data to support purposes of general interest. However, more information need to be provided on the specifics of such organizations. Would these organizations act as controller or processor? What is the legal status of them and should they be allowed to charge a fee for their service? Should they be allowed to share the data with other entities? These issues and open questions could provide an opportunity to more clearly define the objectives of data altruism and its differentiation from the current processing for public interest. Additionally, this provides an opportunity to harmonize the different approaches towards consent that also relate to the role of the individual in the concept of data altruism.

Bias in Training Data for AI

Context: As also reflected in Fig. 1 and elaborated upon by Hagendorff [33] two of the most pressing ethical issues in machine learning are fairness and non-discrimination in data processing.

Ethical Issue: Goodman and Flaxman [30] define the right to non-discrimination as the absence of unfair treatment of a natural person based on the belonging to a specific group, such as a religion, gender or race. Thus, in their opinion, society exhibits exclusion, discrimination and inequality per definition, so a sufficient preparation of data is a crucial step when designing non-discriminatory AI [8]. In the following, we will have a closer look at the issues caused by insufficient data preparation and data bias.

Example Gender Bias: On of the most frequently mentioned issues with regard to discriminatory and unfair AI is the gender bias. For instance, Madgavkar [52] report about the google translator service where sentences from gender-neutral languages like Farsi or Turkish result in gender stereotypical translations. They provide the example that "This person is president, and this person is cooking" will result in "He's president and she's cooking". This shows very well a bias in the training data resulting in a not gender neutral translation. The bias in such AI reflecting the values of the society and/or its creators [18]. Leavy [47] identified five reasons for gender bias in language and text that are naming, ordering, biased descriptions, metaphors and presence of women in text. For example, she summarizes that the male is always named first when pairs of each gender are named resulting in a social order bias [60]. Moreover, men are more often described based on their behavior while women are described based on their sexuality and external appearance. This will result in a bias of adjectives when used for AI training [10]. A methodology on how to maintain desired associations while removing gender stereotypes is provided by Bolukbasi et al. [7].

Example Ethical Affiliation Bias: Closely related and as frequently discussed as gender bias are ethical affiliation bias. One of the most prominent examples is Microsoft's AI chat bot Tay. After learning from tweets of other users, Tay was shut down after one day because of "obscene and inflammatory tweets" [65]. Finally, Tay mirrored the racism that was picked up from the users. Neff and Nagy [65] also stress that the case of Tay shows very well how not only programmers but also users can assign agency and personality to AI. This example very well clarifies that not only a robust design but also monitoring over the whole life-cycle is required.

Example Uncertainty Bias: Another bias to be considered is the uncertainty bias. In their example of loan payment prediction, Goodman and Flaxman [30] illustrate that a simple under-representation of a group below a certain value will lead to a systematic discrimination in risk avers AI applications. Moreover, they declare that while for geography and income such bias might be easy to detect, more complex correlations such as between race and IP addresses it might not.

Example Indirect Bias: Although a sensitive attribute is not in the dataset, the above mentioned biases can still be indirectly correlated to other attributes. A prominent example for this is the criminal risk assessment tool COMPAS that predicts the risk that a defendant commits a misdemeanor or felony within 2 years. Although no attributes about race were in the data, the algorithm was found to be racial biased [2,21].

Risk Assessment and Discussion: The observed examples demonstrate that biases in data can have manifold reasons and are therefore not always easy to detect. A careful data preparation and problem analysis is therefore key when developing an AI application. However, in specific circumstances, as with the example of the chat bot Tay, the data bias evolves over time. In such cases, only the constant monitoring of the AI's behavior can spot data bias issues. Finally, as already stated by Hall and Gill [34] the key countermeasures to spot and prevent data bias are interpretability, accountability and transparency which goes hand in hand with the results from the Commission et al. [15]. Although these countermeasures aim to avoid bias in data, Caliskan et al. [11] argue that such debiasing is just a "fairness through blindness" [11] what gives the AI an incomplete understanding of the world. They argue that the AI will suffer from debiasing in meaning and accuracy. In their opinion, long-term interdisciplinary research is required to enable AI to understand behavior different from its implicit biases.

Model Reflecting Reality

Context: To evaluate a model, a variety of methods exist to spot different unintentional behavior. But how to define unintentional behavior and how to test it is still a decision often made by a small group of developing experts.

Ethical Issue: Leavy [47] argue that e.g., the problem of gender bias was identified and is in most cases addressed by women. While developers are overwhelmingly male, this can cause a restricted view on the reality. Moreover, she argues that diversity in the area of AI is important because it improves the assessment of training data, incorporation of fairness and assessment of potential bias.

Example: A straightforward example for a developer diversity issue was reported by Dailymail [46] in 2017. A soap dispenser did not recognise hands of people with dark skin so for them no soap was released. One reason for this issue could be an ethical affiliation bias with only white hands in the training data. The problem seems to be obvious and one would expect it to be detected latest during the testing but it was not. In this case, the problem could have been easily avoided if the development team had been more diverse and would have considered different skin colors from the beginning.

Risk Assessment and Discussion: Although we do not want to play down the ethical affiliation bias in the soap dispenser example, its consequences are only annoying. For example, people loose their jobs such as when Uber driver's cares were locked because the face recognition algorithm had problems to identify black and Asian people [5]. Having similar issues in privacy and security areas might raise serious security risks. But also with a diverse team of developers, the question when to know that the dataset is complete is not easy to answer. Löbner et al. [48] argue that a transparent development, providing interpretability in each step of model design can help do identify unfair treatment in the model itself. Finally, this issue relates to the issue of quality control and the degree of investment for quality, which is competing with requirements like saving resources and time-to-market.

4.2   Aggregation

In the second step of digital service chains, data and information from different sources, such as multiple data subjects or organizations, are aggregated. In this step, the trade-off between data anonymization and data quality was identified as an ethical issue.

Anonymization vs. Data Quality

Context: Personal data requires the data controller to get the persons' consent to process their data in most circumstances. This also holds if the data allows to link it without disproportionate effort to the person. Since it is not possible or often not desired to request each person's consent, data sets are anonymized respectively de-identified. For a proper anonymization it is often not sufficient to just delete a person's name or identifier (cf. Sweeney [81]). Thus, other data fields need to be changed to prevent a re-identification of the respective person. Moreover, numbers might need to be truncated, rounded or noise is added, other data fields might be masked, scrambled or blurred.

Ethical Issue: When changing the data to anonymize it, it might prevent that the data is used for the desired purpose or might lead to false results. Therefore, a trade-off between privacy of the persons in the data set and the precision of the calculations on the data set emerges [29]. One major problem in this trade-off is that for cases where it is easier to identify people because the anonymity set is (too) small, changes to protect the persons' identity will have a large impact on the data quality. On the other hand, when changes to guarantee the persons' identity will have only minor impact to the data quality, then often the privacy of the persons is already in good shape, e.g. because the number data in the data set is already huge and it would be hard to identify specific persons.

Example: Collecting data for security purposes might cause privacy problems if the persons are identifiable. This is in particular the case for intrusion detection systems (cf. [66]) or mobile trajectories of persons which might be used for research or urban planning in smart cities (cf. [88]).

Risk Assessment and Discussion: The trade-off between the persons' privacy and the goal of the data evaluation needs to be done by the person setting up the system. Depending on the system's goal, beneficence (of the user) may be in opposition to non-maleficence (if a user suffers any kind of harm from the miscalculations due to the anonymization of the data) or explicability (if systems can not be protected sufficiently). On the other hand, if the users are pushed to give their consent – perhaps with the argument that if they don't provide their data they would put someone at risk – their autonomy is endangered. As a further observation, we can conclude that this is in particular an issue for small data sets: Small data sets increase the likelihood that someone can be identified while changes within the data set to anonymize participants will have a more significant effect on the data. When the data set is large, it can be considered to be more difficult to extract data on a specific subject and on the other hand, changes will in general have a smaller affect on the quality of the data set.

4.3 Distribution

The third step of a digital service chain relates to the distribution of a service on a suitable system such as a dedicated server for a software solution. Data that is placed on such a solution might not be available for all entities, leading to power asymmetries in the distribution phase.

Power Asymmetries

Context: Data and the information and insights that can be gathered from it are not equally distributed. While individuals typically have only access to personal data that relate to themselves, organizations gather data to create or improve their products and services. Depending on the business model and the size of the organization, the amount of data that an organization possesses differs greatly. For instance, with the rise of "Big Tech", multinational organizations such as Google, Meta, Amazon or Alibaba did not only gain tremendous financial power, but also access to a wealth of data from their customers. Indeed, excessive gathering data is seen as a major business model in "surveillance capitalism" [92] in which a power asymmetry is created between different entities. Network effects only increase the amount of data and the market power of these organizations as "knowledge is power" Bacon [3]. These factors lead to the development of natural monopolies in which one organization maintains control over the wealth of information. This market power then allows organizations to distribute information and services to their own choosing, with little oversight by regulators.

Ethical Issue: Power asymmetry can manifest itself in different forms, from the asymmetric amount of data to an asymmetric distribution and access of data. More precisely, organizations may have more data at their disposal than others and are free to distribute the data to their liking. This results in different ethical issues, from competitive advantages between organizations to questions of autonomy and sovereignty for individuals and organizations alike.

Example: An example of power asymmetry are social media networks whose business model relies on the gathering of data to attracts advertisers to their platforms. The more data on its users a social network possesses, the higher the value for its advertisers. The social network is free to distribute "its" information to the advertisers of choice, while individuals do not know based on what decisions and algorithms advertising is shown to them and to others. The GDPR and other data protection regulation aim to overcome this loss of autonomy by obliging organizations to make the processes behind such distribution of data transparent. Nonetheless, the sharing of data remains problematic as organizations might be pressured from governments or agencies to share the data, or distribute the data their choosing. Similarly, this issue enables industrial espionage if organizations obtain data of their competitors through agencies or other means of "involuntary" sharing of data.

Risk Assessment and Discussion: It can be seen that the sharing of data naturally poses the risk of a loss of autonomy or digital sovereignty. While this risk might be small in cases where entities retain a balance of power, it increases with power and information asymmetry. Especially individuals and smaller organizations cannot be certain that large, multinational organizations process personal data lawfully. Given this risk, organizations and individuals might be inclined to not share their data anymore, stop using certain services or stop working with particular organizations or states with which they feel a power asymmetry exists. Another consequence might be the emergence of the "chilling-effect", whereby individuals start to behave in conformity with behavior they feel are expected from them, as they feel they are being under constant surveillance [12]. This demonstrates that multiple ethics principles in cybersecurity, namely nonmaleficence, explicability, justice and autonomy are endangered. While regulation such as the GDPR rightfully intends to put an end to the unlawful processing of personal data that is the consequence of information asymmetry, this asymmetry itself continuous to remain as organizations continue to hold and gather ever more data. Multiple measures that could and should be combined exist, that provide starting points to mitigate this issue. Regulators and governments should aim to foster competition by strengthening the role of smaller organizations, decreasing lock-in effects and breaking up monopolies, to rectify power asymmetry between organizations in general. European Competitors and a European data ecosystem should be fostered to promote the fair and ethically compliant use of personal data, communicating such usage as a competitive advantage to end-users. Continuous power asymmetries should be transparently communicated to increase trust. A first step in this direction might be the introduction of legislation comparable to the "Freedom of Information Act" in Germany which enables citizens to request information in possession of German authorities [42]. Nonetheless, such measures will ultimately rely on individuals trust in the lawful application of such regulation as well as in the authorities and organizations themselves.

4.4 Data Transport

The original definition of data transport by Voudouris [86] refers to the transport of data through satellite or terrestrial broadcasting such as cables. The ethical issues identified in this step demonstrate that individuals as well as whole regions or countries might be cut off from services or each other through means that were originally introduced to safely protect data during the transport phase.

Restriction of Data Transport

Context: The internet was designed to allow people to peacefully collaborate with each other. However, as the internet matured and gained widespread adoption, criminals, or nation states who attack users to enrich themselves financially or to spy on the users entered the ecosystem. As a consequence firewalls and filters were developed and set up with the aim to block attacks and protect individuals and organizations alike.

Ethical Issue: Firewalls and filters can not only be used to secure a network, but also to lock up users. This can either be done nation wide to suppress opinions or information, or to lock users up in a certain business model, e.g. by not counting certain traffic. Thus, a technology which was designed to protect networks and manage and shape traffic, can be used against the users of the network.

Example: The Great Firewall of China [89] is an example where users free speech and accessibility of information is limited (Justice) by restricting access to services, to the disadvantage of the users. Zero-Rating [62] is an example where the company aims to improve their financial benefits (Beneficience) by nudging users' to use or not use certain services.

User Empowerment

Context: In many contexts the users shall be empowered to enforce their rights, e.g. to protect their privacy or take informed decisions. This has also been the objective of the introduction of the GDPR in Europe. This empowerment may simply go together with changing some settings or even using specific software or services such as anonymization services.

Ethical Issue: Companies may shift tasks to the responsibility of the user. For instance, instead of offering privacy friendly services, they refer to tools, plugins, etc. the user can install. Sometimes these tools come with disadvantages or perceived disadvantages for the user.

Example: Users of the anonymization service Tor[8] hesitate to use the service since they are afraid that this could make them look suspicious, and they will therefore be observed by secret services or the police [41]. These concerns effectively prevent users from using services that let them manage their data privacy preferences.

Risk Assessment and Discussion: Ethical principles concerned are the users' right of self defence and privacy (Justice), the users' informed consent, privacy settings (Autonomy) versus the users' trust in the company and the users' well being (Beneficence) since taking responsibility and getting information can be a burden to the users.

4.5   Digital Experience

In the last step of a digital service chain, the service, that has been created in the prior steps, is experienced by the users. As these services largely rely on personal data of data subjects, the identified ethical issues relate to the value of the data. This includes how to ethically price the data and how to value services that were obtained through the combination of data. Lastly, the ethical implications of paying with personal data for services are discussed.

The Value of Data - Inferences

Context: Privacy, and the protection of personal data, constitute a fundamental human right, recognized in the UN Declaration of Human Rights [64, Art. 12], accentuating the enormous qualitative value typically assigned to personal data. However, no legislation so far offers distinct guidance on how best to determine the monetary value of data. Data subjects are often unaware of the value of

---

[8] https://www.torproject.org/.

personal data in general as there exist no established pricing mechanism for data. While data subjects might possess a feeling of ownership of personal data that relates to them specifically, the true value of data is not derived from a single data point alone. Oftentimes, data is gaining in value through the combination of personal and non-personal data and the inferences that can be drawn from the data [87]. The value of the collected data is not known at the time of the collection of it, but rather after it has been processed, that is after it was combined and analysed. Technologies such as machine learning, artificial intelligence and big data analytics create new opportunities to draw inferences from personal data, collected from numerous data sources. The value of data therefore varies greatly, not only in the type of data that is gathered but also in the amount of data and the combination of data from different sources.

Ethical Issue and Example: Wachter and Mittelstadt [87] argue that, depending on the definition used, such inferences can be regarded as personal data and should be protected more strongly than it is the case at the moment. For instance, an organization might use an algorithm that creates inferences, out of gathered data, about a specific person: *"Person X is not a reliable borrower as there is a high probability that X has an undiagnosed medical condition."* Such sensitive information surprisingly receive only very limited protection under the GDPR, constituting to both a legal and ethical issue. Inferences can be seen as "new" data, created through the combination of (personal) data of different types and sources. Inferences can also be targeted at de-identified data [49,73] when combining the existing data set with another set to re-identify users. The ethical issue is now how these inferences should be treated under consideration of all circumstances, that is the different entities, creator, data subjects, involved, the type of data as well as its purpose and processing.

Risk Assessment: Art. 15 GDPR, the right of access, grants data subjects the right for confirmation whether personal data regarding the data subject was used by a controller. Data subjects also have the right to obtain a copy of the specific data used for a type of processing. However, a data subject might be denied a copy of inferences drawn about the data subject if they constitute a trade secret or an intellectual property in the Trade Secrets Directive [71] as is likely the case with customer data, preferences and predictions. Thus, the right of access is limited with regards to inferences even if they are seen as personal data. A similar problem can be observed with the right to data portability that only applies to data "provided by" the data subject, which is not the case with inferences. Similarly, Art. 16 GDPR, the right to rectification and Art. 17 GDPR, right to erasure are not tailored towards inferences and therefore not directly applicable for this type of data[9]. This issue poses the ethical questions whether the type of personal data that provides an organization with the most value should solely be under control of the controller. Although inferences are created

---

[9] See the Joined Cases C-141/12 and C-372/12 and Case C-434/16 by the European Court of Justice.

by the controller, the base of the processing are personal data from a data subject that is often not aware of this increase in economic value in the data. A first step towards an ethical solution to this problem might there-fore be a "right to reasonable interference" [87]. Such a right could enable data subjects to challenge unreasonable inferences and would require controllers to ex-ante disclose why certain sensitive types of data are acceptable for inferences, why the inferences are necessary and disclose the statistical reliability of the techniques and data upon which inferences are created. However, the fact that the true value of data remains unknown.

The Value of Data - How to Price Data

Context: When discussing the value of personal data, one needs to define personal data first. Art. 4(1) GDPR defines personal data as "any information which are related to an identified or identifiable natural person." According to Art. 8(1) of the Charter of Fundamental Rights of the European Union and Art. 16(1) of the Treaty on the Functioning of the European Union, both of which are explicitly mentioned in Recital 1 of the GDPR, in the EU personal data protection constitutes a fundamental right. This approach to informational privacy demonstrates that personal value possesses a qualitative value in society. This qualitative term, the differing functions and objectives for which personal data can be used, can be extended by a quantitative, monetary, term to enable a pricing mechanism for data.

Ethical Issue: The ethical issue with regards to the pricing of data is the following: Is it ethically acceptable, and possible, to put a price on personal data? As the protection of personal data constitutes a fundamental human right, putting a price on such data seems legally and ethically challenging, although the value of the data economy, and the services that can be bought with data, can indeed be priced.

Example: Suppose a data subject would like to sell his/her personal data, containing all the information contained on a personal computer, such as browser history, purchased gooods and service as well as pictures and other information. Would it be possible, and ethically acceptable to put a price on this data?

Risk Assessment and Discussion: While valuations for the EU data economy and data market exist [58], extant legislation offers no guidance on how to determine the monetary value of a specific set of personal data. From an economic perspective personal data can furthermore be considered as a discrete object that can be produced on site, by an individual, an organization or a third party. It can be transferred between entities that can in turn transform and process the data and/or transfer it again to other entities. Data has been titled "the new oil" or a currency, demonstrating the economic value for organizations that are actively taking an effort to obtain, create and process personal data. Personal data is for instance used in marketing and business intelligence in order to market to, and obtain, new customers for a product or service. Data is also currently being used as de-facto means of payment for access to specific services on the internet, as discussed in this document and the legal evaluation on counter-performance practices in the critical analysis.

Given this economic reality, the current situation therefore requires an ethical consideration on how personal data could and should be valued as there is no established pricing mechanism for personal data.

In his Theory of Communicative Action, Habermas [32] provides a framework within which different areas of law come into place that also apply to personal data. Individuals are seen to behave in a sphere of private autonomy. Here, individuals can choose to do what they like, including buying and selling personal data under the agreed upon conditions, i.e., price and amount of data. In this context, property rights come into place. Property rights concede a basic recognition of ownership, providing a stabilizing condition in a private autonomy. Naturally, different types and forms of property rights exist, for instance depending on the type of economic good, be it a commodity or an intellectual property. The simple absence of property rights for the commercialization of data does not mean that commercialization of data is not possible. Data could still be commercialized in private autonomy, only without property rights put into place to regulate the transfer. Before creating a property right, regulators should be clear on the objective that is to be achieved with the right. What kind of right should be implemented? Should it be a right for intellectual property or rather an object? Lawmakers and regulators might also want to intervene by limiting the capacity of individuals to commercialize data in their private autonomy. Here, fundamental rights come into play, providing individuals with equal opportunities and restrictions. The GDPR clearly granted individuals with fundamental rights related to personal data and the use of it through other entities. However, it is less clear whether and to what extend the GDPR restricts commercialization and propertization of personal data [83].

Valuation Methods. It is not that fundamental rights and property rights need to contradict each other. Instead, property rights, granting and quoting data a definable, monetary, value, could add to the bargaining power of individuals, thereby extending their fundamental rights. There are however other options and tools besides rights that could help in defining the value of personal data. Malgieri and Custers [54] state that *"[a]ttaching a monetary value to personal data requires some clarity on (1) how to express monetary value, (2) which object is actually being priced, and (3) and how to attach value to the object, i.e. the actual pricing system"*. Personal data should be valued in a currency, per a specified time frame and per person. Factors to be considered are the completeness, relative rarity of data as well as the level of identifiability [54]. The pricing could be based on a market valuation or individual valuation method. A market-based valuation would price personal data according to its costs or benefits for market participants, as observed in illegal data markets[10] or data breaches. An indi-

---

[10] For an exemplary pricing of data records such as passwords and accounts, see keepersecurity.com/how-much-is-my-information-worth-to-hacker-dark-web.html.

vidual valuation method could be based on individuals' willingness to pay for data protection and privacy [22]. Both approaches remain incomplete as market valuation methods rely on indicators that are insufficiently precise while individual valuation methods are no incentive compatible. Defining the value of personal data therefore remains an ethical, legal and practical challenge without an apparent optimal solution. To overcome this epistemic uncertainty, more research into fair and ethical pricing mechanisms is needed to educate individuals on the value of personal data. As technology and the data economy are under constant change, the exact value of data at the point of collection is likely to continue to be unknown for most parties involved in the transfer of the data. Thus, the most probable and promising route would aim at developing adequate proxies and indicators that allow for an approximation of the data's value. Renewed legislation could provide examples and frameworks for measuring the value of data in order to compensate data subjects.

The Value of Data - Counter-Performance Practices

Context: Currently, it is unclear whether or not a form of trade that does not involve money transfers but rather the monetarization of the data, i.e., the process of converting personal data into currency, is lawful [83]. As the value of the EU data economy is continuing to grow [23] and many internet service providers are opting to monetise personal data instead of charging a fee for their service or platform [78], this matter also requires ethical consideration.

Ethical Issue and Example: Presently, individuals oftentimes pay with personal data for the usage and experience of digital products and services. An example are popular social media or communication services such as Facebook, WhatsApp or TikTok. While these services are advertised as "free" to individuals, they are paying indirectly by consenting to the processing of their personal data by the service providers. Most often, users do not have the chance to chose between paying with money or their data and personal information. Indeed, it is possible that individuals are not even aware about this possible choice or would simply opt for the payment using personal data as they do not have the means to pay with money, while still relying on the service or product. The ethical issue lies therefore in the question whether personal data should be accepted as a form of payment and under what considerations.

Risk Assessment and Discussion: Kitchener [43] identified several moral principles that can serve as ethical guidelines for this issue. The principles are defined as *beneficence, non-nmaleficence, autonomy, justice* and *fidelity*. As the principle of fidelity does not fit the context of counter-performance practices, the principle of *explicability* is used instead, which has already been used in related work on ethics in AI [26]. It can be seen that data as counter-performance for a service contributes to the welfare of the individual, satisfying the beneficence criterion. Similarly, *non-maleficence* be seen as fulfilled, assuming that the service provider does not offer the service to intentionally harm the individual or others. In relation to fundamental right for privacy, a service provider needs to take measure to prevent accidental or deliberate harm to the data subject when processing personal data. Regulation such as the GDPR acts therefore as a control mechanism for the non-maleficence principle.

The principle of *autonomy* relates to independence, allowing an individual freedom of choice in its actions. In this case, individuals are, in principle, free to choose a service that asks for data as counter-performance for a service. Individuals could decline such an offer, choose no service at all, or search for other service providers that offer the same or a similar service for a monetary fee. To do so, individuals must firstly understand how their decisions impact them and others in a society. Secondly, this decision must be able to be sound and rational, that is, children for instance can-not be expected to make a sound and rational decision on this matter. The Covid-19 crisis demonstrated that access to services that gather personal data as payment is not always a free choice but a necessity. During worldwide lockdowns, especially school-children and students were forced to use services to connect with each other as well as with education institutions in order, as the alternative would have been to not receive any kind of education. For children and students from less fortunate households and countries, a paying-with-money option would not have been a better alternative, given that many individuals were not even able to afford laptops, let alone a functioning working and learning environment. Additionally, individuals are often not aware of the value of their data, as discussed in other sections of this work, or unaware of the potential implications and processing activities that are conducted with personal data. As data can be stored indefinitely, individuals might forget about consent that they gave in the past, preventing them to exercise their right of erasure or to withdraw their consent. Thus, the use of data as counter-performance for a service can therefore not be considered a completely autonomous decision in many circumstances. This however does also apply to instances in which individuals consent to the processing of data for a service. According to the GDPR, consent has to be freely given to act as a legal basis for the processing of personal data. If an individual is not able to use a service or product without consenting to the processing of their personal data, this consent is not freely given. Oftentimes, for instance in the case of website cookies or ubiquitous internet services, individuals are not able to effectively withdraw their consent. There are a number of reasons for this. Especially in the case of cookie notifications, organizations use techniques such as nudging and dark patterns to push individuals into accepting them. While the opt-in choice is easy to choose, finding an opt-out choice is often a tedious and frustrating task. Organizations might also decline website visits or only offer limited functionality if individuals not fully consent to the whole cookie policy. The recent EDPB Statement 03/2021 on the ePrivacy Regulation reiterates the importance of enforcing more strict consent requirements for cookies and similar technologies in the upcoming ePrivacy regulation [6]. However, individuals might have no other option than to consent to the processing of data as they effectively need, feel or are obliged to use a product or a service. This could be because individuals are socially pressured in the case of monopolistic or oligopolistic services or because individuals are not able to use costly alternatives that collect no or less personal data, demonstrating that individuals are often unable to take autonomous decisions on the processing of personal data in general.

Kitchener [43] defines justice as "treating equals equally and unequals unequally but in proportion to their relevant differences". Treating individuals differently therefore requires a rationale that explains the appropriateness of this treatment to promote fairness and impartiality [27]. In principle it could be argued that individuals could receive different degrees of services for their data, depending on how the service providers values the data. Similarly, the justice principle could also encompass the option of giving individuals the option to pay with data or with money for a specific service. However, this could not be regarded as fair practice given the power imbalance be-tween individuals and service providers in instances outlined above. The ethical is-sues related to the use of data as counter-performance for a service are however not automatically solved if the provider of a service gives the individual the option to pay with money for this particular service. Less wealthy individuals are likely to always prefer data as payment, as money could be used for other goods and services while the same type of data could be used to "pay" for multiple services. Similarly, as the value of data is oftentimes not observable at the time of data collection, but through the combination with other data points, a price discrimination between individuals cannot satisfy the justice principle in this case.

Finally, *explicability* acts as an enabler for the aforementioned principles by promoting intelligibility, accountability and transparency. Individuals should be enabled to understand what data is being processed, how exactly it is being processed, by whom and for how long. Only then can individuals gain an understanding on the current and future value of their data. Service providers need to be held accountable for their processing activities. Again, current regulation such as the GDPR aim to increase explicability by fostering transparency and accountability when personal data is being processed. Under the condition that regulation allows for data as payment for a service and regulates it, the explicability principle can be affirmed.

Overall, the use of data as payment for a service poses both, ethical and legal issues. From an ethical point of view, the simple prohibition of this matter does not solve the underlying power imbalance between individuals and service providers. Instead, it may hinder individuals in gaining an understanding over the value of personal data. Clear contractual agreements and regulation could allow for data as payment while complying with legal and ethical requirements.

5 Discussion

Based on the analysis of the ethical issues identified and elaborated upon in the prior section, Table 2 provides an assessment of the ethical principles of cybersecurity potentially violated in each step of a digital service chain. Moreover, for each ethical issue the negatively affected party as well as the party that could potentially resolve the issue is identified. These parties are namely the user, or individual, or the organization that is providing a specific service to a user. We deliberately decided not to include the state, that could introduce additional legislation to overcome ethical issues, in the table. Instead, the aim of this work is to assess whether and how organizations and individuals may overcome these ethical issues without further regulation.

Table 2. Ethical issues and potentially violated ethical cybersecurity principles in digital service chains

Stage in Service Chain	Ethical Issue	Non-Maleficence	Beneficence	Autonomy	Justice	Explicability	Affected Party	Potential Resolver
Content Creation	Defining Fairness	✓	✓		✓	✓	User	Organization
Content Creation	Data Altruism		✓	✓	✓	✓	Both	Organization
Content Creation	Bias in AI Training Data	✓	✓		✓	✓	User	Organization
Content Creation	Model Reflecting Reality	✓	✓		✓	✓	Both	Organization
Aggregation	Anonymisation vs. Quality	✓	✓	✓		✓	Both	Organization
Data Transport	Power Asymmetries	✓		✓	✓		User	Organization
Data Transport	Restriction of Data Transport	✓	✓				User	Organization
Data Transport	User Empowerment	✓	✓	✓			User	Both
Digital Experience	Inferences	✓			✓		User	Organization
Digital Experience	How to price Data	✓			✓	✓	User	Both
Digital Experience	Counterperformance Practices	✓	✓	✓			User	Organization

The results suggest that different ethical issues in different steps of digital service chains affect different ethical cybersecurity principles. Consequently, there cannot exist a one-size-fits-all solution to solve these ethical issues. Moreover, in all cases, the individual is the entity negatively affected through the specific ethical issue. Organizations are largely found to be potentially in the position to resolve or mitigate ethical issues, although there exist issues were both entities may be negatively affected or able to resolve an issue. We find that each cybersecurity ethics principle is violated through at least one ethical issue identified in this work. Similarly, for each step in the digital service chain, at least one ethical issue could be identified. As discussed in the beginning of this work, the objective has not been to provide a comprehensive list of all ethical issues but to focus on the ones derived through the methodology of this work.

Schoentgen and Wilkinson [77] noted that while digital technologies should be used for the benefit of individual people and the society, most of them are rather designed for commercial benefits. They sketch the transition of digital services prioritising ethics through a feedback loop. In order to have companies incorporating ethics, it is essential that they are rewarded for their efforts, i.e.

benefits need to exceed costs. To benefit from ethical services, it is necessary that customers notice that organizations take ethical compliance serious and that individuals benefit from this compliance. Increased ethical awareness can be achieved through increased transparency and accountability, but requires ethics to be measurable to allow customers to compare digital services on their ethical conduct.

Consequently, stronger ethical conduct can build users' trust which in turn will increase engagement and consumption of digital technologies which could reward the company. These observation are in line with findings of Hagendorff [33] who concluded that there are currently no consequences if an organization is not considering ethical issues when developing and offering their services.

However, Schoentgen and Wilkinson [77] also note that users of digital services face the ethical dilemmas of self-responsibility and choice making and that the best way to drive awareness of ethics is education and data literacy. In particular for privacy enhancing technologies, this is not new, as for Tor[11] and Jondonym[12], two tools safeguarding against mass surveillance, trust in the technology has been shown to be one of the major drivers [37–39,41]. The trust in the technology was driven by online privacy literacy [40] supporting Schoentgen and Wilkinsons' theory. In accordance with Schoentgen and Wilkinson [77] is also the result of a study [35] investigating incentives and barriers for the implementation of privacy enhancing technologies from a corporate view where ethics and reputation of the company were among the named incentives. Another incentive mentioned is to charge for more privacy friendly services. This is a business model which is currently popular among German publishers who require online users to either pay a fee or agree to accept cookies for targeted advertising. However, besides the question whether users are willing to pay [36], offering privacy-friendly services only with additional charge may amplify other ethical issues. In particular, if users can opt-out from their data being used if they pay for it, this will most likely cause biased data since one will expect that only more wealthy people would afford to pay for their privacy. As sketched in the previous section any bias in the data, which might be used to train machine learning models, may cause algorithms to fail causing other problems.

Nonetheless, even if an organization wants to provide services in an ethical way, the resulting trade-offs are sometimes difficult to overcome. Examples are the storage of personal data, where it is not per se clear if data on a local device is necessarily more secure than if stored in the cloud [69]. Although it might seem logical that the users keeps as much data as possible on their devices, with manufactures not providing updates for still used devices and current malware targeting mobile users, it may be that data stored in a trustworthy environment, such as a cloud, where professionals operate and secure the systems might be more secure. Another example is the provision of open data for the benefit of the society. While it might allow the creation of new services, research or just transparency, it might on the other hand threaten the users' privacy if its possible

---

[11] https://www.torproject.org/.

[12] https://anonymous-proxy-servers.net/.

to link the data with existing datasets [70]. Thus, even well-intentioned ideas might backfire to the disadvantage of the users. For instance, questioning users directly on their preferences might be an obvious ethical solution. However, this solution requires well-educated users being able to make informed decisions and being willing to take the time and effort necessary to do so, which can not be assumed in any context [44].

6   Conclusion and Future Work

This work demonstrates the importance of the consideration of ethical issues in digital service chains. As such service chains strongly rely on data and information for the creation, aggregation, distribution, transport and experience of an organizations' products and services, ethical issues are highly related to the data and information that is used in these steps. Using workshops and encounters with ethical experts as well as experts in data protection from both, a technological and a legal point of view, multiple ethical issues were identified. When analyzing these ethical issues it became apparent that ethical issues arise particularly in the steps of data creation and aggregation as well as in the last step, digital experience. While the first steps need to carefully consider how data is obtained, created and combined, the last step of a digital service chain needs to consider how the service, and its underlying use of data and information are to be valued. Following the classification of Hagendorff [33], all ethical cybersecurity principles were at least once potentially violated in the ethical issues identified in this work. The analysis of the differing ethical issues demonstrated that their exists no one-size-fits-all solution to solve these ethical issues. Various different ethical frameworks for cybersecurity as well as different approaches to overcome or mitigate the ethical issues exist. Prior research indicated that different approaches can lead to differing and conflicting solutions. In this work, we did not focus on the introduction of additional regulation to overcome ethical issues but aimed to elaborate on them in the context of digital service chains. Here, organizations create content and information by aggregating and processing personal data to offer new, digital services to users. Not surprisingly, we find that in particular users are the ones that may be harmed through the identified issues while organizations are in the position to overcome these issues.

Limitations and Future Work. The objective of this work has not been to develop or list all possible ethical issues with regards to cybersecurity and digital service chains. While experts were asked to state their most pressing issues, there might exist other ethical issues that were not discussed in this work. Moreover, changes and advancements in technology could lead to the rise of other, more pressing, issues, constituting a limitation of this work. Additionally, we did not discuss potential solutions to the ethical issues but rather aimed to create awareness on them in the context of digital service chains and cybersecurity. Several opportunities for future work could be identified. Further research could build up on the results of this work by developing a framework on how best to overcome the identified ethical issues. Here, it could be assessed whether the violation of different ethical principles, as outlined in the previous section, could require differing approaches to mitigate the identified ethical issues. Such frameworks should incorporate and assess economic benefits for organizations to comply with ethical principles [77]. Lastly, future work might focus on the empowerment of users in the context of digital service chains as the mere awareness and education on ethical issues could lead to a change in behavior and might help in mitigating the identified ethical issues.

Acknowledgements. This work was supported by H2020 Science with and for Society Programme's projects PANELFIT (grant no. 788039) and CyberSec4Europe (grant no. 830929).

References

1. Act, D.G.: Proposal for a regulation of the European Parliament and the Council on European data governance (Data Governance Act). EUR-Lex-52020PC0767 (2020)
2. Angwin, J., Larson, J., Mattu, S., Kirchner, L.: Machine bias: there's software used across the country to predict future criminals. And it's biased against blacks. ProPublica (2016). https://www.propublica.org/article/machine-bias-risk-assessments-in-criminal-sentencing. Accessed 1 Feb 2022
3. Bacon, F.: Meditationes sacrae (1597). The Works of Francis Bacon **14**, 149 (1864)
4. Barocas, S., Selbst, A.D.: Big data's disparate impact. Calif. L. Rev. **104**, 671 (2016)
5. Bateman, T.: Uber's 'racist' facial recognition software is firing black and Asian drivers, former driver claims. euronews.next (2021). https://www.euronews.com/next/2021/10/06/uber-s-racist-facial-recognition-software-is-firing-black-and-asian-drivers-former-driver-. Accessed 1 Feb 2022
6. European Data Protection Board: Statement 03/2021 on the ePrivacy Regulation (2021)
7. Bolukbasi, T., Chang, K.W., Zou, J.Y., Saligrama, V., Kalai, A.T.: Man is to computer programmer as woman is to homemaker? Debiasing word embeddings. In: Advances in Neural Information Processing Systems, vol. 29, pp. 4349–4357 (2016)
8. Brunet, M.E., Alkalay-Houlihan, C., Anderson, A., Zemel, R.: Understanding the origins of bias in word embeddings. In: International Conference on Machine Learning, pp. 803–811. PMLR (2019)
9. Bundestag, D.: Entwurf eines gesetzes zum schutz elektronischer patientendaten in der telematikinfrastruktur (patientendaten-schutz-gesetz-pdsg). Deutscher Bundestag, Berlin (2020)
10. Caldas-Coulthard, C.R., Moon, R.: 'Curvy, hunky, kinky': using corpora as tools for critical analysis. Discourse Soc. **21**(2), 99–133 (2010)
11. Caliskan, A., Bryson, J.J., Narayanan, A.: Semantics derived automatically from language corpora contain human-like biases. Science **356**(6334), 183–186 (2017)
12. Cas, J.: D4.1 issues and gap analysis on security and cybersecurity ELI in the context of ICT research and innovation (2020). https://www.panelfit.eu/wp-content/uploads/2020/11/D41-Issues-and-gap-analysis-on-Security-and-Cybersecurity-ELI-in-the-context-of-ICT-research-and-innovation.pdf. Accessed 1 Feb 2022

13. Christen, M., Gordijn, B., Loi, M.: The Ethics of Cybersecurity. Springer, Cham (2020). https://doi.org/10.1007/978-3-030-29053-5
14. European Commission: Communication from the commission to the European Parliament, the Council, the European economic and social committee and the committee of the regions a European strategy for data (2020). https://ec.europa.eu/info/sites/default/files/communication-european-strategy-data-19feb202_en.pdf. Accessed 1 Feb 2022
15. European Commission: Directorate-General for Communications Networks, Content and Technology, Ethics guidelines for trustworthy AI. Publications Office (2019)
16. EUHealthSupport Consortium: Assessment of the EU member states' rules on health data in the light of GDPR (2021). www.ec.europa.eu/health/sites/default/files/ehealth/docs/ms_rules_health-data_en.pdf. Accessed 1 Feb 2022
17. Corbett-Davies, S., Pierson, E., Feller, A., Goel, S.: A computer program used for bail and sentencing decisions was labeled biased against blacks. It's actually not that clear. Washington (2016). https://www.washingtonpost.com/news/monkey-cage/wp/2016/10/17/can-an-algorithm-be-racist-our-analysis-is-more-cautious-than-propublicas. Accessed 1 Feb 2022
18. Crawford, K.: Artificial intelligence's white guy problem. New York Times (2016)
19. European Union Agency for Cybersecurity: Glossary. https://www.enisa.europa.eu/topics/threat-risk-management/risk-management/current-risk/risk-management-inventory/glossary. Accessed 1 Feb 2022
20. Dorne, R., Voudouris, C., Lesaint, D., Owusu, G.: Service Chain Management: Technology Innovation for the Service Business. Springer, Heidelberg (2008). https://doi.org/10.1007/978-3-540-75504-3
21. Dressel, J., Farid, H.: The accuracy, fairness, and limits of predicting recidivism. Sci. Adv. 4(1), eaao5580 (2018)
22. Organisation for Economic Co-Operation and Development: Exploring the economics of personal data: a survey of methodologies for measuring monetary value. OECD Publishing (2013)
23. European Commission: Communication from the commission to the European Parliament, the Council, the European economic and social committee and the committee of the regions "building a European data economy" (2017). https://eur-lex.europa.eu/legal-content/EN/TXT/?uri=COM:2017:9:FIN. Accessed 1 Feb 2022
24. European Data Protection Board, European Data Protection Supervisor: Joint opinion on the proposal for a regulation of the European Parliament and of the Council on European data governance (Data Governance Act) (2021). https://edps.europa.eu/data-protection/our-work/publications/opinions/edpb-edps-joint-opinion-proposal-regulation-european_en. Accessed 1 Feb 2022
25. FIDIS, I.: Information technology - security techniques - information security risk management ISO/IEC 27005:2018 (2018)
26. Floridi, L., et al.: AI4people-an ethical framework for a good AI society: opportunities, risks, principles, and recommendations. Mind. Mach. 28(4), 689–707 (2018). https://doi.org/10.1007/s11023-018-9482-5
27. Forester-Miller, H., Davis, T.E.: A Practitioner's Guide to Ethical Decision Making. American Counseling Association Alexandria (1995)
28. Formosa, P., Wilson, M., Richards, D.: A principlist framework for cybersecurity ethics. Comput. Secur. 109, 102382 (2021)
29. Ghinita, G., Karras, P., Kalnis, P., Mamoulis, N.: A framework for efficient data anonymization under privacy and accuracy constraints. ACM Trans. Database Syst. (TODS) 34(2), 1–47 (2009)

30. Goodman, B., Flaxman, S.: European Union regulations on algorithmic decision-making and a "right to explanation". AI Mag. **38**(3), 50–57 (2017)
31. Grace, K., Salvatier, J., Dafoe, A., Zhang, B., Evans, O.: When will AI exceed human performance? Evidence from AI experts. J. Artif. Intell. Res. **62**, 729–754 (2018)
32. Habermas, J.: The Theory of Communicative Action: Volume 1: Reason and the Rationalization of Society. Beacon Press (1985)
33. Hagendorff, T.: The ethics of AI ethics: an evaluation of guidelines. Minds Mach. **30**(1), 99–120 (2020). https://doi.org/10.1007/s11023-020-09517-8
34. Hall, P., Gill, N.: An Introduction to Machine Learning Interpretability. O'Reilly Media Incorporated, Sebastopol (2019)
35. Harborth, D., Braun, M., Grosz, A., Pape, S., Rannenberg, K.: Anreize und hemmnisse für die implementierung von privacy-enhancing technologies im unternehmenskontext. In: Sicherheit 2018: Sicherheit, Schutz und Zuverlässigkeit, Beiträge der 9. Jahrestagung des Fachbereichs Sicherheit der Gesellschaft für Informatik e.V. (GI), Konstanz, 25–27 April 2018, pp. 29–41 (2018). https://doi.org/10.18420/sicherheit2018_02
36. Harborth, D., Cai, X., Pape, S.: Why do people pay for privacy-enhancing technologies? The case of Tor and JonDonym. In: Dhillon, G., Karlsson, F., Hedström, K., Zúquete, A. (eds.) SEC 2019. IAICT, vol. 562, pp. 253–267. Springer, Cham (2019). https://doi.org/10.1007/978-3-030-22312-0_18
37. Harborth, D., Pape, S.: Examining technology use factors of privacy-enhancing technologies: the role of perceived anonymity and trust. In: 24th Americas Conference on Information Systems, AMCIS 2018, New Orleans, LA, USA, 16–18 August 2018. Association for Information Systems (2018). https://aisel.aisnet.org/amcis2018/Security/Presentations/15. Accessed 1 Feb 2022
38. Harborth, D., Pape, S.: JonDonym users' information privacy concerns. In: Janczewski, L.J., Kutyłowski, M. (eds.) SEC 2018. IAICT, vol. 529, pp. 170–184. Springer, Cham (2018). https://doi.org/10.1007/978-3-319-99828-2_13
39. Harborth, D., Pape, S.: How privacy concerns and trust and risk beliefs influence users' intentions to use privacy-enhancing technologies - the case of Tor. In: 52nd Hawaii International Conference on System Sciences (HICSS) 2019, pp. 4851–4860, January 2019. https://scholarspace.manoa.hawaii.edu/handle/10125/59923. Accessed 1 Feb 2022
40. Harborth, D., Pape, S.: How privacy concerns, trust and risk beliefs and privacy literacy influence users' intentions to use privacy-enhancing technologies - the case of Tor. In: ACM SIGMIS Database: The DATABASE for Advances in Information Systems, vol. 51, no. 1, pp. 51–69 (2020). https://dl.acm.org/doi/abs/10.1145/3380799.3380805
41. Harborth, D., Pape, S., Rannenberg, K.: Explaining the technology use behavior of privacy-enhancing technologies: the case of Tor and JonDonym. In: Proceedings on Privacy Enhancing Technologies (PoPETs), vol. 2020, no. 2, pp. 111–128, May 2020. https://content.sciendo.com/view/journals/popets/2020/2/article-p111.xml. Accessed 1 Feb 2022
42. Government Federal Ministry of Justice: Federal Act Governing Access to Information held by the Federal Government (Freedom of Information Act) (2013). https://www.gesetze-im-internet.de/englisch_ifg/. Accessed 1 Feb 2022
43. Kitchener, K.S.: Intuition, critical evaluation and ethical principles: the foundation for ethical decisions in counseling psychology. Couns. Psychol. **12**(3), 43–55 (1984)

44. Kröger, J.L., Gellrich, L., Pape, S., Brause, S.R., Ullrich, S.: Personal information inference from voice recordings: user awareness and privacy concerns. In: Proceedings on Privacy Enhancing Technologies (PoPETs), vol. 2022, no. 1, pp. 6–27, January 2022. https://www.sciendo.com/article/10.2478/popets-2022-0002. Accessed 1 Feb 2022
45. Kusner, M.J., Loftus, J.R., Russell, C., Silva, R.: Counterfactual fairness. arXiv preprint arXiv:1703.06856 (2017)
46. Lazzaro, S.: Soap dispenser only responds to white skin. Dailymail.com (2017). https://www.dailymail.co.uk/sciencetech/article-4800234/Is-soap-dispenser-RACIST.html. Accessed 1 Feb 2022
47. Leavy, S.: Gender bias in artificial intelligence: the need for diversity and gender theory in machine learning. In: Proceedings of the 1st International Workshop on Gender Equality in Software Engineering, pp. 14–16 (2018)
48. Löbner, S., Tesfay, W.B., Nakamura, T., Pape, S.: Explainable machine learning for default privacy setting prediction. IEEE Access **9**, 63700–63717 (2021)
49. Löbner, S., Tronnier, F., Pape, S., Rannenberg, K.: Comparison of de-identification techniques for privacy preserving data analysis in vehicular data sharing. In: Brücher, B., Krauß, C., Fritz, M., Hof, H., Wasenmüller, O. (eds.) CSCS 2021: ACM Computer Science in Cars Symposium, Ingolstadt, Germany, 30 November 2021, pp. 7:1–7:11. ACM, November 2021. https://dl.acm.org/doi/10.1145/3488904.3493380
50. Loi, M., Christen, M.: Ethical frameworks for cybersecurity. In: Christen, M., Gordijn, B., Loi, M. (eds.) The Ethics of Cybersecurity. TILELT, vol. 21, pp. 73–95. Springer, Cham (2020). https://doi.org/10.1007/978-3-030-29053-5_4
51. Macnish, K., van der Ham, J.: Ethics in cybersecurity research and practice. Technol. Soc. **63**, 101382 (2020)
52. Madgavkar, A.: A conversation on artificial intelligence and gender bias (2021). https://www.mckinsey.com/featured-insights/asia-pacific/a-conversation-on-artificial-intelligence-and-gender-bias. Accessed 1 Feb 2022
53. Malgieri, G.: The concept of fairness in the GDPR: a linguistic and contextual interpretation. In: Proceedings of the 2020 Conference on Fairness, Accountability, and Transparency, pp. 154–166 (2020)
54. Malgieri, G., Custers, B.: Pricing privacy-the right to know the value of your personal data. Comput. Law Secur. Rev. **34**(2), 289–303 (2018)
55. Manjikian, M.: Cybersecurity Ethics: An Introduction. Routledge, London (2017)
56. Mason, R.: Policy for ethical digital services. J. Assoc. Inf. Syst. **22**(3), 11 (2021)
57. Mehrabi, N., Morstatter, F., Saxena, N., Lerman, K., Galstyan, A.: A survey on bias and fairness in machine learning. ACM Comput. Surv. (CSUR) **54**(6), 1–35 (2021)
58. Micheletti, G., Pepatou, C.: The European data market monitoring tool: key facts & figures, first policy conclusions, data landscape and quantified stories (2019). https://datalandscape.eu/sites/default/files/report/D2.6_EDM_Second_Interim_Report_28.06.2019.pdf. Accessed 1 Feb 2022
59. Morgan, G., Gordijn, B.: A care-based stakeholder approach to ethics of cybersecurity in business. In: Christen, M., Gordijn, B., Loi, M. (eds.) The Ethics of Cybersecurity. TILELT, vol. 21, pp. 119–138. Springer, Cham (2020). https://doi.org/10.1007/978-3-030-29053-5_6
60. Motschenbacher, H.: Gentlemen before ladies? A corpus-based study of conjunct order in personal binomials. J. Engl. Linguist. **41**(3), 212–242 (2013)

61. Mozer, M.C.: Neural network music composition by prediction: exploring the benefits of psychoacoustic constraints and multi-scale processing. Connect. Sci. **6**(2–3), 247–280 (1994)
62. Muller, A., Asakura, K.: The Telenor case: the (in) compatibility of zero-rating with the net neutrality principle. Eur. Competition Reg. L. Rev. **5**, 59 (2021)
63. Nabbosa, V., Kaar, C.: Societal and ethical issues of digitalization. In: Proceedings of the 2020 International Conference on Big Data in Management, pp. 118–124 (2020)
64. United Nations: Universal declaration of human rights (1948). https://www.un.org/en/about-us/universal-declaration-of-human-rights. Accessed 1 Feb 2022
65. Neff, G., Nagy, P.: Automation, algorithms, and politics: talking to Bots: symbiotic agency and the case of Tay. Int. J. Commun. **10**, 17 (2016)
66. Niksefat, S., Kaghazgaran, P., Sadeghiyan, B.: Privacy issues in intrusion detection systems: a taxonomy, survey and future directions. Comput. Sci. Rev. **25**, 69–78 (2017)
67. Nissenbaum, H.: Where computer security meets national security. Ethics Inf. Technol. **7**(2), 61–73 (2005). https://doi.org/10.1007/s10676-005-4582-3
68. Nissenbaum, H.: Privacy in Context. Stanford University Press, Redwood City (2009)
69. Pape, Sebastian, Rannenberg, Kai: Applying privacy patterns to the Internet of Things' (IoT) architecture. Mob. Netw. Appl. **24**(3), 925–933 (2018). The Journal of Special Issues on Mobility of Systems, Users, Data and Computing. https://doi.org/10.1007/s11036-018-1148-2
70. Pape, S., Serna-Olvera, J., Tesfay, W.: Why open data may threaten your privacy. In: Workshop on Privacy and Inference, Co-Located with KI, September 2015
71. European Parliament: Directive (EU) 2016/943 of the European Parliament and of the Council of 8 June 2016 on the protection of undisclosed know-how and business information (trade secrets) against their unlawful acquisition, use and disclosure (2016)
72. van de Poel, I.: Core values and value conflicts in cybersecurity: beyond privacy versus security. In: The Ethics of Cybersecurity, p. 45 (2020)
73. Rannenberg, K., Pape, S., Tronnier, F., Löbner, S.: Study on the technical evaluation of de-identification procedures for personal data in the automotive sector. Technical report, Goethe University Frankfurt, May 2021. http://publikationen.ub.uni-frankfurt.de/frontdoor/index/index/docId/63413. Accessed 1 Feb 2022
74. Repetto, M., Carrega, A., Rapuzzi, R.: An architecture to manage security operations for digital service chains. Future Gener. Comput. Syst. **115**, 251–266 (2021). https://www.sciencedirect.com/science/article/pii/S0167739X20303290. Accessed 1 Feb 2022
75. Repetto, M., Striccoli, D., Piro, G., Carrega, A., Boggia, G., Bolla, R.: An autonomous cybersecurity framework for next-generation digital service chains. J. Netw. Syst. Manag. **29**(4) (2021). Article number: 37. https://doi.org/10.1007/s10922-021-09607-7
76. Royakkers, L., Timmer, J., Kool, L., van Est, R.: Societal and ethical issues of digitization. Ethics Inf. Technol. **20**(2), 127–142 (2018). https://doi.org/10.1007/s10676-018-9452-x
77. Schoentgen, A., Wilkinson, L.: Ethical issues in digital technologies (2021)
78. Schreiner, M., Hess, T.: Why are consumers willing to pay for privacy? An application of the privacy-freemium model to media companies. Published in Twenty-Third European Conference on Information Systems (ECIS), Münster, Germany (2015)

79. Selbst, A.D., Boyd, D., Friedler, S.A., Venkatasubramanian, S., Vertesi, J.: Fairness and abstraction in sociotechnical systems. In: Proceedings of the Conference on Fairness, Accountability, and Transparency, pp. 59–68 (2019)
80. Stevens, S.: A framework for ethical cyber-defence for companies. In: Christen, M., Gordijn, B., Loi, M. (eds.) The Ethics of Cybersecurity. TILELT, vol. 21, pp. 317–329. Springer, Cham (2020). https://doi.org/10.1007/978-3-030-29053-5_16
81. Sweeney, L.: k-anonymity: a model for protecting privacy. Int. J. Uncertain. Fuzziness Knowl. Based Syst. **10**(05), 557–570 (2002)
82. Timmers, P.: Ethics of AI and cybersecurity when sovereignty is at stake. Minds Mach. **29**(4), 635–645 (2019). https://doi.org/10.1007/s11023-019-09508-4
83. Tronnier, F.: D3.1 issues and gap analysis on data commercialisation in the context of ICT research and innovation (2020). https://www.panelfit.eu/wp-content/uploads/2020/11/D31-Issues-and-gaps-analysis-on-Data-Commercialisation-in-the-Context-of-ICT-Research-and-Innovation.pdf. Accessed 1 Feb 2022
84. Vacca, J.R.: Computer and Information Security Handbook. Newnes (2012)
85. Vallor, S., Green, B., Raicu, I.: Ethics in technology practice. The Markkula Center for Applied Ethics at Santa Clara University (2018)
86. Voudouris, C.: Defining and understanding service chain management. In: Voudouris, C., Lesaint, D., Owusu, G. (eds.) Service Chain Management, pp. 1–17. Springer, Heidelberg (2008). https://doi.org/10.1007/978-3-540-75504-3_1
87. Wachter, S., Mittelstadt, B.: A right to reasonable inferences: re-thinking data protection law in the age of big data and AI. Colum. Bus. L. Rev. 494 (2019)
88. Wang, H., Gao, C., Li, Y., Wang, G., Jin, D., Sun, J.: De-anonymization of mobility trajectories: dissecting the gaps between theory and practice. In: The 25th Annual Network & Distributed System Security Symposium (NDSS 2018) (2018)
89. Weinberg, Z., Barradas, D., Christin, N.: Chinese wall or Swiss cheese? Keyword filtering in the great firewall of China. In: Proceedings of the Web Conference 2021, pp. 472–483 (2021)
90. Wirth, R., Hipp, J.: Crisp-DM: towards a standard process model for data mining. In: Proceedings of the 4th International Conference on the Practical Applications of Knowledge Discovery and Data Mining, vol. 1, pp. 29–39. Springer, London (2000)
91. Zafar, M.B., Valera, I., Rogriguez, M.G., Gummadi, K.P.: Fairness constraints: mechanisms for fair classification. In: Artificial Intelligence and Statistics, pp. 962–970. PMLR (2017)
92. Zuboff, S.: The Age of Surveillance Capitalism: The Fight for a Human Future at the New Frontier of Power. Profile Books (2019)

Author Index

Printed in the United States
by Baker & Taylor Publisher Services

Printed in the United States
by Baker & Taylor Publisher Services